Implementing Email Security and Tokens: Current Standards, Tools, and Practices

Sean Turner
Russ Housley

WILEY

Wiley Publishing, Inc.

Implementing Email Security and Tokens: Current Standards, Tools, and Practices

Published by
Wiley Publishing, Inc.
10475 Crosspoint Boulevard
Indianapolis, IN 46256
www.wiley.com

ISBN: 978-0-470-25463-9

Manufactured in the United States of America

10 9 8 7 6 5 4 3 2 1

For general information on our other products and services or to obtain technical support, please contact our Customer Care Department within the U.S. at (800) 762-2974, outside the U.S. at (317) 572-3993 or fax (317) 572-4002.

Wiley also publishes its books in a variety of electronic formats. Some content that appears in print may not be available in electronic books.

Library of Congress Cataloging-in-Publication Data is available from publisher.

Wiley also publishes its books in a variety of electronic formats. Some content that appears in print may not be available in electronic books.

Dedicated to all those who helped develop the Internet and those who will help develop it in the future.

— S.T. and R.H.

Thanks for the loving support from Sue, Ryan, and Patrick.

— R.H.

Thanks for all the support Mom and Dad.

— S.T.

About the Authors

Sean Turner — Mr. Turner is vice president and a co-founder of International Electronic Communications Analysts Inc. (www.ieca.com), a Virginia-based consulting services firm that specializes in information security, protocol design, and technical standardization for both the government and commercial sectors. His consulting efforts draw on his vast experience in secure systems analysis, architecture, design, and engineering of email, public key infrastructures, and key management systems. He assists clients with Service Oriented Architecture concepts, developing certificate policies, applying security to web services, and addressing issues of security policy and access control. He has been active in technical standards efforts in the IETF for over 12 years, and he is the author of numerous RFCs. He has been the S/MIME WG co-chair since mid-2003.

Mr. Turner holds a bachelor's degree in Electrical Engineering from the Georgia Institute of Technology. He has been an IEEE member since 1995.

Russ Housley — Mr. Housley is owner and founder of Vigil Security, LLC (www.vigilsec.com), a very small firm that provides computer and networking security consulting. He has contributed to the development of many standards, including PKIX Part 1, Privacy-Enhanced Mail and S/MIME. He began participating in the development of Internet security specifications in 1988 as a member of the Privacy and Security Research Group. He was the chair of the IETF S/MIME WG when it was formed, passing the reigns to Sean

Turner and Blake Ramsdell when he accepted the position as IETF Security Area Director. Mr. Housley is now serving as the chair of the IETF. He is the author of more than 30 RFCs.

Mr. Housley holds a bachelor's degree in Computer Science from Virginia Tech and a master's degree in Computer Science from George Mason University. He has been a member of ACM and IEEE since 1987.

Credits

Executive Editor
Carol Long

Development Editor
Julie M. Smith

Production Editor
Angela Smith

Copy Editor
Foxxe Editorial Services

Editorial Manager
Mary Beth Wakefield

Production Manager
Tim Tate

Vice President and Executive Group Publisher
Richard Swadley

Vice President and Executive Publisher
Joseph B. Wikert

Project Coordinator, Cover
Lynsey Stanford

Proofreader
Sossity Smith

Indexer
Johnna VanHoose Dinse

Contents

Acknowledgments

All the mistakes and incorrect reading of our Magic 8 Ball belong to the authors. Numerous people have contributed to this book, directly and indirectly. Most notably, we could never have completed the book without the patience and support of one wife (Sue), one girlfriend (Alexis), and two loving families.

Some friends and colleagues provided review, and other provided technical input. Thank you for the help: Chris Bonatti, Richard Guida, Cindy Cullen, Randy Sabett, George Rathbun, Jon Weisberg, Bill Bialick, John Marchioni, Bill Price, Barbara Keller, and Tim Polk. We'd also like to thank Carol Long for her hard work, and Julie Smith for cracking the whip.

Finally researchers, standards developers, and application developers have been developing this technology for the last 50 years. Our intent was to provide all appropriate credit to those who came before us. We hope that no one was inadvertently omitted.

Email and Security
Background

Introduction

In the early days of the Internet, no one worried about security. Those days are long gone. Today, everyone uses the Internet, and electronic mail is used for both business communication and personal communication. Much of it is sensitive, making security necessary. Secure electronic mail is available, yet very few people use it.

Many people are under the mistaken impression that email is point-to-point communication protocol. It is not. Many servers are involved, and each one of them can mess with the messages — unless you protect them. You do not want the messages read by anyone other than the intended recipient. You do not want anyone to change the message content. And, you do not want others to masquerade as you. Luckily, the tools are all readily available for providing these protections.

In this book, we explain security tools, including cryptography, security protocols, tokens, and hardware security modules to protect your email. You do not need to be an expert in these technologies to secure your email. Products are available that can help you. This book provides the information needed to first select wisely from these security offerings and then successfully deploy them. The case studies at the end of the book allow you to emulate the successes and avoid the potholes found by others.

How This Book Is Organized

We organized this book in to six sections. The later sections build on material presented in the earlier ones. A person familiar with email and who understands fundamental security services may be able to skip the earlier parts, but most readers will want to read the book from beginning to end.

We start by introducing Internet email, which is what we want to secure. Next, we provide motivation for why you should want to secure your email from prying eyes and then show you how to do it. Finally, we discuss the mechanism necessary to secure email. Three case studies give you hands-on lessons concerning these programs that will prove invaluable to you. Finally, we provide our Magic 8 Ball predictions for the future. Obviously, only time will tell if our Magic 8 Ball was lying.

Part I: Email and Security Background

Part I contains four chapters, including this one. Chapter 2, "Understanding Email," explains the Internet electronic mail transport and content standards. We use postal service analogies, hoping to make it easier to understand by leveraging things that you already know about the postal service (sometimes called snail mail). Chapter 3, "Security Fundamentals," explains who might want to read your email, how they might try to do it, and what you can do to stop them. Chapter 4, "Cryptography Primer," introduces the basics of cryptography, which is one of the key arrows in your quiver for thwarting the attackers introduced in Chapter 3.

Part II: PKI Basics

Part II contains only one chapter, dealing with Public Key Infrastructure (PKI). Chapter 5, "Understanding PKI," explains who should be trusted to properly perform specific activities in a PKI. It describes the most common PKI architectures, explains the public key certificates, and elucidates the certificate revocation lists structures produced by a PKI.

Part III: Secure Email

Part III contains two chapters, both detailing the ins and outs of email security. Chapter 6, "Protecting Email Message Contents," provides a history of email security mechanisms and explains the most common mechanism to protect your emails' contents, whereas Chapter 7, "Protecting Email Passwords, Message Headers, and Commands," explains how to make sure that your passwords aren't disclosed to attackers and how to protect the email message headers and commands.

Part IV: Tokens

Part IV also contains a single chapter. Chapter 8, "Tokens and Hardware Security Modules," describes the different types of devices that can be used to store and protect your private keys. We also discuss the ways that these devices are evaluated by professionals in certified laboratories.

Part V: Case Studies

Part V contains three chapters, one for each case study. Each chapter describes an implementation that includes secure email, PKI, and tokens. Chapter 9, "Signatures and Authentication For Everyone," describes the SAFE program in the pharmaceutical community, which interconnects the PKIs from many members of that community to support secure email, as well as other applications that make use of digitally signed documents. Chapter 10, "Department of Defense Public Key Infrastructure, Medium Grade Service, and Common Access Cards" describes PKI, Medium Grade Service (MGS), and Common Access Card (CAC) programs of the U.S. Department of Defense. Chapter 11, "National Institute of Standards and Technology Personal Identity and Verification," describes the smart-card-based standard developed by the National Institute of Standards and Technology (NIST) and the way that it is being used to fulfill the requirements in HSPD12.

Part VI: Expectations for the Future

Part VI contains a single chapter. Chapter 12, "Future Developments," offers predictions for developments in each of the areas discussed in this book.

Appendices

We provide supplemental information in four appendices. Appendix A, "ABNF Primer," provides an introduction to Augmented Backus-Noir Form, which is the formal language used to describe the syntax for character-based protocols, such as electronic mail. Appendix B, "ASN.1 Primer," provides an introduction to Abstract Syntax Notation One, which is the formal language used to describe the syntax in many binary-oriented protocols. Appendix C, "MIME Primer," explains how arbitrary data is included in character-based email messages using Multipurpose Internet Mail Extensions. We provide sufficient detail for reading and understanding the structures used in this book, but you'll need to look elsewhere for a complete coverage of these topics. Appendix D, "RFC Summaries," provides a summary of the Requests for Comments (RFCs) that are referenced in this book.

Who Should Read This Book

This book is intended for the chief technology officer (CTO) or perhaps the person whom the CTO assigns to implement an enterprise secure email solution, including PKI and tokens. It will also help people who want to buy the various components of such a system, but who may not have the expertise to do so confidently.

Keep in mind that this is not a guide for developers. However, developers of one component within an overall email security system will find it useful to understand how their component interacts with the rest of the system. It is not possible to include every detail of every component in this book. Therefore, we recommend that developers refer to the Internet Engineering Task Force (IETF) standards for details on the syntax and semantics of email-related protocols and PKI-related protocols.

You are presented with many choices when implementing an email security system. We hope that this book will help you wade through these options and achieve the benefits of secure email.

CHAPTER 2

Understanding Email

Before you can run, you have to walk, and before that you have to crawl. Likewise, before we explain how to secure email, you first have to understand the origins of email.

Email has evolved into one of today's most powerful and oft-used communication tools. In some circles, it has supplanted speech as the primary mode of communication. How many times have you seen someone on their "Crackberry" or heard someone else laugh out loud while staring at a computer screen? How many times has it been you? Email didn't just appear; it has developed over a number of years (roughly 40). It is important that you have a basic understanding of when and why email was developed and where and how it has evolved to provide background for how to better secure your email. Of course, email is still evolving, and security is sure to play a big role in its evolution.

It's slightly more complicated to give a definition of email today. Bear with us, though, because we promise to do it. As you might have guessed, there are a lot of parts that work together to move the message you typed or scribbled on your computer, phone, or personal data assistant (PDA) to your coworker, boss, friend, or mom. When you get to the end of this chapter, you will know how email messages are formatted and how email messages get from here to there. We are going to make Alice, Bob, and others do all the work. Obviously, to fully implement email you'll need to refer to the interoperability specifications for each of the parts; for that, we provide references at the end of the book.

History and Evolution

Email has been around for a very long time. It's been around almost as long as computers or at least shortly after there was more than one program and one user on a computer. In the beginning, engineers and computer scientists used a form of email to leave messages for one another, but they could only leave messages on the same computer. Remember, there weren't many computers around in the 1960s, and very few of them had a communications link to another computer. Once computer networks began to emerge, email really took off.

One early network was called the Advanced Research Projects Agency Network (ARPANET), and it is this network that later evolved into the Internet. According to [ISOC00], the engineers and computer scientists were motivated to develop email so that they could coordinate amongst each other. Personally, we think Dilbert and his followers would be shocked to know that email evolved because they needed an easy way to schedule meetings — the horror!

WHY TEXT MESSAGES?

So why is email based on text messages? Why not voice? Sure, speech would have been great, but the microphones to capture the sound; the speakers to play it back; and the processing power to capture analog voice, convert it to digital, and then back again were not readily available. In the 1960s, the human user interacted with computers through connected teletype machines. The keyboard was the readily available human input device, and a typewriter-style printer was the readily available output device, which made the text-based message the natural choice. In fact, it was the only choice.

The initial email application supported sending and receiving small messages that were composed entirely of alphanumeric characters. Sending and receiving a message was a lot like moving a file from one computer to another. It was not until the next phase in email evolution (developed by Lawrence R. Roberts) that email added, among other things, the ability to read messages in any order, to forward messages, and to reply to messages. Email has continued to evolve ever since by adding many other features including:

- Carbon Copy (CC)
- Blind Carbon Copy (BCC)
- Lowercase letters
- Character sets (for non-English languages)
- Attachments

- Notifications
- Importance
- Size restrictions
- Security

Features were not added willy-nilly. You can't do this with computers because it won't work. Imagine if you started making up words and using them with the people around you; the words would mean something to you but absolutely nothing to anybody else, unless they had a babelfish. Coordination and documentation of what the new word(s) and their meaning is needed to make changes successful. Luckily, the folks developing the APRANET knew this. They had meetings to discuss, agree, and document the agreements. From these documented agreements, people developed computer programs that would talk with programs developed by others. In other words, implementers use standards to develop computer programs that are interoperable; sometimes these agreements are referred to as interoperability standards.

Today, the Internet Engineering Task Force (IETF) has filled the role as the organization that develops interoperability standards related to the Internet. Email is just one of the important protocols specified in these standards. Table 2-1 lists some of the important interoperability standards that we will discuss later in the chapter.

Table 2-1 Important Internet Standards*

RFC NUMBER	TITLE
RFC 791	Internet Protocol
RFC 793	Transmission Control Protocol
RFC 1035	Domain Names - Implementation and Specifications
RFC 1939	Post Office Protocol - Version 3
RFC 2045-2049	Multipurpose Internet Mail Extensions
RFC 2131	Dynamic Host Configuration Protocol
RFC 2821	Simple Mail Transfer Protocol
RFC 2822	Internet Mail Transfer Protocol
RFC 3501	Internet Message Access Protocol - Version 4rev1

*It's important to note that some of these are updates of earlier RFCs, making the earlier work obsolete. Yet, backward compatibility is always a consideration.

INTEROPERABILITY STANDARDS

Many of the standards referenced in this book were developed by the IETF. It is an organization made up of individuals that meet, discuss, and agree on interoperability standards that are relevant to the Internet. For a more complete coverage of the Internet Standards process we suggest [RFC2026], where Scott Bradner describes the process by which an idea becomes an Internet Standard. While there have been other email "standards," the Internet Standard is the most important.

The number of individuals that attend the IETF has grown over the years from less than 50 to around 3000 and settled down to around 1200 participants nowadays. Obviously, to focus this number of participants, some organizational structure is needed. The IETF is organized into areas of interest, including Applications, Routing, Security, and Transport. Within these broad areas, specific topics are discussed in working groups.

The standardization process begins with a document called an Internet Draft (ID), and results in a document called a Request for Comment (RFC). Don't get hung up on this name. The name doesn't really align with the standards process used today, but it would be too painful to change, so everyone lives with the name. Even the standardization process is published in an RFC. RFCs are on different tracks, but in this case we are almost exclusively interested in standards track RFCs. To keep things simple, the RFCs are sequentially numbered, started at 1, and total just over 5000 now. That's about 125 per year since 1969. Over 400 were published in 2006!

It is not all hard work. The powers that be serve cookies at meeting breaks, and there are a long line of "April Fools" RFCs, such as the one that describes how carrier pigeons can be used to carry Internet traffic. And, yes, people took the joke to the next level; it has been implemented.

Everyone on a mainframe computer used email to communicate with other users on the same mainframe, but up to this point (the mid-1980s) you probably would never have heard of email because it was almost exclusively used by researchers at universities and government agencies. In the late 1980s, MCIMail was the first commercial email provider; others followed. Email use increased as businesses began to use it. When service providers like CompuServe and America Online (AOL), which were originally glorified Bulletin Board Systems (BBSs), were created they brought email to the masses.

BULLETIN BOARD SYSTEMS

Yes, there was life before the World Wide Web. Before the Web there was the Bulletin Board System (BBS). The BBS allowed users to dial in over Plain Old Telephone System (POTS) and share information: pictures, software, news, and messages. Initially many BBSs were run by hobbyists and were free of charge.

(continued)

> **BULLETIN BOARD SYSTEMS** *(continued)*
>
> When commercial companies like CompuServ and AOL arrived, they charged a fee for their "content." Content is information created for your consumption. It includes catalogues for online shopping.

So at this point many people had email at work, and some had it at home through various service providers, and then along comes the World Wide Web. Companies like Excite, AltaVista, Yahoo!, and later Google began to provide free webmail. Combine free email with the spread of wireless technologies to laptops, PDAs, and cell phones, and you have a recipe for an almost viral-like growth of email.

Now people give out email addresses instead of phone numbers, put email addresses on their business cards, and send billions of emails every year. Life has changed.

Internet Email

As we mentioned earlier, email has many moving parts. This is because engineers and computer scientists break complex problems down into smaller more manageable problems. We are going to follow this same philosophy and explain the technical parts of email in two manageable byte-sized pieces. The first is the process and format of email, and the second is the system that moves the email.

Wow! Email Is Just Like Snail Mail

With a name like email, you shouldn't be surprised that email is a lot like regular postal service mail. The process, formats, and commands for email have postal service analogies.

Process

To email or not to email: that is the question. If you are like Alice and Bob, then email it is. For Alice to send an email message to Bob, the steps are similar to using snail mail. Alice, Bob, and some infrastructure in the middle need to work together. Table 2-2 highlights the similarities in the snail mail and email process. Alice and Bob are the same in both, but in the email process the Simple Message Transfer Service, which we will shorten to the Mail Transfer Service (MTS), replaces the postal service. In the real world, there are many MTSs run by each service provider (such as your company, Google, and Yahoo!).

More complicated work flows are permitted. For example, Alice and Pat work together, but they are really busy and are senior enough to have an assistant, Doug. Alice and Pat can compose an email together during one of their arduous retreats in Palm Springs, and then they get Doug to send it to Bob.

Table 2-2 Snail Mail and Email Process Similarities

STEP	SNAIL MAIL	EMAIL
Compose	Alice pulls out pen and paper and writes her letter.	Alice either starts a dedicated email application or a web browser to compose her email message.
Submit	Alice pulls out pen and addresses, stamps, and stuffs her envelope. Alice drops the letter in to the mailbox. Postal Service checks for stamp and accepts snail mail.	Alice's email application or web browser submits the email message to MTS. MTS accepts email from Alice.
Transfer	Postal Service examines envelope, determines the location of Bob's mailbox, and transfers letter from post office to post office until it reaches the post office serving his neighborhood.	MTS determines location of Bob's electronic mailbox and transfers email to the part of the MTS servicing Bob.
Deliver	Bob's post office delivers snail mail to Bob's personal mailbox.	MTS delivers mail to Bob's personal electronic mailbox.
Retrieve	Bob walks, wheels, hops, or skips over to get his mail.	Bob either starts his dedicated email application or web browser to retrieve his email.
Read	Bob opens envelope, pulls out letter, and reads it.	Bob selects the email message in his personal electronic mailbox, displays it, and reads it.

Formats

Figure 2-1 shows the two parts of a snail mail that Alice sends to Bob and Matt. The first part of the snail mail is the letter, which includes: Alice's name, address, and signature; Bob's name and address; Matt's name; the date Alice wrote the letter; the subject of the letter; and the body of the letter. The second part of the snail mail is the envelope which, unfortunately for Alice, is the regular envelope and not the flying variety from Hogwarts. Alice's envelope includes a stamp, her name and address, and Bob's name and address. You should notice that some of the fields appear in both the letter and on the envelope. Also shown in Figure 2-1 is Bob's reply to Alice.

Figure 2-2 shows a simple version of Alice's email message. You'll see that the information used in email is similar to the information used in snail mail. It shows what Alice sends and what Bob and Matt receive. Like snail mail, email has two main parts, an envelope and the content, each of which also has subparts, as described below.

Alice Adams
123 Politics Street
Washington, DC 20001
11 February 2008

Bob Burton
509 Golden Beaches
Pleasantville, CA 99999

Dear Bob,

SUBJECT: MEETING DATE AND TIME

Can we meet on Tuesday 1 April 2008?

Sincerly,

alice

Alice Adams

CC: Matt

Bob Burton
509 Golden Beaches
Pleasantville, CA 99999

Alice Adams
123 Politics Street
Washington, DC 20001

Dear Alice,

SUBJECT: RE: MEETING DATE AND TIME

Sure we can. How about 1 p.m.? I've also included a map to get you to our offices.

Sincerly,

Bob

CC: Matt

Alice Adams
123 Politics Street
Washington, DC 20001

Stamp

Bob Burton
509 Golden Beaches
Pleasantville, CA 99999

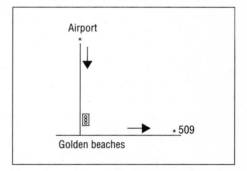

Bob Burton
509 Golden Beaches
Pleasantville, CA 99999

Stamp

Alice Adams
123 Politics Street
Washington, DC 20001

Figure 2-1 Snail Mail: Letters and Envelopes

```
Date: Mon, 11 Feb 2008 09:55:06 -0400
From: Alice <aadams@washington.dc.us>
Subject: Meeting Date and Time
To: Bob <bburton@pleasantville.ca.us>
Cc: Matt <mrogers@pleasantville.ca.us>
Message-ID: <1234@washington.dc.us>

Bob,

Can we meet on Tuesday 1 April 2008?

Alice
```

```
Received: from 123.123.12.1  (EHLO
washington.dc.us) (123.123.12.1)
by pleasantville.ca.us with SMTP; Mon,
11 Feb 2008 09:55:07 -0400
Date: Mon, 11 Feb 2008 09:55:06 -0400
From: Alice <aadams@washington.dc.us>
Subject: Meeting Date and Time
To: Bob <bburton@pleasantville.ca.us>
Cc: Matt <mrogers@pleasantville.ca.us>
Message-ID: <1234@washington.dc.us>

Bob,

Can we meet on Tuesday 1 April 2008?

Alice
```

Figure 2-2 Alice's Message

Envelope.   The email envelope is composed of fields that are mostly behind the scenes, but they are the workhorse fields that make email go. Envelope fields are used by the MTS to get the email from Alice to Bob and Matt, and they are a combination of data passed in protocol commands and fields in the email message. Alice, Bob, and Matt do not see the email envelope; it is usually removed (or hidden) by the email application in the same way that a secretary might remove the envelope from executive correspondence. The email envelope has two parts:

The protocol commands (see the next section for more information). Those that are part of the envelope are MAIL FROM: and RCPT TO:. They are defined in [RFC2821]. MAIL FROM: provides the sender information and RCPT TO: provides the recipient information. The information passed in the commands is normally derived from the message's content.

Two envelope fields, Received: and Return-Path:, from [RFC2822] are added to the message as the message moves around the MTS. These are akin to every person in the postal service marking Alice's letter as it moved through their possession from Washington to Los Angeles (i.e., just like the United Parcel Service).

NOTE Some argue that the design of email should have a clean break between the envelope and content fields. We will leave that argument for the zealots and focus on more important things. We do, however, note that some information is repeated in both the envelope and content.

Content.   The email content is the information Alice wants to send to Bob and Matt, and it all goes in the DATA: command defined in [RFC2821].

The content has a header and a body, but technically only the header is required:

Header.   The header is composed of fields that provide a service, user information, and transaction information. From [RFC2822], the header fields are listed below. `Date:` and `From:` or `Sender:` are the only required fields, but typically most emails also include `To:`, `Subject:`, and `Message-ID:`. Many mail applications only show the `Date:`, `From:`, `To:`, `Cc:`, and `Subject:` fields, and Bob would need to hunt in his email program to see the other fields, because most people really do not care about the other fields.

`Date:` Alice uses this field to indicate the date and time at which she considered the message complete and ready for the MTS. That is the date and time when she hit send. This field is almost always filled in by Alice's email program.

`From:` Alice uses this field to indicate that she authored the message. In our example there is only Alice, but more than one author can be included.

`Sender:` Doug, if he was acting on behalf of Alice, would use this field to indicate that he and not Alice sent the message. In most cases, Alice is both author and sender, then only the `From:` field is used.

`Reply-To:` Alice uses this field to indicate where replies should be sent. For example, if Alice cannot be bothered to read the replies, she puts her assistant Doug's email address here. In most cases, this field is absent and replies are sent to the email address in the `From:` value.

`To:` Alice uses this field to indicate the primary recipient(s) of the message, which in this case is Bob.

`Cc:` Alice uses this field to indicate the carbon copy recipients (sometimes called a courtesy copy), which in our case is Matt.

`Bcc:` Alice uses this field to indicate the blind carbon copy recipient(s), those the other recipients do not know about; in this case there are none.

`Message-ID:` Alice uses this field to indicate a unique message identifier that refers to a particular version of a particular message. This field is almost always filed in by Alice's email program when she hits send;

`In-Reply-To:` If Alice is responding to a previous message, she uses this field to indicate the unique message identifier of that message, in this case there are none.

References: Alice uses this field to refer to a thread of conversations; in this case there are none.

Subject: Alice uses this field to indicate what the message is about. If Bob replies to Alice's message, his email program will add "Re:" to the beginning of the subject provided by Alice.

Comments: Alice uses this field to indicate additional comments on the contents of the message; in this case there are none.

Keywords: Alice uses this field to add words she thinks Bob might find useful; in this case there are none.

Resent-Date:, Resent-From:, Resent-Sender:, Resent-To:, Resent-Cc:, Resent-Bcc:, and Resent-Message-ID: These fields are added by Alice if she has to resend the message to Bob and Matt. These fields are almost always filled in by Alice's email program when she hits send.

Body.   The body, which is optional, is either a text message or a structured message.

Text.   This is limited to the ASCII characters minus the Carriage Return (CR) and Line Feed (LF).

Structured messages.   These use the Multipurpose Internet Mail Extensions (MIME) standards [RFC2045-2049]. MIME has three main features. First it defines the encoding for arbitrary data in plaintext, which is sometimes referred to as ASCII Armor. Second, it allows multipart messages, which allows you to have text, video, audio, and other attachment types in one message. Third, message type indicators, which allow email applications to determine whether they support the attachment type. Appendix C provides a detailed explanation of ASCII Armor. Figure 2-3 shows Bob's reply message, which is a multipart message.

The RFCs referenced in this section have many formatting and processing rules, and they should be consulted if you are going to write code for an email program. The general rule in these implementations, though, is to be liberal in what you receive and conservative in what you send. This philosophy helps various implementations interoperate.

Commands

Email protocol commands are used to move the message around the MTS much like the postal workers move snail mail around the postal system. Email commands (i.e., the email system language) are defined by the Simple Mail Transfer Protocol (SMTP) [RFC2821]. SMTP involves an SMTP client that makes requests of an SMTP server and the SMTP server responding to the request. SMTP is all about SMTP clients asking SMTP servers to transmit their messages. SMTP servers can become SMTP clients as they transmit the message through a network of SMTP servers. The protocol commands are:

EHLO or HELO: Asserts to the SMTP server the identity of the SMTP client.

MAIL FROM: Tells the SMTP server the source of the email message.

RCPT TO: Tells the SMTP server the destination of the email message. If there is more than one recipient, then multiple commands are issued.

DATA: Provides the email message content.

RESET: Aborts the current transaction with the SMTP server.

VERIFY: Asks the SMTP server to confirm a user or mailbox.

EXPN: Asks the SMTP server to confirm a mailing list, and if it does, to return the membership of that list.

HELP: Asks the SMTP server to send helpful information to the SMTP client.

NOOP: Asks that the SMTP server send an OK reply.

QUIT: Tells the SMTP server to send an OK reply and then close the transmission channel.

```
Date: Mon, 11 Feb 2008 09:57:06 -0400

From:  Bob <bburton@pleasantville.ca.us>
To: Alice <alice@washington.dc.us>
Cc: Matt <matt@pleasantville.ca.us>
Subject: Re: Meeting Date and Time
Message-ID: <5678@pleasantville.ca.us>
In-Reply-To: <1234@washington.dc.us>
MIME-Version: 1.0
Content-Type: multipart/mixed;
        boundary="notice the boundry"

--notice the boundary
Content-type: text/plain; charset=us-ascii

Alice,

Sure we can. How about 1 p.m.?  I've also
included a map to get you to our offices.

Bob
--notice the boundary
Content-type: image/jpeg

Converted map picture goes here
--notice the boundary
```

Figure 2-3 Bob's Reply

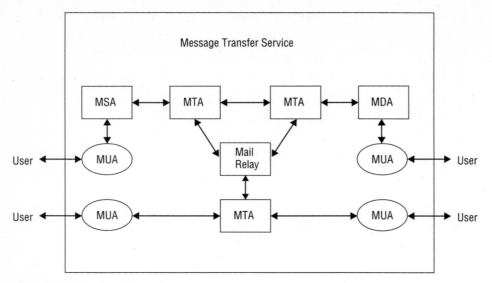

Figure 2-4 Email Architecture

Response Codes. These tell the SMTP client the status of the previous command. Every command results in a response code, which is a three-digit code. The digits provide an increasing level of granularity: the first digital indicates whether the response is good, bad, or incomplete, the second digit provides information on where the error occurred, and the third digit is reserved for the most granular error.

Figure 2-4 provides an illustration of a successful SMTP client-server interaction. In Listing 2-1, S stands for server and C stands for client. Response Codes returned are: 220 SMTP server ready for SMTP commands, 250 SMTP server successfully completed request, 254 SMTP server waiting for DATA: command, and 221 SMTP server is closing transmission channel.

```
S: 220 pleasantville.ca.us
C: EHLO washington.dc.us
S: 250-pleasantville.ca.us greets washington.dc.us
S: 250-8BITMIME
S: 250-SIZE
S: 250-DSN
S: 250 HELP
C: MAIL FROM: <aadams@washington.dc.us>
S: 250 sender <aadams@washington.dc.us> OK
C: RCPT TO:<bburton@pleasantville.ca.us>
S: 250 recipient <bburton@pleasantville.ca.us> OK
C: RCPT TO:<mrogers@pleasantville.ca.us>
S: 250 recipient <mrogers@pleasantville.ca.us> OK
```

Listing 2-1 SMTP client-server interaction

```
C: DATA
S: 354 Start mail input; end with <CRLF>.<CRLF>
C: Date: Mon, 11 Feb 2008 09:55:06 -0400
C: From: Alice <aadams@washington.dc.us>
C: Subject: Meeting Date and Time
C: To: Bob <bburton@pleasantville.ca.us>
C: Cc: Matt <mrogers@pleasantville.ca.us>
C: Message-ID: <1234@washington.dc.us>
C:
C: Bob,
C:
C: Can we meet on Tuesday 1 April 2008?
C:
C: Alice
C: .
S: OK
C: QUIT
S: 221 pleasantville.ca.us closing transmission channel
```

Listing 2-1 *(continued)*

Also note that other commands have been defined, but they are no longer used (e.g., SEND, SOML, and SAML). Further, commands can be defined for bilateral use. You may have also noticed the 250 response codes from the server. These are SMTP service extensions [RFC1869]. The full list of SMTP service extensions are found in [IANAM]. They are:

- SIZE [RFC1870] indicates the maximum message the SMTP server supports.

- 8BITMIME [RFC1652] indicates the SMTP server supports relaying SMTP content body consisting of text containing octets outside of the US-ASCII character set.

- DSN [RFC1891] indicates the SMTP server supports Delivery Status Notifications (DSN).

Mail Transfer System Architecture

The MTS can be characterized as transactional store-and-forward message exchange architecture. Just like in the postal service, there are different entities that perform the steps in the email process (see Table 2-2). There is the email application that Alice uses to compose her message, but depending on which email application she is using, it may or may not include an SMTP client to submit to the MTS. Once the MTS has the email message, it has delivery responsibility for the message. The MTS delivers it to Bob and Matt, but if not able to do so directly, it sends the message on to the next SMTP server and so on until the reaches an SMTP server that does have delivery responsibility for the recipient's mailbox. To abstract out the MTS functionality, the following terms are used:

WARNING Do not get hung up on trying to split the functions between the MUA and MTA. Even the interoperability standard, [RFC2821], which defines the MTS indicates "the implied boundaries between MUAs and MTAs often do not accurately match common, and conforming, practices with Internet mail." If those authors are not hung up on this split, then you shouldn't be either.

Message User Agent (MUA).   This provides access to the MTS for users and are the sources and targets of email. Users can be humans like Alice, Bob, and Matt or nonhuman like sensors. Users are categorized in three ways:

Originators.   These are the sources of email messages. In this example, Alice is the originator.

Recipients.   These are the destination of email messages. In this example, both Bob and Matt are recipients.

Senders.   These are the sources of email messages. They are a special case in which they did the sending but not the composition of the email. There is no sender in our example.

Message Transfer Agent (MTA).   These submit, transfer, and deliver email. MTAs implement SMTP. Implementers have made special case MTAs that partially support the functions:

Message Submission Agent (MSA).   These accept email from MUAs and submit it to the MTS.

Message Delivery Agent (MDA).   These deliver email from the MTS to the MUAs.

Mail Relay.   These transfer the email from MTA to MTA. It does not deliver the message the final MTA.

Mail Gateway (not shown).   These act as an interface to a separate MTS that support different formats and transport mechanisms.

There are number of ways to construct an MTS. If there are limited numbers of users with no need to interact with the outside world, there's no need for an MSA or MDA and perhaps a single MTA would work. For large systems that interact with the outside world, an MSA is a good idea because the MSA can implement security policies, which we will get to later. For a more detail analysis of an MTS architecture, we suggest Marshall Rose's book *The Internet Message* [ROSE92].

SECURITY OBSERVATIONS

Regardless of how the email system is implemented there are a few observations that need to be made:

◆ The email envelope is seen by every MTA (regardless of type) that handles the email message.

◆ The email headers are seen by every MTA (regardless of type) that handles the email message. The `Date:`, `From:`, `To:`, `CC:`, and `Subject:` are available to the MTAs.

◆ The user's mailbox is on an MTA and at some point the mailbox will contain email.

The importance of all these observations will be explained in the security chapters.

Emailing

The email steps in Table 2-2 rely on many different peer-to-peer pairings (i.e., hops) to get the email in, around, and out of the MTS. There are also other interoperability standards that are necessary to get access to the network. The following highlights the protocols that the email peer-to-peer pairings use:

Network.   Internet Protocol (IP) and Transmission Control Protocol (TCP)

Network Access.   Dynamic Host Configuration Protocol (DHCP)

Address Translation.   Domain Name Service (DNS)

Submit, Transfer, and Deliver.   Simple Mail Transfer Protocol (SMTP) and Enhanced SMTP (ESMTP)

Retrieve.   Post Office Protocol (POP) or Internet Mail Access Protocol (IMAP)

Alice is now going to compose an email, send it to Bob, and copy Matt (i.e., make Matt a carbon copy recipient). A scenario is provided for each of the two most common email applications, email client and webmail.

Email Client

Assuming that Alice has opened her email application and drafted her email message, she now needs to submit the email message, but before she can do that her computer needs to have an IP address to use the network. Her computer's DHCP client automatically obtains an IP address from the DHCP server operated by her Internet service provider (ISP). Once she has an IP address she can use SMTP/ESMTP to submit the email message. Normally, she is submitting the email to an MSA that is operated by her ISP, which will check that she is allowed to submit email. ISPs do not want to be the source of spam, so they generally check that the email message is coming from one of their customers. The MSA will often pass all email downstream to a downstream MTA for further handling. The MTA will use DNS client to obtain Bob and Matt's email host IP addresses, and then use SMTP/ESMTP to transfer the message to one or more MTAs that are responsible for Bob and Matt. The MTA serving Bob and MTA serving Matt will transfer the message to the appropriate MDAs for delivery. Bob and Matt will use the same process to get an IP address and then use POP or IMAP to retrieve the email from their MDA.

Webmail

For webmail, Alice needs to obtain an IP address; again DHCP is used. Alice will use a browser to open navigate to her provider's website using HTTP; she will click to open her web browser and get to the compose mail interface. She will type the email message and upload it with HTTP. When she is done she hits send and the web server uses SMTP/ESMTP to submit the email to her MSA. At the receiving end, Bob and Matt use their web browsers to access a web server that is usually running in the same computer room as their MDA. The web browser and server act together to be a distributed MUA.

CHAPTER 3

Security Fundamentals

Chapter 2 provided some security observations and an explanation of the insecure Mail Transfer Service (MTS). You're probably ready to learn how to secure your email system; however, before we tell you about email security, we need to help you figure out which security services are necessary and relevant in an email environment by asking you some questions. To get into the right frame of mind, you might need to put on your thinking cap and take a conservative viewpoint when you're thinking about these questions and their answers.

Here are the kinds of questions you should be asking yourself, in no particular order:

- How valuable is your information?
- Who wants to read your email?
- Where can they get at your email in the network?
- How can they read your email?
- What can they do to the MTS?
- Can someone else damage my reputation by sending email that appears to come from me?

What's with all the questions? Answering questions like these can help you determine your *risk*, and the process itself is called a *security assessment*. Risk is calculated by determining *threats* and *vulnerabilities*, so that you can determine the appropriate approach for your security solution. Just as you wouldn't protect a penny — unless it's a buffalo penny — with an army of security guards, likewise you may not need a lot of security if your MTS is on your desktop and you aren't connected to the Internet. But it's more likely that your email goes over the Internet and that you sometimes use a wireless network. If this sounds like you, well, then you really ought to start asking yourself these questions. For more detailed examination of risk management concepts we suggest Andy Jones and Debi Ashenden's book *Risk Management for Computer Security* [RISK] and for security assessment we suggest Douglas Landoll's book *Performing an Information Security Risk Assessment* [ASSESS].

We can't really help you determine the value of your information. It's hard to put a value on business-related information or personal communications, but you might be able to guess at the value. Ask yourself, how much time went into the development of your business plan, chip design, or screenplay? Remember from Chapter 2, that email heading fields (for example, From, To, and Subject), contents, and attachments are all available to prying eyes from the outside world in an insecure MTS.

In this chapter, we'll help you answer the previous questions, and then we'll describe some security services and mechanisms that you can use to protect your email. Taken together, the technical term for these services and mechanisms is *countermeasures*.

Who Wants to Read Your Email?

As long as there has been mail, there has been somebody trying to read it. Just envision diplomatic correspondences between heads of state, and you get the idea. As Bruce Schneier pointed out in [SCHN00], there are all kinds of organizations and individuals — we'll call them *attackers* in this book — that want to read your email. To be honest, the attackers that Bruce described in 1995 haven't changed much, except that there are now more of them and they are more sophisticated (see Figure 3-1).

The amount of damage an attacker can cause varies with their individual skills, intelligence, motivation, and resources. Also, attackers can either be passive or active. *Passive attackers* just listen, while *active attackers*, as its name implies, do something to the emails. This "something" will be discussed in later sections. We'll begin by describing the different kinds of attackers to be found when dealing with email security.

Governments

Governments are arguably at the apex of predators. They have smart, specialized, and dedicated employees backed by enormous sums of money. They are motivated to protect the nation's interests. Governments also have one thing that other attackers lack: the authority to be attackers.

One national interest is to protect the nation from attack by another state, and this involves monitoring other countries' military capabilities. The five-cent term for this is state-sponsored espionage, but most of us just call it spying.

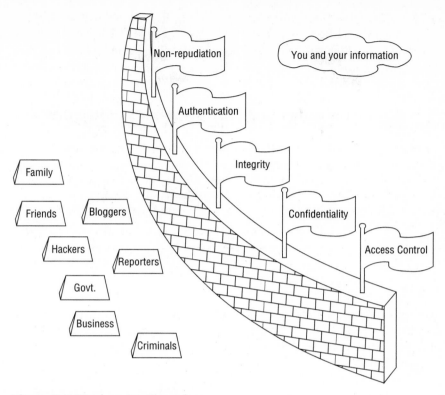

Figure 3-1 Attackers Are Everywhere

You can pretty much bet that if a country has a military capability, whether it's a developing country or an already highly developed country, some part of that military capability is spying on the capabilities of its neighbors. Nations with a larger reach look farther afield, and their spy agencies are made famous in the movies (and sometimes the news): Russia had the KGB, the United States has the NSA, Great Britain has MI6, and France has DGSE. We don't want to pick on any one country in particular, but the point is, do not be a fool; they do exist, and they are out there looking and listening and reading email.

So now you're thinking "I'm not in the military; why would I care about governments spying on me?" Another national interest, which governments do not openly discuss, is to spy on businesses from other countries to gain competitive advantage. That is, one country might spy on companies based in another country and then give the information to a similar company based in their own country. While government might not openly discuss this policy, there are many unsubstantiated stories. We'll let you Google for one about your favorite government's spy agency and its industrial espionage exploits.

Yet another national interest is to maintain law and order, which sometimes means monitoring citizens. Obviously, in a perfect world, the monitored citizens would all be criminals, but because we don't live in a perfect world, you could unwittingly be targeted. Stop to think about the number of state, local, and federal agencies involved in law enforcement. With a court order, in most cases, these agencies can get access to just about anything, including your email.

FREEDOM

In countries where freedom of speech is severely limited by the government, you need to think about keeping your email private from prying eyes to avoid repercussions. Depending on which country you are in, you could find yourself censured, in cuffs and heading to jail, or with your head on a chopping block. Needless to say we support free speech, and we thought it important enough to highlight this issue here.

Businesses

Businesses spy on one another just like countries do, although they call it market research or business intelligence. For a good read on this topic, we recommend Adam Peneberg and Marc Barry's book *Spooked: Espionage in Corporate America* [SPOOK]. Regardless of what it's called, the whole point of "business intelligence" is to collect information about competitors. Most businesses are legitimate and ask consumers, vendors, and clients to fill out surveys, but there are certainly less legitimate businesses out there that stoop to attacking the email communications of a competitor.

Why do they do this? Competitive advantage. Think about it. Your company just spent $500,000 on developing a product, brand, or customer list. If another company stole the plans, tagline, or list that you just emailed to your coworker, then they would only be out the cost of the attack in order to obtain the very same information.

Sometimes the value of information comes from the damage that could be done to one's reputation if it is not adequately protected. Lawyers need to keep their legal arguments safe from the opposition. Medical professionals are required by law to protect medical records. The bottom line: make the bad guys work hard to steal your information. It is probably worth spending some money to secure your email.

Businesses spy on their employees too. Sometimes the purpose of the monitoring is to enforce the proper use of company assets, but there are cases where companies have done much, much more. Remember the HP board room scandal that forced the resignation of the CEO and other top officials [HP]? The CEO wanted to figure out who was leaking board discussions, so she ordered electronic surveillance of board members, which included "bugging" emails.

COKE AND PEPSI RIVALRY

How much would Pepsi like to know Coca-Cola's secret formula? Most of us would think that would be invaluable to Pepsi. Well we'd be very wrong. In 2006, a Coke employee stole Coke's crown jewel and tried to sell it to Pepsi, but Pepsi did the right thing and called the FBI. The conspirators were arrested, charged, and found guilty [DOJ]. We are glad to see that some companies have enough integrity to keep them from perpetrating these nasty attacks on their competition. Sadly, not all companies have high integrity.

Criminals

It should come as no surprise that criminals want to read email for easy, ill-gotten gains. They have moved from their brick-and-mortar environment to the world of ecommerce, just like legit businesses have. Sending your personal identification numbers (PINs), Social Security number (SSN), and passwords over an insecure MTS is not only dangerous, it's downright foolish. A book to read on the topic is Judith Collin's *Investigating Identity Theft: A Guide for Businesses, Law Enforcement, and Victims* [IDTFT]. These criminals often use a technique referred to as *phishing*, whereby the attacker tricks the email recipient into divulging personal information about him- or herself. For more information on phishing, we recommend Rachael Lininger and Russell Dean Vines' book *Phishing: Cutting the Identity Theft Line* [PHISH].

Criminals do not just go after personal information; they are just as likely to be targeting your business to learn information about what's in that next shipment coming from or going to your facility. I bet Jimmy Conway from the movie *Goodfellas* would rather hijack a truck full of high-end electronics than a truck full of Styrofoam pellets; I mean forgettaboutit. Likewise, I bet he would've loved to have gotten his hands on your customer database with names, credit card numbers, expiration dates, and addresses, which you just sent to your coworker to review.

Hackers

Some might consider hackers a subset of criminals, but the difference is that these attackers have always been part of the ecommerce world. They wear different-colored hats: white hats are good, black hats are bad, and gray hats are both at different times. Sometimes they hack systems for financial gain, sometimes for notoriety, and sometimes just because it's cool. You can even read on of those "Dummy" books and hack like Kevin Beaver and Stuart McClure's book *Hacking For Dummies* [HACK]. Hackers have penetrated systems just to expose insecurity numerous times; they publish the account names and passwords just to prove it can be done. Hackers penetrated the cell phone of Paris Hilton, and then posted her cell phone address book, making many celebrity phone numbers and email addresses public. This was certainly not done for financial gain. Needless to say, with a little more security planning, this might be harder for them to pull off.

Reporters and Bloggers

Old school reporters and new school bloggers want to do the same thing: publish information. Their credo is "freedom of the press," and while reporters do sometimes exercise restraint, they probably wouldn't hesitate to publish an email that had multiple sources to back it up. Bloggers may have even less restraint and print just about anything. Imagine what would happen if an email describing the personal exploits of a public figure got out; it would get published no doubt. If you need proof, remember Michael Brown, the former head of FEMA, and his emails begging to quit [BROWN], and the uproar it caused.

Friends and Family Members

If busybody, control freak, nosy, or jealous are adjectives that have been applied to any of your friends or family members, you may have to worry about them reading your email. They might not have the resources of any of the other attackers, but they may be more motivated. You probably don't need to protect your tee times from your significant other, but if you're complaining about your father-in-law or trying to surprise your significant other with a vacation, then you probably have something to worry about.

Where They Can Read Your Email

There are a couple of places an attacker can get at your email:

- **As Alice types it:**   Eve, our evil attacker, can simply look over Alice's shoulder. She could also be in the building across the street with a pair of binoculars, looking through a pinhole camera in the A/C vent, or by installing a keystroke logger. This book does not address physical security, but it pays to think about who is around and which way your screen faces.
- **As Alice sends it:**   Eve can monitor the network, which we will address in the very next section.
- **As it traverses the MTS:**   Eve could own an MTS and be able to watch every message as it passes through.
- **As Bob retrieves it:**   Eve can monitor the network, which we will address in the very next section.
- **As Bob reads it:**   Eve could glance at Bob's screen as she walks by or Bob could leave a copy on the printer for Eve to intercept.

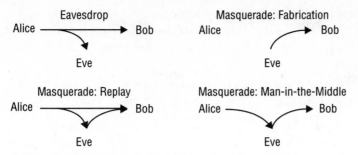

Figure 3-2 Eavesdrop and masquerade attacks

How They Can Read Your Email

Now you know where criminals can attack your email. Here are the two main types of attacks against insecure email, as shown in Figure 3-2.

Eavesdrop

This is a passive attack where Eve collects, intercepts, snoops, or sniffs communications unbeknownst to the communicating parties (Alice, Bob, and Matt). This is surprisingly easy to do with a $29.95 program off the Internet. The program works by turning your computer, which normally only listens for its own network traffic, into a capture device that collects all the data traversing the network. If you are furiously typing your email to send it before you get on a plane from an airport hotspot, then when you hit send, Eve could simply capture everything you send. Once the message has been collected, an *unauthorized disclosure* has occurred. Additionally, Eve can perform *traffic analysis* on the message, because she knows all the message's originators and recipients. By watching the email over time, Eve learns who you talk to, and how often you talk to them.

Masquerade

This is an active attack where Eve impersonates one or more of the communicating parties, and which is sometimes called *spoofing*. Obviously, this is only a successful attack if the communicating parties do not detect the attack, but if successful, Eve can insert herself between Alice and Bob and intercept the message. Masquerade attacks can be categorized in three ways:

■ **Fabrication:** This is the generic masquerade attack where Eve originates the message for Bob acting as Alice or for Alice acting as Bob. This attack is as simple as changing the "FROM:" address in the email message header field (many ISPs now check for this).

- **Replay:**   A specific type of masquerade attack where Eve collects messages (i.e., she eavesdrops) and then resends them. This can be done by capturing the email asking for $50 dollars and then resending your request 50 more times.

- **Man-in-the-middle:**   A specific type of masquerade attack where Eve has fooled Alice into thinking she is Bob and Bob into thinking she is Alice.

What Else Can They Do to the MTS?

The one other major attack that Eve can perform is referred to as a *denial of service* (DoS) attack or *distributed denial of service* (DDoS) attack. The intent is to foul up the MTS somehow and interrupt the system to keep it from doing its job. With DDoS, Eve uses many computers to mount the attack. Shutting down one of the computers has little impact; the attack continues. There are two main ways to do this:

Hacking.   Eve somehow, some way, some time gets into the computer that runs the MTS or the network connecting the MTS to the rest of the world, and then she makes it stop working. Maybe Eve was eavesdropping on the network administrator and captured his or her username and password, thereby allowing unfettered access to the SMTP server program files and configuration.

Flooding.   Eve sends so many requests or responses to the MTS that it overwhelms the SMTP server either slowing the process down or stopping it altogether. Eve may queue up thousands of computers, each sending thousands of messages at the same time to the SMTP server.

How You Can Stop Them

Hopefully, the last couple of sections have not depressed you. Be assured, all is not lost. You, Alice, Bob, and anybody else who wants to secure their email have many available countermeasures to stop would be attackers. Next, we'll describe the *security services* (or properties) that can counteract the attacks we have described, and then describe some basic and cryptographic tools that implement these services. These cryptographic tools are called *security mechanisms*. As you'll see, some of the service names correspond to the mechanism that is often used to implement them, but more often they correspond to the protection that is provided.

Security Services

Some would say that all of the security services are fundamental, but we're going to divide them into two categories: fundamental and derivative. Fundamental security servers are those that are required to make all the other services work in a secure manner. Derivative services are those services that are made possible by the fundamental services. We're not going to try to list all the possible derivative services, because depending on whom you talk to almost everything is a derivative service. [ISO74982] is considered by many as the definitive source for the security service definitions, so we'll use it as our reference. That standard defines an abstract security architecture for communications systems and describes security services and mechanisms. The thing to remember about these services is that you may not need all of these services all of the time, but you need most of them at one time or another.

Fundamental Services

There are few types of fundamental services, including access control, authentication, confidentiality, integrity, and non-repudiation. We'll define each of these in this section.

Access Control

Access control is a service that controls and logs access to systems, resources, and applications and protects against their unauthorized use. While access control makes the decision, which is called an *access control decision*, and provides access to the system, resource, and application, for the decision to be a "good" decision the input ought to include an authenticated identity to ensure that only those authorized gain access.

Authentication

Authentication is a service that protects against masquerade attacks. *Peer entity authentication* corroborates a user identity and *data origin authentication* corroborates the source of data. One integral mechanism for this service is *digital signatures*, which we'll describe later on in the chapter.

WARNING Authentication by itself does not protect against unauthorized modification. Additionally, it does not protect against replay attacks.

Identity authentication.   There are two ways to authenticate identities: unilateral or mutual authentication. In *unilateral authentication* only one party verifies the identity (e.g., the SMTP server authenticates the SMTP client). In *mutual authentication* both parties verify each other.

> **NOTE** Identification and authentication (I&A) are often discussed as one service because it is normally of little use to have an unauthenticated identity. Technically, identification could be defined as a separate service where the identities could be authenticated or unauthenticated.

Confidentiality

Confidentiality is the service that protects against unauthorized disclosure. Confidentiality can be applied to data in transit and storage. It protects the communication channel between clients and servers, protects against passive attackers, and, depending on a number of factors, from active attackers as well. Don't worry, we will address these various factors as we come to them. Encryption, a cryptographic tool described later, implements this service.

Integrity

Integrity is the service that protects communications from unauthorized, undetectable modification. One-way hash functions, a cryptographic mechanism described later, are used to implement this service.

Non-repudiation

Non-repudiation is the service that prevents either the sender or receiver from denying the content of a transmitted message. When the recipient has proof that the sender sent the content, this is called *non-repudiation with proof of origin*. When the sender has proof that the recipient has the content, then it is called *non-repudiation with proof of delivery*. A lot of parts are needed to implement either non-repudiation service, but the fundamental mechanism necessary to implement non-repudiation is digital signatures.

> **WARNING** Non-repudiation can be a volatile subject for some and has probably consumed hundreds of man hours debating what non-repudiation means and how it can be implemented. The basic point to remember is that anything and everything can be repudiated. To determine whether the claim is actually repudiated, it is up to an arbiter or judge to sift through the proof presented by each party and the relevant facts to decide on a claim. The point of the non-repudiation service is to generate this proof.

Derivative Services

There are few types of derivative services, including accountability, authorization, availability, and notary. We'll define each of these in this section.

Accountability

Accountability is a service that ensures that a user's actions can be accurately linked to that user and that holds that user responsible for their actions. Accountability uses logging tools to store the information about the actions.

Authorization

Authorization is the service that grants a user's request to perform a requested action. It is invoked as part of the Access Control.

> **WARNING** Authentication and authorization are often confused; they do not provide the same service. Just because a user has been identified doesn't mean they are authorized to perform every function.

Availability

Availability is a service that ensures a system, resource, or application is available upon request to authorized users. This service can only really be provided if access control is implemented.

Notary

Notary is a service — provided by a trusted third party — that can attest to the origin, destination, and integrity of a particular content. Additionally, the notary service can attest to the time of origin and receipt.

Cryptographic Mechanisms

Cryptographic mechanisms are important tools; they are part of your arsenal against attackers. This section introduces the cryptographic mechanisms, while Chapter 4 will provide a more detailed explanation.

Encryption

The best way to make sure that your communications are not disclosed to unauthorized individuals is to not talk to anyone, but this really isn't very practical. To send communications without fear of disclosure, you can use an encryption algorithm. Encryption algorithms vary in complexity, but the basic concept is that the message is scrambled so that only the communicating parties can unscramble the message.

Digital Signatures

One mechanism used to implement the authentication security service is the digital signature algorithm, which is the digital equivalent of a wet signature that Alice applied to the message in Figure 2-1. The process uses public key cryptography, and it relies on the basic concept of keeping a private key to yourself while providing wide distribution to the corresponding public key.

> **NOTE** One of the primary themes in this book is the protection of private keys. If you cannot keep the key private, then the basis for most of the security is lost.

One-Way Hash Functions

One mechanism to implement the integrity security service is the symmetric integrity function. These functions produce a fingerprint of the data, and any change in the data will yield a different fingerprint. It is astronomically difficult to find two email messages that have the same fingerprint. So, if the fingerprint is not as expected, you'll know you are being attacked.

Basic Security Tools

Cryptographic mechanisms are very powerful, but they are not the only tool in your toolbox. The following set of basic security tools can be employed in conjunction with cryptography to better protect your email. Luckily for you, many of these services are already built into security protocols that we will describe later.

Access Control Lists

Access Control Lists (ACLs) are lists that can be used to check a user's identity before access to a system, resource, or application is granted. Depending on the policy of the system, resource, or application, the identity presented may be a username and password or a piece of data digitally signed by the user. The service implementing the ACL then authenticates the user's identity, evaluates the user's authorizations (for example, Alice is allowed to send email through this server because she has an account here), provides access to the system, resource, or application (like email), and logs positive and negative outcomes of these events.

Fake Traffic

If you have encrypted your email or the connection on which your email flows, attackers may still be able to determine how much email is being sent and then possibly determine where your email is going. One countermeasure for this type of passive attack is to send dummy network traffic on the connection or to the recipients. If the connection always has the same amount of traffic or if the recipient always gets the same amount of email, an attacker cannot determine whom is talking to who, or how often.

Logs

Logs are linked to accountability. If you don't keep track of who is doing what and when, then it's hard to figure out what went wrong and what or who might have caused it to go wrong. Obviously, these logs are very important and need to be protected (just like your email), and at a minimum they should be stored in an integrity-protected file.

Nonces

Nonces are a technique that we can use to deter attackers from replaying messages. The concept is simple: include some information in the message that is sent that must be repeated in the message that is returned. If the nonces do not match, ignore the response. This technique is sometimes called *cookies*.

Signed Receipts

One way to make sure that the recipient got the message is to ask explicitly for a signed receipt. If the signed receipt includes some information from the original message, then the originator of the first message will know the recipient actually got the intended message. If the receipt isn't signed, then it could be Eve masquerading as Bob sending the unsigned receipt.

Sequence Numbering

Sequence numbers are a technique for receivers to determine whether messages arrived in order or whether the message sequence has been modified. This is important if a process requires a particular order of messages.

Time

A time server provides an indication of the time. It can be used to prove at a later date that the message existed before a particular time or that an action occurred at a particular time.

More Attacks

Just when you thought it was safe to send email, your adversaries developed a new set of attacks, all of which are based on the tools you just employed. This cat and mouse game will never end, because it's really no different than bank robbers developing new techniques when banks get better vaults. So, get used to it. Assuming that you have implemented some cryptographic mechanisms, your attackers will no doubt employ cryptanalysis, which is well beyond the scope of this book but it is discussed in David Kahn's book *The Codebreakers: The Story of Secret Writing* [KAHN]. We will, however, explain three different kinds of cryptography — specifically symmetric, symmetric integrity, and asymmetric — in greater detail in the next chapter. These cryptographic mechanisms will be one of your main defenses against the attacking horde.

CHAPTER 4

Cryptography Primer

This book is not about cryptography; however, you must have a fundamental understanding of cryptography to fully understand secure email. For this reason, we include this primer. For a more complete coverage of cryptography, we have a few suggestions for further study. Kahn [KAHN67] provides a remarkably complete history of cryptography, from its origins to the middle of the twentieth century. Menezes, van Oorschot, and Vanstone [MENE97] provide an encyclopedia of known techniques with an emphasis on both the secure and the practical. Schneier [SCHN96] provides a complete discussion of the applications of cryptography with a focus on engineers and computer programmers.

The word *cryptography* means hidden or secret writing. Cryptography is generally thought of as the scrambling, and the unscrambling, of private messages. A message is scrambled to keep it private; it provides *confidentiality*. Modern cryptographic techniques are also used to determine whether a message has been changed since it was created and to identify the message's sender. An unaltered message has *integrity*. Knowledge of a message's origin is *authentication*.

A *cryptographic algorithm* defines the series of steps that a sender takes to scramble a private message and the series of steps that a receiver takes to unscramble it. Most cryptographic algorithms use two inputs to scramble the message, protect its integrity, or authenticate its source. The first input is the message content, and the second is a secret value known as a *key*. There are several different types of cryptographic algorithms that are differentiated by the security services that they provide and the type of keys that they employ.

Symmetric Cryptography

In symmetric cryptography, both the sender and the receiver use the same key value. As a result, symmetric key systems are sometimes called *shared secret key systems*. When Alice wants to send a private message to Bob, she selects an encryption algorithm and a key that Bob knows. Alice encrypts the plaintext message using the encryption algorithm and the key, obtaining ciphertext. Alice sends the ciphertext to Bob. Bob uses the decryption algorithm and key to recover the plaintext from the ciphertext (see Figure 4-1).

For an attacker, Eve, to obtain the plaintext, she must guess or intercept the key. The most difficult keys to guess are random bit strings. Eve may use a computer to try all possible key values. Such a brute-force attack will take centuries on many cooperating fast computers if the key is long. To make it difficult for Eve to intercept the key during distribution, it must be encrypted during transmission. Secure key distribution of shared secret keys is a difficult task, and some of the tools needed to do it are discussed later in this chapter.

Types

There are two primary symmetric encryption algorithm types: *stream ciphers* and *block ciphers*. Stream ciphers operate on the plaintext 1 bit at a time. (A few stream algorithms operate an octet at a time, but they are not the normal case.) RC4 is a well-known stream cipher. Block ciphers operate on a group of bits called a *block*.

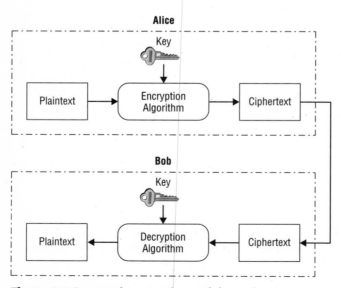

Figure 4-1 Symmetric encryption and decryption

Algorithms

The Data Encryption Standard (DES), also known as the Data Encryption Algorithm (DEA), is the most well-known symmetric block cipher. The U.S. Government made DES a standard in 1977, and many people adopted DES because the U.S. Government supported it. DES is published as FIPS PUB 46 [FIPS46] and ANSI X3.92 [X392]. It uses a 56-bit key, and encrypts a 64-bit block with each operation. Many cryptographers are concerned about the DES key length; they believe that a longer key is needed to provide security. Computing power has increased many fold since DES became a standard in 1977, and a 56-bit random key is no longer sufficient to protect against a brute-force attack [EFF98]. In plain English: do not use DES!

Using the DES encryption multiple times can increase the effective key size [TUCH79, X952] and thus its strength. Triple-DES involves the encryption with one key, followed by the decryption of the resulting ciphertext with a second key, followed by the encryption of the result with a third key. This is called *Three-Key Triple-DES*. If the same key value is used for the first and third keys, the algorithm is called *Two-Key Triple-DES*. Both Two-Key Triple-DES and Three-Key Triple-DES are significantly stronger than DES.

The *Advanced Encryption Standard* (AES) has replaced DES as the U.S. Government's symmetric cipher. Rijndeal (the author's original name for the cipher that became AES) was developed by two Belgian scientists, Dr. Joan Daemen and Dr. Vincent Rijmen. It was evaluated against a number of other algorithms, and it won an open competition held by the U.S. National Institute of Standards and Technology (NIST), based on its combination of security, memory requirements, hardware and software performance, efficiency, ease of implementation, and flexibility. AES is published in [FIPS197]. It supports key sizes of 128, 192, and 256 bits, and it has a block size of 128 bits.

HOW SECURE IS AES?

The U.S. Government is confident enough in AES that it recommends using it to protect classified information up to the TOP SECRET level, based on which key size you use [CNSS]. This is the first time a publicly available algorithm has been approved for this kind of use.

Modes

In order to encrypt arbitrary messages with a block cipher, the blocks must be processed one after another. The handling of the blocks is called the *mode of operation*. [SP800-38] defines eight common modes of operation:

- Electronic Codebook (ECB)
- Cipher Block Chaining (CBC)

- Cipher Feedback (CFB)
- Output Feedback (OFB)
- Counter (CTR)
- Cipher Based-MAC (CMAC)
- Counter with CBC-MAC (CCM)
- Galois Counter Mode (GCM)

CBC encryption is by far the most common, and it works as follows. The message is broken into a sequence of blocks, with the last block padded to create a complete block if necessary. A random block, called the *initialization vector* (IV), is then generated. Each block is XORed (that is, bitwise exclusive OR) with the ciphertext from the previous block before it is encrypted. The IV serves as the previous ciphertext block for the first plaintext block. The IV need not be kept secret. All of the encryption and decryption operations are performed with the same key. If one block obtains an error in transmission, the decryption will synchronize after two garbled blocks. When the message is decrypted, only the block that contains the transmission error and the block that follows will be garbled (see Figure 4-2).

TWO BIRDS: ONE STONE

The CCM and GCM are new. They are authenticated encryption modes, which means that the mode provides both confidentiality and authentication. They provide both of these security services by producing two outputs: the encrypted data and an authentication tag. The authentication tag can cover additional data, such as packet headers or message attributes. These modes require a large cipher block, so to date they have primarily been used with AES.

Symmetric Key Management

The trick to being successful with symmetric cryptography is to distribute the shared symmetric key without the attacker getting it too. The key is fairly small, so distributing it is easier than distributing an entire message that you want to keep private.

When Alice wants to encrypt a message for Bob, the two parties must first share the same symmetric key value. The creation, distribution, use, archive, and destruction of that key is called *key management*. If Alice wants to send the same encrypted message to multiple people she has two choices:

Individual Keys.   Alice shares a different key with each recipient. That is, Alice has one key she uses with Bob, another one she uses with Matt, another for Pat, and so on. In this case, Alice will need to separately store each key. The creation, distribution, and storage techniques must protect the keys from disclosure, and they must ensure that the keys remain associated with the correct party. If Bob's key and Matt's key are swapped in Alice's protected key storage, then Matt may be able to decrypt messages that Alice intended only for Bob.

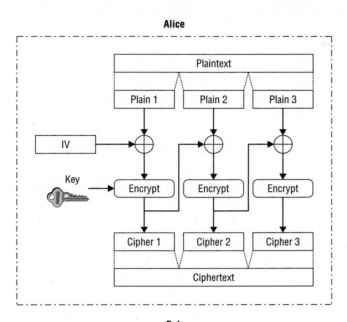

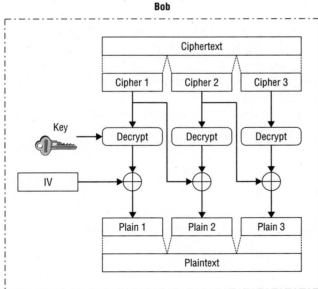

Figure 4-2 Cipher block chaining (CBC) mode

Group Keys.   Alice shares the same key with each recipient. If Alice uses a group or net key, then she does not need to store each separate key. Of course, there is no way to tell from the key whether Alice, Matt, Pat, or anybody else with the group key sent the message.

WHERE'S THE BEEF?

We can't stress enough that the security of symmetric cryptography is about keeping the key(s) secret. Also, designing a key management system that is based solely on symmetric key cryptography is challenging because you need authentication to make sure that each key goes to the right person and that it *came* from the right person. You can do this distribution through physical means, but if the keys are short lived you're going to rack up a lot of frequent flyer miles.

You can avoid many of the complexities associated with the distribution and storage of symmetric keys by using asymmetric cryptography to provide *just-in-time* key establishment, which we'll discuss shortly.

Symmetric Integrity Functions

A value that is carried with the message and used to ensure that the message sent by Alice is the message received by Bob can be called an *Integrity Check Value* (ICV), a *Message Integrity Check* (MIC), an *Authentication Tag*, or a *Message Authentication Code* (MAC). Unfortunately, all of these terms are in common use.

AES MAC uses AES encryption in CBC mode to provide integrity. An IV of all zero bits is used, which is the same as having no IV at all. Instead of transmitting the ciphertext blocks, all except the last one are discarded. Alice transmits this last block, or a portion of it, along with her message to Bob. Bob performs the same encryption on the received message. If the received MAC and the locally computed one match, Bob can be sure that the received message was not altered (see Figure 4-3).

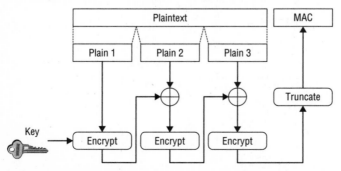

Figure 4-3 Message Authentication Code (MAC)

If Alice wants to provide confidentiality by encrypting with AES CBC, and authentication and integrity by computing an AES MAC, independent keys must be used for the two operations. Furthermore, it is generally best to compute the MAC, and then encrypt the message as well as the MAC.

Since both Alice and Bob have access to the key, either party can compute a MAC. The MAC ensures that Eve, the attacker, cannot alter the message without Bob detecting it. However, the MAC is not helpful in resolving disputes between Alice and Bob. Using the key, either Alice or Bob can generate an altered message and an associated valid MAC. Alice and Bob can each provide a different message to a judge, and both messages will have a valid MAC. In addition, the symmetric key must be provided to the judge for him or her to validate the MAC. This disclosure permits the judge to generate another altered message with a valid MAC.

One-way hash functions may also be used to provide integrity. One-way hash functions operate on an arbitrary-length-input message and produce a fixed-length output. Many functions have this property, but a one-way hash function must also have two additional properties:

- It is computationally infeasible to recreate the input message from the hash value.

- It is computationally infeasible to construct two different input messages that produce the same output hash value.

Any weakness in these properties may result in weakness in the integrity and authentication mechanisms that depend on the one-way hash function.

The Secure Hash Algorithm 1 (SHA-1) is the most well-known one-way hash function. It is published as FIPS PUB 180-1 [FIPS180a] and ANSI X9.30-2 [X9302]. It produces a 160-bit output. There have been a number of attacks against hash algorithms recently [NIST1], and current guidance recommends the U.S. Government stop using SHA-1 for applications that require collision resistance as soon as possible [NIST2]. It may be used after 2010 for limited purposes.

WARNING You can continue to use SHA-1 for as long as you'd like, but it ought to strike you as odd to ignore advice given by the people who invented the algorithm.

The replacement for SHA-1 is the SHA-2 family of one-way hash functions published as FIPS PUB 180-2 [FIPS180b]: SHA-224, and SHA-256, SHA-384, SHA-512. The new algorithms provide longer hash values for the purpose of offering integrity and authentication functions that are of comparable strength to the AES encryption algorithm.

The hash-based message authentication code (HMAC) [KRAW97, FIPS198] function is the most common method of using a shared secret, or key, with a one-way hash function for creating an integrity check value (see Figure 4-4). This method applies the one-way hash function twice.

HASH CHALLENGE

If "Hash Challenge" causes you envision two chefs from the Food Network battling it out while preparing some mouthwatering breakfast food, you'd be hungry just like me. With all the recent attacks against hash algorithms, NIST is increasingly interested in investigating other hash algorithms. They've sponsored two workshops, one in November 2005 and the other in April 2006. Their intent was to allow cryptographers to publish and discuss possible new hash algorithms. The timeline for publishing the successor to FIPS 180-2 is 2012, and NIST is planning to hold a competition for future one-way hash function standards in a manner similar to the competition that resulted in AES [NIST3]. The hash competition hasn't been formally announced yet, but in addition to the technical discussions about hashes, you can only hope they're going to have a Food Network star there to prepare some delicious breakfasts for you.

Alice has the same problem with symmetric integrity functions as she does with symmetric cryptography; namely, when Alice wants to MAC a message being sent to Bob, the two parties must first share the same symmetric key value. They key management issues have not gone away, and in some respects they are worse because Alice can't use a MAC to provide confidentiality of the key during distribution.

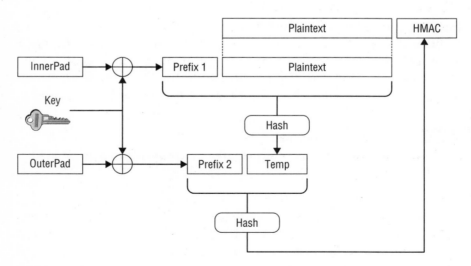

HMAC = Hash ((Key XOR OuterPad) || Hash ((Key XOR InnerPad) || Plaintext))

Figure 4-4 Keyed Hashing for Message Authentication (HMAC)

Asymmetric Cryptography

Asymmetric cryptography is also called *public key cryptography* because there are two distinct keys: one that must be kept private and one that can be made public. The two keys are complementary, but the value of the private key cannot be determined from the public key. Public key cryptography greatly simplifies the management of symmetric keys used for encryption or integrity by significantly reducing the number of keys that need to be stored for an extended period. Generally, the symmetric keys are used for a short period of time and are then discarded. Only the private key must be protected for an extended period. Furthermore, public keys can be distributed openly since they do not need to be kept secret. Public key cryptography supports both encryption and digital signatures.

> **HONEY, HAVE YOU SEEN MY KEYS?**
>
> One of the main points, if not *the* main point, of asymmetric cryptography is to keep the private key secret. You could print it out and keep it in your sock drawer, but that would make it more difficult to ensure that you typed it in properly every time — even worse if you have fat finger syndrome. You could keep the naked file on your computer, but how secure is your computer? In our opinion, it is far better to store it on a personal portable cryptographic token, which we'll discuss in Chapter 8.

Public Key Encryption

Public key cryptography supports encryption, but it is not generally used to encrypt user data. Public key algorithms require significantly more computational power than comparable symmetric encryption algorithms. Thus, the expensive public key operations are performed infrequently for the establishment of symmetric keys, and the efficient symmetric algorithm is used to encrypt the bulk of the data.

There are two key management public key algorithm types:

Key agreement. With key agreement algorithms, Alice and Bob exchange public keys and then combine their own private key with the public key of the other party to compute a symmetric key that is known only to the two parties. The Diffie-Hellman algorithm [DIFF76] (see Figure 4-5) is the most well-known key agreement algorithm.

Key transport. With key transport algorithms, Alice creates a symmetric key and encrypts it with Bob's public key. Bob then uses his own private key to decrypt the value and recover the symmetric key. The RSA algorithm [RIVE78] (see Figure 4-6) is the most well-known key transport algorithm.

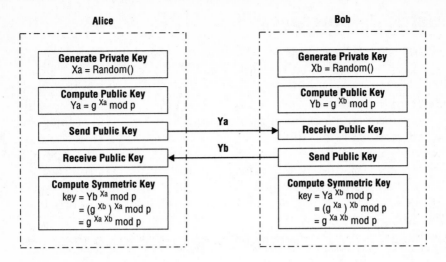

Alice and Bob have prior agreement on the generator, g, and the prime modulus, p.
Alice and Bob compute the same symmetric key, $g^{Xa\,Xb} \bmod p$.
An eavesdropper cannot derive the key value from Ya and Yb.

Figure 4-5 Diffie-Hellman key agreement

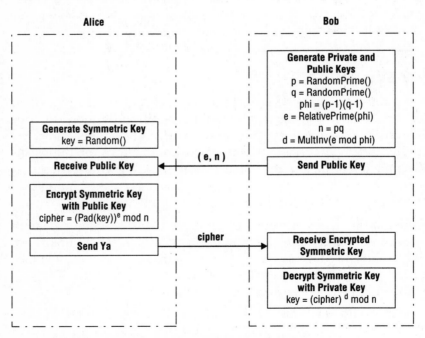

The symmetric key generated by Alice is securely transferred to Bob.
An eavesdropper cannot derive the key value from e, n, and cipher.

Figure 4-6 RSA key transport

EMERGING PUBLIC KEY ENCRYPTION ALGORITHMS

As the attackers evolve, so do the algorithms. New algorithms almost always add more security, which is always good, but one way to measure an algorithm is based on the amount of time it has been studied, attacked, and survived.

Diffie-Hellman (DH) and RSA might be most famous; here are some other algorithms creeping (or being dragged kicking and screaming based on your point of view) into the world:

> **RSA Optimal Asymmetric Encryption Padding (RSA-OAEP).**   Eliminates the vulnerability to adaptive chosen ciphertext attacks that is in the form of RSA that is widely used today.

> **RSA Key Encapsulation Method (RSA-KEM).**   Eliminates structures that might aid cryptanalysis by always encrypting a completely random value of the largest possible size for the recipient's public key.

> **Elliptic Curve Diffie-Hellman (ECDH).**   Same as traditional Diffie-Hellman, except that elliptic curve is used instead of discrete logarithms, resulting in smaller key sizes for the same security and faster computations.

> **Elliptic Curve Menezes-Qu-Vanstone (ECMQV).**   Like ECDH, elliptic curves are used. At the cost of additional computation, ECMQV offers improved authentication.

There will always be new algorithms that come along, hopefully the ones you implement have been vetted by experts and have withstood many years of attackers attempting to break them.

Authentication of the public key is needed with both key agreement and key transport algorithms. Alice must know that the public key she is using corresponds to the private key known only to Bob. If this is not the case, then Alice ends up sharing a symmetric key with an unknown party. In a few circumstances, this situation is desirable, but in general, this situation is completely unacceptable. Alice needs an additional mechanism to complement key agreement and key transport algorithms. Alice needs a mechanism that connects the public key to the user who holds the corresponding private key.

Digital Signatures

Public key cryptography also provides the basis for *digital signatures*. The private key is used to generate signatures, and the public key is used to validate them. In real-world applications, messages are not digitally signed directly. Rather, the message is hashed using a one-way hash function, and then the resulting hash value, also called a *message digest*, is signed.

Unlike symmetric integrity functions, digital signatures can provide important evidence in a dispute. If Alice uses her private key to sign a message, Bob can validate it with her public key. Since Bob does not need Alice's private key to validate the signature, he does not have the information he needs to generate a valid signature on an altered message. Furthermore, the judge can use Alice's public key to validate the signed message.

There are two digital signature public key algorithm types:

Digital signature with message recovery.   With these algorithms, Alice signs by encrypting the message digest with her own private key. Bob validates the signature by comparing a message digest that he computes locally with one that is obtained by decrypting the signature value with Alice's public key. If the two message digest values match exactly, then the digital signature is valid. The RSA algorithm [RIVE78] (see Figure 4-7) is the most well-known digital signature with message recovery algorithm.

Digital signature without message recovery.   With these algorithms, Alice uses her private key and the message digest to generate the signature value. Alice may also need to provide additional parameters, such as a unique random value. Bob validates the signature value with Alice's public key and a locally computed message digest and gives it to the verify function. The verify function returns a result of either valid or invalid, rather than the message digest. The Digital Signature Algorithm (DSA) [FIPS186a] (see Figure 4-8) is the most well-known digital signature algorithm that does not provide message recovery.

EVOLVING DIGITAL SIGNATURE ALGORITHMS

As you may have guessed, digital signature algorithms are evolving, too.

RSA Signature Scheme with Appendix Probabilistic Signature Scheme (RSASSA-PSS).   This was developed in an effort to have more mathematically provable security. It is specified in [RFC3447].

Elliptic Curve Digital Signature Algorithm (ECDSA).   As with ECDH, ECDSA takes advantage of the smaller key size and faster computation offered by elliptic curve cryptography. It is specified in [FIPS186b, X942, SEC1].

Again, implement only those algorithms that have been vetted by experts and have stood the test of time.

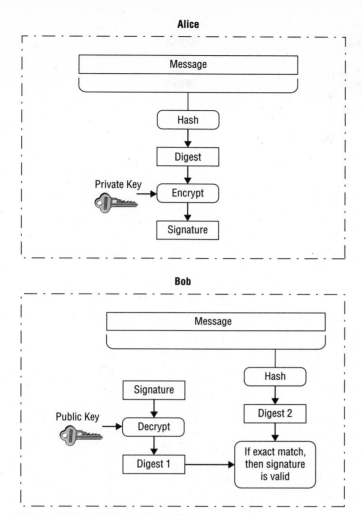

Figure 4-7 RSA Digital Signature

Authentication of the public key is needed with all digital signature algorithms. Bob must know that the public key he is using corresponds to the private key known only to Alice. If this is not the case, then Bob has no proof of the origin of the message. Bob has evidence that the message has not been modified since the signer signed it, but he does not know who signed it. As with key management, Bob needs an additional mechanism to complement digital signature algorithms. He needs a mechanism that connects the public key to the user who holds the corresponding private key.

Alice

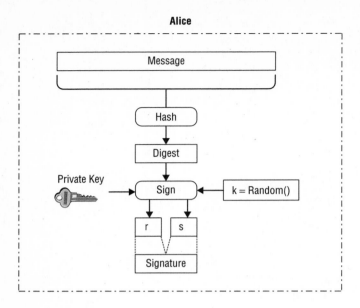

Bob

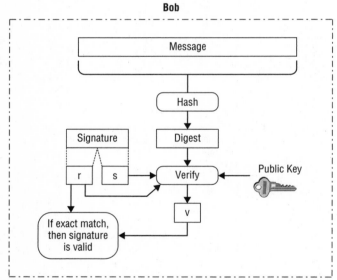

Figure 4-8 DSA Digital Signature

Public key certificates are the solution. As you will see in Chapter 5, certificates are used to bind an identity to the public key. By using certificates, Bob can be sure that he is using Alice's public key and, therefore, that Alice signed the message.

Asymmetric Key Management

Key management, well at least the distribution part, for public keys is easy to grasp: distribute the public part as widely as possible and keep the private key to yourself. Don't share it with anyone, even your spouse. The other aspects of creating, storing, use, and destruction can be accomplished by a couple of techniques. But, public key certificates and the supporting Public Key Infrastructure (PKI) are the most widely implemented asymmetric key management technique. Add in a security token, and you are on your way to securing your email.

PKI Basics

Understanding Public Key Infrastructure

Now that you understand email from your reading of Chapter 2 and have the security fundamentals mastered from Chapter 3, it's time to start doing some security. You learned in Chapter 4 that cryptography is a powerful tool that you can use to provide access control, authentication, confidentiality, integrity, and non-repudiation services. There is always a catch, and when using cryptography the catch is key management. This chapter is going to focus on the most widely used of the three key management techniques, which is by far, asymmetric key management systems.

There are number of ways to distribute public keys, such as with public key servers or a direct exchange between Alice and Bob, but using a *Public Key Infrastructure* (PKI) is arguably the most widely deployed because it offers greater scalability. For email, we need a key management solution that scales to billions of users. PKI is used to solve the asymmetric key management problem by distributing public keys in *public key certificates*. Going forward, we simply call these certificates.

Certificates include more information than just the public key, and it's all digitally signed to ensure that the key and other information are unaltered. A third party, called a *certification authority*, or CA, issues certificates to Alice and Bob, and both Alice and Bob have confidence in the content of the certificate because they have chosen to rely on this CA. To support email, the CA issues certificates that bind the public key to the appropriate email address. We'll describe the functions of a CA in much more detail later in this chapter.

That's the basics, but we're going to go in to more depth. We can't address every PKI issue in this chapter, but we cover the fundamentals. For complete coverage of a PKI, we suggest Housley and Polk's *Planning for PKI* [HP] and

Adams and Llyod's *Understanding PKI: Concepts, Standards, and Deployment Considerations* [AL]. Both books offer comprehensive coverage, and they are the number one and number two selling books on PKI.

Trust

The reliance on the CA is what makes a PKI work. The CA is a *trusted third party*. Alice and Bob are relying on the CA to ensure that the person asserting that they control the private key that corresponds to the public key in the certificate actually does control it and that their email address is correct. Obviously, the more rigorous the checking performed by the CA, the more confidence Alice, Bob, and others can place in the certificate. For example, the CA can have greater confidence in Alice's identity if she presents a government-issued passport instead of her Mickey Mouse Club Card.

CERTIFICATE POLICIES AND CERTIFICATION PRACTICE STATEMENTS

How do Alice and Bob know what the CA is doing to earn their trust? The CA has a Certification Policy (CP) that spells out in detail (and yes it can be very long) what the CA must do to check that the person with the private key has the key, the ways that person must identify themselves to the CA, how the CA protects the private key used to sign certificates, and so on. (The CA has six fundamental responsibilities, which we'll discuss later in this chapter.) The CA also has a Certification Practice Statement (CPS) that reveals how the CA implemented the CP. The CP and the CPS can be in the same document or in separate documents. These documents allow Alice, Bob, and others to determine how much they should trust the CA. One shouldn't trust the CA very much if its private key is stored in the CA operator's sock drawer.

Often, CPs will define a set of criteria to get a certificate issued under policy A and then more rigorous set of criteria to get a certificate issued under policy B. Sometimes A and B are named by numbers; other times, they are named by colors: A = 0 and B = 1 or A = bronze and B = gold. If you're picking the name for a policy, don't pick low and high; nobody will want to be associated with a policy called low.

Another part of trust is the belief by Alice and Bob that at the time the private key was used the binding was still considered valid. If Alice is using her public key certificate to sign something that is validated by Bob, then Bob needs to ask two questions:

- **Is Alice's certificate still okay?**   The signature on the certificate must be good, and the certificate must not have expired. Additionally, the CA can indicate problems with the certificate, usually through a *certificate revocation list* (CRL).

- **Is Alice's signature okay?** Bob checks the digital signature to see if it is *valid*. To be valid, the digital signature check must be performed with a public key from a valid certificate.

Answering both these question is a process called *digital signature verification*. When Bob checks that Alice's certificate is valid, it called *certificate validation*. The process of collecting the certificates is called *certificate path building* or *certificate path construction*. The process of checking each certificate in the certificate path is called *certification path validation*.

PKI Architectures

If there was only one CA in the world, then that CA would be very busy. Luckily, there is more than one CA. There can be multiple CAs to serve various user communities. PKIs can be organized to support simple user requirements and more complex enterprise requirements. Each of the architectures described in the following sections has strengths and weaknesses. Each is appropriate for some environments and inappropriate for others.

Single CA

The most basic PKI architecture is a single CA that provides all the certificates and CRLs for a community of users. In this configuration, all users trust the CA that issued their own certificate. By definition, new CAs cannot be added to the PKI. Since there is only one CA, there are no CA trust relationships. The user accepts only certificates and CRLs issued by their CA. As a result, certification paths can be built with a single certificate and a single CRL. Since all certificates are user certificates, path analysis will not include information that describes or limits CA trust relationships. Certificate path construction and analysis can't get any easier than that.

> **NOTE** This architecture is only really applicable to a single enterprise that does not need to communicate with the outside world. It is included here for completeness.

Figure 5-1 depicts a single CA — the Fox Consulting CA — which issues certificates to the employees of the Fox Consulting company. Alice and Bob are two of those employees. Alice trusts the Fox CA, so she can easily build and validate Bob's certification path.

While it's the simplest to implement, this architecture does not scale easily to support very large or diverse use communities. As Alice and Bob expand their set of secure applications, they may need to communicate with Carol at Hawk Data. The Fox CA only offers services to Fox Consulting employees,

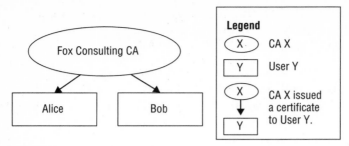

Figure 5-1 A PKI with a single CA

so Carol must get her certificate from another CA. Alice and Bob need an architecture that incorporates additional CAs to communicate with Carol.

The single CA PKI presents a single point of failure. Compromise of the CA invalidates the trust point information and all certificates that have been issued in this PKI. Every user in the PKI must be informed about the compromise immediately, or they may establish security based on unreliable information. To reestablish the CA, all certificates must be reissued and the new trust point information must be distributed to other users.

Trust Lists

The *trust list* is the most straightforward way to handle more than a single CA, as described previously. In this architecture, more than one CA provides PKI services, but there are no trust relationships between CAs. In this model, Alice maintains a list of CAs that she trusts. She trusts valid certificates issued by any of them. New CAs can be added to the PKI by modifying the trust list. As with a single CA, there are no trust relationships. The users accept only certificates and CRLs issued by CAs in their trust list. As a result, one certificate and one CRL are all that is needed for any user. However, this is complicated slightly by the increase in the number of trust points. There are no CA certificates, so complex certificate extensions do not appear. Certificate path construction and analysis are very easy.

In Figure 5-2, Carol has obtained certificates for Hawk Data Company CA. There is no trust relationship between the Fox CA and the Hawk CA. Alice wants to communicate with Carol securely, but there is no certificate path beginning with Fox CA (whom Alice trusts most) that ends with Carol's certificate. Alice needs to add a new CA to her trust list. Once Hawk CA is added to her trust list, Alice can verify Carol's certificate.

The primary advantage of this architecture is simplicity, because there are no certification paths, just single certificates. In addition, the mechanism of adding a new CA to the PKI is very straightforward; Alice simply adds one more CA to her list of trusted CAs.

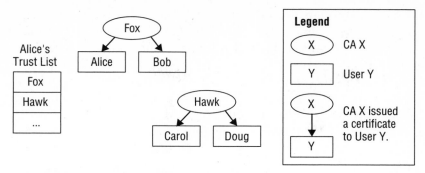

Figure 5-2 Supporting multiple CAs through a trust list

There are important disadvantages, however. Alice added the new CA to her trust list out of expediency because she wanted to communicate with Carol. However, Alice really should have investigated the Hawk CA before she added it to her trust list. In addition, Alice should maintain critical information about every CA that she trusts. As this number grows, it will be very difficult for her to keep this information up to date.

CA compromise is very difficult to handle with trust lists. If the Hawk CA private key is compromised, then it will probably notify all its users immediately. However, the Hawk CA does not have a direct relationship with Alice; the Hawk CA probably does not even know that it is a member of Alice's trust list. Alice will continue to trust certificates issued by the compromised CA.

Hierarchical PKI

The traditional PKI architecture is hierarchical PKI. In this architecture, multiple CAs provide PKI services, and the CAs are related through superior-subordinate relationships. In this architecture, all users trust the same central *root CA*. With the exception of the root CA, all the CAs have a single superior CA. CAs may have subordinate CAs, issue certificates to users, or both. Each CA trust relationship is represented by a single certificate. The issuer is the superior CA, the subject is the subordinate.

To add a new CA to the PKI, one of the existing CAs issues a certificate to the new CA. The new CA is grafted directly under the CA of the existing PKI, and the new CA becomes the subordinate of the issuing CA. Two hierarchical PKIs may be merged in the same fashion.

Certification paths are easy to develop in a hierarchy because every CA has a single superior CA. There is a simple, obvious, and deterministic path from a user's certificate back to the single trust point at the root. The certification paths are relatively short. The longest path is equal to the depth of the tree: a CA certificate for each subordinate CA, plus the user's certificate. Superior CAs may impose restrictions upon the subordinate's actions. These restrictions could be maintained through procedural mechanisms or imposed through the certificates themselves. In the last case, the CA certificate will contain additional information to describe these restrictions. (The types of restrictions are discussed later in this chapter.)

In Figure 5-3, the R&D, Legal, and Ops CAs have joined a small hierarchical PKI. The root CA is the HQ CA. Alice sets her trust point to HQ, even though she obtained her certificate from the R&D CA. Alice can easily construct Carol's certification path, which contains a single certificate. The path contains more certificates, and the CA certificates contain additional information that must be processed.

Hierarchical PKIs handle the compromise of a single CA within the infrastructure easily, as long as it is not the root CA. If a CA is compromised, its superior CA simply revokes its certificate. The superior issues a new certificate to the CA, containing the new public key and bringing it back into the hierarchy. Once the CA has been reestablished, it issues new certificates to all of its users. In the interim, transactions between any two users outside the compromised part of the PKI can proceed. Of course, users in the compromised part of the hierarchy lose all services.

On the other hand, the compromise of a root CA has as catastrophic an impact as in the single CA architecture. It is critical to inform all the users in the hierarchical PKI that the root CA has been compromised. Until the root CA is reestablished, issues new certificates to its subordinates, and distributes the new trust point information, users cannot use the PKI to establish secure communications. There is one advantage in comparison to a PKI consisting of a single CA: The root CA will have to reissue a much smaller number of certificates. In addition, the root CA can operate offline, significantly reducing the likelihood of key compromise.

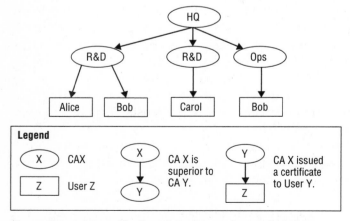

Figure 5-3 A hierarchical PKI for Alice, Bob, Carol, and Doug

Mesh PKI

The mesh PKI architecture is the primary alternative to a hierarchy. This architecture is also referred to as the network PKI or a web of trust. In this architecture, multiple CAs provide PKI services, and the CAs are related through peer-to-peer relationships. Each user trusts a single CA; however, the trust point is not the same for all users.

In general, users will trust the CA that issued their certificate. CAs issue certificates to each other; a pair of certificate describes their bidirectional trust relationship.

A new CA can easily be added to a mesh PKI. The new CA issues a certificate to at least one CA that is already a member of the mesh, and it issues a certificate to the new CA. However, path construction is particularly difficult in a mesh PKI. In a hierarchy, building a certification path from a user's certificate to a point of trust is deterministic. In a mesh, this process is nondeterministic. Path discovery is more difficult since there are often multiple choices. Some of the choices lead to a valid path, but others result in useless dead ends. Even worse, it is possible in a mesh PKI to construct an endless loop of certificates. The length of a path may be longer than in a typical hierarchical PKI. In the worst case, the path length can approach the number of CAs in the PKI.

Certificates issued in a mesh PKI are also more complex. Since the CAs have peer-to-peer relationships, they cannot impose conditions governing the types of certificates other CAs can issue. If a CA wishes to limit the trust, it must specify these limitations as certificate extensions in the certificates it issues to all of its peers.

Mesh PKIs are very resilient since there are multiple trust points. Compromise of a single CA cannot bring down the entire PKI. CAs that issued certificates to the compromised CA simply revoke them, thereby removing the compromised CA from the PKI. Users associated with other CAs will still have a valid trust point, and can communicate securely with the remaining users in their PKI. In the best case, the PKI shrinks by a single CA and its associated user community. At worst, the PKI fragments into several smaller PKIs. Recovery from a compromise is simpler in a mesh CA than in a hierarchy PKI, primarily because it affects fewer users.

In Figure 5-4, the CAs are incorporated into a mesh PKI. Alice and Bob trust the R&D CA, Carol trusts the Legal CA, and Doug trusts the Ops CA. It is more difficult for Alice to find and analyze a certification path for Carl than in a hierarchical PKI. The certification path may contain two or three certificates. It contains two if the path from the R&D CA directly to the Legal CA is used. However, it contains three certificates if the path through the Ops CA to the Legal CA is used. While attempting to find one of these valid paths, Alice may also follow other paths that result in dead-ends. For example, Alice might try a path that includes the HQ CA. The certificates will also be more complicated to process, since all limitations in trust relationships are expressed as additional information in the certificate.

Cross-Certified PKIs

If two user communities have an ongoing requirement for secure communications, their PKIs may wish to establish peer-to-peer trust relationships. In Figure 5-5, Alice's CA has cross-certified with the Hawk hierarchical PKI's root CA, and R&D CA in the Dove, Inc. mesh. In addition, these CAs have cross-certified with each other.

Each user can maintain a single trust point. Alice, Bob, and Doug trust the CA that issued their certificates, and Carol trusts her root CA. While the cross-community relationships are peer-to-peer, it is either peer-to-peer or hierarchical relationships that relate CAs within the PKI.

Unlike with the trust list, Alice cannot add a new PKI on her own. CA administrators must renew the policies and practices of another CA before they cross-certify. On the other hand, the CA administrators are probably better qualified than Alice to determine if a CA or PKI is trustworthy. Once the CAs are cross-certified, Bob can also validate user certificates in the other PKI. Therefore, one administrator action enables secure communications for the whole user population. With the trust list architecture, both Bob and Alice need to update their own trust lists.

Certification paths in this environment may be quite complex. Since the resulting PKI includes both mesh and hierarchical sections, the path building algorithms must combine both hierarchical and mesh certification path-building techniques to perform efficiently in this architecture. Certificates may be quite complex, and finding a valid path may be difficult. On the plus side, Alice is building paths from a single trust point.

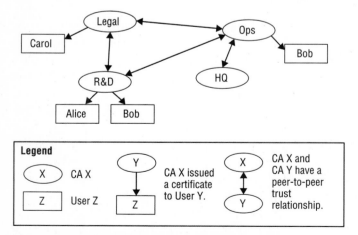

Figure 5-4 A mesh PKI for Alice, Bob, Carol, and Doug

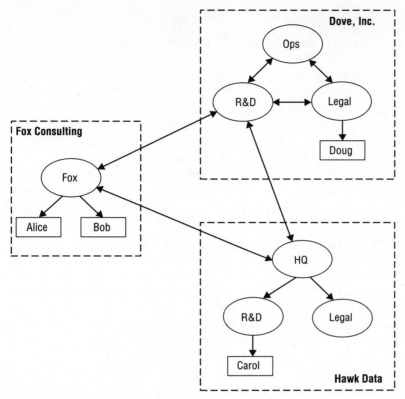

Figure 5-5 Three cross-certified PKIs

Many of Alice's problems with CA compromise are resolved by this architecture. Alice is maintaining a single trust point, and she has a direct trust relationship with that CA. She can expect immediate notification if her own CA is compromised. Alice's CA has a direct relationship with the three cross-certified CAs. If either is compromised, Alice's CA will be notified and will revoke the appropriate certificate. In addition, if CAs within the other PKIs are compromised, they will be handled as discussed earlier.

The architecture is an appropriate solution when a small number of PKIs must establish trust relationships. In Figure 5-5, three peer-to-peer relationships and six CA certificates were required to establish these relationships. However, this number grows rapidly as the number of PKIs increases. Cross-certifying n PKIs requires $(n^2 - n)/2$. For example, if there are 8 PKIs, then cross-certifying each pair requires 28 peer-to-peer relationships and 56 CA certificates. Since establishing these relationships requires a time-consuming review of policies and practices, this architecture rapidly becomes an intractable problem.

Bridge CAs

The bridge CA architecture was designed to address the shortcomings of the trust list and cross-certified PKI architectures. The user cannot be expected to maintain current information on a large number of trust points. One the other hand, CA administrators need a mechanism for establishing trust relationships with other PKIs in a more efficient fashion.

The bridge CA meets these requirements, acting as sort of arbitrator. Unlike a mesh CA, the bridge CA does not issue certificate directly to users. Unlike a root CA in a hierarchy, the bridge CA does not issue certificates directly to users. All PKI users consider the bridge CA as an intermediary. The bridge CA establishes peer-to-peer relationships with different PKIs. These relationships can be combined to form a *bridge of trust* that connects the users from the different PKIs.

If the trust domain is implemented as a hierarchical PKI, the bridge CA will establish a relationship with the root CA. If the domain is implemented as a mesh PKI, the bridge CA will establish a relationship with only one of its CAs. In either case, the CA that enters into a trust relationship with the bridge CA is termed the *principle CA*.

In Figure 5-6, the bridge CA has established relationships with three PKIs. The first is Bob and Alice's CA, the second is Carol's hierarchical PKI, and the third is Doug's mesh PKI. None of the users trusts the bridge CA directly. Alice and Bob trust the CA that issued their certificates, they trust the bridge CA because the Fox CA issued a certificate to it. Carol's trust point is the root CA of her hierarchy; she trusts the bridge CA because the root CA issued a certificate to it. Doug trusts the CA in the mesh that issued his certificate; he trusts the bridge CA because there is a valid certification path from the CA that issued him a certificate to the bridge CA. Alice (or Bob) can use the chain of valid certificates, which includes certificates to and from the bridge CA, to establish relationships with Carol and Doug.

The trust relationship between the bridge CA and the principle CAs are all peer-to-peer. The trust relationships within the PKIs it connects are determined by their own architecture. Within the hierarchical PKI, trust relationships are superior-subordinate. Within the mesh PKI, the trust relationships are peer to peer.

It is easy to add new CAs, or entire PKIs, to a bridge-connected PKI. The change is transparent to the users, since no change in trust points is required. As the PKI grows, the number of trust relationships that must be established is far more manageable. In Figure 5-6, three trust relationships were established for three PKIs. This is the same as the cross-certified example shown in Figure 5-5. However, a bridge CA with PKIs will require 8 trust relationships, rather than the 28 required by the cross-certified example.

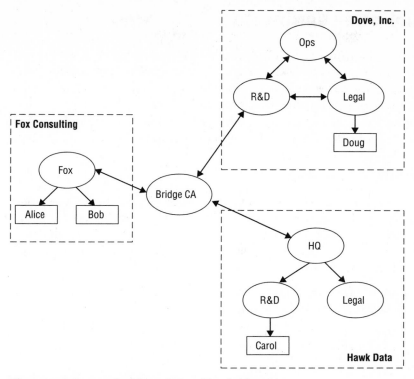

Figure 5-6 Connecting three PKIs with a bridge CA

The bridge CA does not resolve the certification path construction or validation problem. Path construction is just as complex as in a mesh PKI, since some of the PKIs are themselves a mesh. Certificates issued to and by the bridge may be very complex to ensure that the trust relationship is accurately conveyed. This increases the complexity of the path validation software.

In a bridge CA architecture, the PKI can easily recover from compromise. If the principle CA from a PKI is compromised, the bridge CA revokes its certificate. This invalidates the trust relationship between that PKI and any other PKIs. The rest of the relationships are not affected. If the bridge CA itself is compromised, it notifies the principle CAs. Since none of the users has the bridge CA as a trust point, the principle CAs simply revoke the certificates they issued to the bridge CA. For completeness, the bridge CA can issue a CRL revoking the certificates it has issued as well. The result is a set of separate PKIs, so users from different PKIs will lose the ability to establish secure services. On the other hand, it is straightforward to reestablish the PKI after rebuilding the bridge CA.

X.509 Public Key Certificates

X.509 Certificates (see Figure 5-7) may be considered as three nested components. The first component is the *tamper-evident envelope*, provided by the *digital signature*. Inside the envelope, we find the *basic certificate content*, which includes the information that must be present in every certificate. The basic certificate content may include an optional set of certificate extensions. The vast majority of certificates generated today will include certificate extensions.

Tamper-Evident Envelope

At the outermost level, certificates have just three fields: the to-be-signed certificate, the signature algorithm identifier, and the signature value. Consider the tamper-evident envelope as a transparent plastic envelope around the certificate content. The message is easily read, but it cannot be modified without tearing the envelope. The fields are defined as follows:

tbsCertificate.   This field contains the signed certificate, and its structure is discussed in the next section.

signatureAlgorithm.   This field contains an AlgorithmIdentifier that identifies an algorithm with an object identifier (OID) and optional

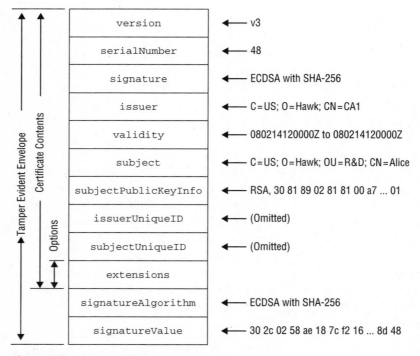

Figure 5-7 X.509 certificate structure

parameters. Here, only the algorithm identifier is included, and it identifies the digital signature algorithm used by the CA to sign the certificate. The optional parameters field is not used to validate the signature because this field is not inside the tamper-evident envelope. The information in this field is repeated in the signature field within the to-be-signed certificate, which is protected.

signatureValue.   This field contains the digital signature. The digital signature is computed using the ASN.1 DER encoded to-be-signed certificate. The resulting signature value is encoded as a bit string, using conventions defined for the specified signature algorithm.

Basic Certificate Contents

The to-be-signed certificate is the real meat of the X.509 certificate; it contains all the basic certificate information. At a minimum, it contains six fields: the serial number, the certificate signature algorithm identifier, the certificate issuer name, the certificate validity period, the public key, and the subject name. The subject is the party that controls the corresponding private key. There are four optional fields: the version number, two unique identifiers, and the extensions. These optional fields appear only in version 2 and version 3 certificates. The fields are described next:

version. The optional version field describes the syntax of the certificate. When the version field is omitted, the certificate is encoded in the original, version 1 syntax. Version 1 certificates do not include the unique identifiers or extensions. When the certificate includes unique identifiers but not extensions, the version field indicates version 2. When the certificate includes extensions, as almost all modern certificates do, the version field indicates version 3.

serialNumber. The serial number is an integer assigned by the certificate issuer to each certificate. The serial number must be unique for each certificate generated by a particular issuer. The combination of the issuer name and serial number uniquely identifies any certificate.

signature. The signature field is an algorithm identifier. It is a copy of the signature algorithm contained in the signature algorithm field; however, the digital signature protects this value.

issuer. The issuer field contains the X.500 distinguished name of the certificate issuer. The Internet Certificate and CRL profile [RFC3280] requires the issuer field to contain a nonempty name. The distinguished name can include any attributes; however, for interoperability, the issuer should be limited to the naming attributes described previously.

validity. The validity field has two components, indicating the dates on which the certificate becomes valid (notBefore) and the date on which the certificate expires (`notAfter`). CAs must encode these fields as UTC time for dates through the year 2049, and generalized time for dates in the year 2050 and beyond.

subject. The `subject` field contains the distinguished name of the holder of the private key corresponding to the public key in this certificate. The subject may be a CA or an end entity. End entities can be human users, hardware devices, or anything else that might make use of the private key. The distinguished name can include any attributes; however, for interoperability, the subject name should be limited to the naming attributes described earlier. In the development of a certification path, the subject names in CA certificates must match the issuer name in the certificate that follows.

subjectPublicKeyInfo. The `subjectPublicKeyInfo` field contains the subject's public key and algorithm identifier. Unlike the signature or signature algorithm fields, which also make use of algorithm identifiers, the parameters within this field convey important information about the public key. For example, the parameters field will contain the domain parameters (p, q, and g) associated with DSA or Diffie-Hellman public keys. If the parameters are omitted, then the subject and issuer have the same public key parameters. *Parameter inheritance* simply reduces the size of certificates by not repeating the same values over and over again.

issuerUniqueIdentifier and **subjectUniqueIdentifier.** These fields contain identifiers, and they only appear in version 2 or version 3 certificates. The subject and issuer unique identifiers are intended to handle the reuse of subject names or issuer names over time. However, this mechanism has proven to be an unsatisfactory solution. The Internet Certificate and CRL profile [RFC3280] recommends omission of these fields. Even so, implementations must parse these fields or reject certificates containing them.

extensions. This optional field only appears in version 3 certificates. If present, this field contains one or more certificate extensions. Each extension includes an extension identifier, a criticality flag, and an extension value. Common certificate extensions are described in the next section.

Certificate Extensions

Early PKI deployments clearly demonstrate that the basic certificate content described earlier is insufficient. Certificate users are unable to determine important information about the issuer, the subject, or the public key itself. The missing information can be divided into five groups. Each group is characterized by the questions that it answers:

Subject type.   Is Bob a CA or an end entity?

Names and identity information. Are alice@fox.com and c=US; o=Fox Consulting; cn=Alice Adams the same person?

Key attributes. Can this public key be used for key transport? Can it also be used to verify a digital signature?

Policy information. Can I trust Alice's certificate? Is it appropriate for large value transactions?

Additional information. Where can I find certificates issued to the Fox Consulting CA? Where can I get CRLs issued by the Fox Consulting CA?

Certificate extensions allow the CA to include information not supported by the basic certificate content. Any organization may define a private extension to meet its particular business requirements. However, most requirements can be satisfied using standard extensions. Standard extensions are widely supported by commercial products. Standard extensions offer improved interoperability, and they are more cost-effective than private extensions.

Extensions have three components: extension identifier, a criticality flag, and extension value. The extension identifier is an OID, and it indicates the format and semantics of the extension value. The criticality flag indicates the importance of the extension. When the criticality flag is set, the information is essential to certificate use. Therefore, if an unrecognized critical extension is encountered, the certificate must not be used. Alternatively, unrecognized noncritical extensions may be ignored.

ITU-T and IETF have defined several extensions for X.509 v3 certificates. They are specified in [X50997], [X50900], [RFC3280], and [RFC3851].

Subject Type Extensions

The inability to determine whether a certificate belongs to a CA or an end entity makes certificate path construction more difficult. When Alice obtains certificates for both Bob and the Hawk Manufacturing CA, she cannot determine from the basic certificate content that Bob is not a CA. Therefore, she may try to use the certificate to construct a certification path. Eventually, she will discover that no certificates chain to Bob's distinguished name. The basic constraints extension resolves this issue.

Basic Constraints. The basic constraints extension indicates whether the subject of the certificate is an end entity or a CA. It also allows a CA to indicate whether subordinate CAs are also allowed to have subordinate CAs.

Name Extensions

In X.509 v1 certificates and X.509 v2 certificates, distinguished names were the only name form available. If a ubiquitous X.500 Directory had quickly emerged, this would be the only name form needed. Every system and user would have an entry in the X.500 Directory, and this name would be a unique identity. However, the global X.500 Directory did not emerge (and will probably never emerge) as a unified system. Further, Internet expansion shows no signs of slowing, and X.500 Directory names are not the preferred name form on the Internet.

Issuer Alterative Name. The issuer alternative name extension provides a list of general names. Generally, the names of CAs are not important to certificate users. The issuer information that is important to certificate users is addressed later in this chapter. However, this extension can advertise the electronic mail address of the CA.

Subject Alternative Name. The subject alternative name extension is extremely useful for end entity certificates. This is the place where electronic mail addresses are placed.

Name Constraints. The name constraints extension allows CA to constrain the names allowed in a certificate. The name constraints extension offers two constraint types: permitted subtrees and excluded subtrees. Permitted subtrees specify acceptable names, and excluded subtrees specify unacceptable names. Permitted subtrees could limit the Hawk Data to distinguished names that begin with C=US, o=Hawk Data, and electronic mail addresses that end with hawk.com. Excluded subtrees could prohibit Hawk Data's use of distinguished names that begin with C=US, o=Fox Consulting, and electronic mail addresses that end with fox.com. A name is acceptable only if it falls within one of the permitted subtrees and is not within any of the excluded subtrees.

Key Attributes

X.509 v1 certificates and X.509 v2 certificates specify the public key algorithm and parameters, but they do not offer any other key attributes. Most CAs and end entities have more than one public/private key pair, and they use different key pairs to implement different security services. To differentiate the public keys in different certificates, CAs employ four standard certificate extensions: key usage, extended key usage, authority key identifier, and the subject key identifier:

Key Usage.   The key usage extension identifies the security services that a public key might provide. This extension offers nine security services, with the CA selecting the appropriate combination.

Extended Key Usage.   The extended key usage extension indicates specific applications for public keys. The extended key usage extension is composed of a sequence of OIDs, where each OID identifies a particular application context in which the public key may be used. For example, the id-kp-serverAuth OID (1.3.6.1.5.5.7.3.1) indicates that the public key may be used by a TLS Web server.

Authority Key Identifier.   The authority key identifier extension provides a means for identifying certificates signed by a particular CA private key. This extension aids certification path construction. If the CA has several certificate signing keys, this extension identifies the correct one to verify a particular certificate signature. Without such a pointer, each public key must be tried in succession until the signature is verified or until all possibilities are exhausted!

Subject Key Identifier.   The subject key identifier extension provides a means for identifying certificates containing a particular public key. The subject key identifier contains a string that names the key. If the subject has multiple certificates — especially if multiple CAs issue them — the subject key identifier provides a means to quickly identify the certificates containing the public key of interest.

Policy

In early PKI implementations using X.509 v1 certificates and X.509 v2 certificates, each CA issued certificates under one and only one policy. The policy was implicit. Implicit policy information proved unacceptable. No single policy fit all needs. Further, it was, and still remains, inefficient to deploy a separate CA for each policy. It was difficult for certificate users to track which policy was used by each CA. Tracking issuer distinguished directory names to policies and policies to application requirements was too complicated; it was not implemented.

Two standard policy extensions fulfill these needs: the certificate policies extension and the policy mapping extension. The *certificate policies extension* indicates the policy or policies under which a certificate was issued. In a CA certificate, this indicates the policies under which the CA operates. In an end entity certificate, this indicates the policy (or policies) under which the certificate was issued. An object identifier, usually referred to as a policy OID, identifies the certificate policy. The *policy mapping extension* translates policy OIDs from one PKI to the equivalent policy OIDs in another PKI.

Certificate Policies.   The certificate policies extension indicates the certificate policies under which the certificate was issued. The CA asserts that the procedures used to issue the certificate satisfy the listed policies. Certificate users must know which policy or policies are acceptable for their application. In end entity certificates, this extension describes the policies satisfied. In CA certificates, this extension defines the set of policies that can be included in subordinate certificates.

Policy Mapping.   The policy mapping extension is used in CA certificates to translate policy information between two policy domains. Generally, certificate users recognize only a handful of policy OIDs. Normally, these are the policy OIDs that appear in certificates issued by their own CA. When two CAs operate under different policies, their users will not be able to use the policy information. A policy mapping extension provides the translation needed to make the remote policy information useful. Policy mapping translates remote policy OIDs into local policy OIDs that the certificate user already knows.

Policy Constraints. The policy constraints extension is used to impose limitations on valid certification paths. This extension can constrain path validation in two ways. First, it can be used to prohibit policy mapping. Second, it can require that each certificate in a path contain an acceptable policy OID. Either restriction can be imposed immediately, or the restriction can begin after the certification path reaches a specified length.

Additional Information

Several standard extensions provide certificate users with pointers to additional information, including issuer certificates, CRLs, delta CRLs, and online certificate status servers. Further, attributes associated with the certificate subject may be included directly in the certificate. The CRL distribution points extension, freshest CRL extension, authority information access extension, subject information access extension, and the subject directory attribute extension provide this additional information.

CRL Distribution Points. The CRL distribution points extension tells certificate users where and how to obtain CRLs needed to determine if the certificate is revoked.

Freshest CRL. The freshest CRL extension could have been named the delta CRL distribution point extension. It identifies how delta CRL information is obtained. The same syntax is used for this extension and for the CRL distribution points' extension described in the previous section. The same conventions apply to both extensions.

Authority Information Access. The authority information access extension tells how to access CA information and services. This information and services may include CA policy data and online certificate status services. However, the location of CRLs is not specified in this extension; that information is provided by the CRL distribution points' extension.

Subject Information Access. The subject information access extension tells more information about the subject. It has the same syntax as the authority information access extension.

S/MIME Capabilities. The S/MIME capabilities extension indicates the cryptographic capabilities of the sender of a signed S/MIME message. Recipients can use this information to select the appropriate cryptographic algorithms in future S/MIME secured exchanges.

X.509 Certificate Revocation Lists

Figure 5-8 illustrates the structure of the X.509 v2 CRL. The tbs prefix means to be signed. Therefore, the to-be-signed certificate list is the portion of the CRL that is ASN.1 DER encoded and digitally signed by the CRL issuer.

The top-level structure of the CRL parallels that described for certificates. The top-level structure of the CRL provides a tamper-evident envelope for the CRL content and is composed of three fields: tbsCertList, signatureAlgorithm, and signatureValue. These fields perform the same function as the fields in the certificate.

Signed Certificate List

The to-be-signed certificate list contains the signature algorithm identifier, the CRL issuer, and the CRL issue date. It should always contain the date by which a new CRL will be issued, even though the syntax specifies the next

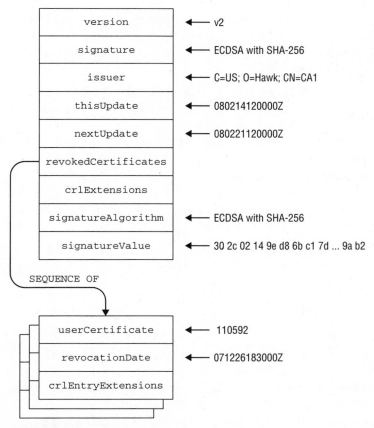

Figure 5-8 CRL structure

update field as optional. Failure to include the next update field significantly complicates validation of a certificate. When there are no revoked certificates, the revoked certificates portion of the structure is absent. When one or more certificates are revoked, each entry on the revoked certificate list is defined by a structure containing the user certificate serial number, revocation date, and optional CRL entry extensions.

The to-be-signed certificate list may also contain CRL extensions. CRL entry extensions provide information about a single revoked certificate, while CRL extensions provide information about the whole list.

The fields within the signed portion of the CRL are described next:

version.   The optional version field describes the syntax of the CRL. When extensions are used, which is usually the case, the field specifies version two (v2). CRL issuers may set the version field to v2 even if extensions are absent, so very few version one (v1) CRLs are actually in use today.

signature.   The signature field contains the algorithm identifier for the digital signature algorithm used by the CRL issuer to sign the to-be-signed certificate list. This field must contain the same algorithm identifier as the signature algorithm field in the top-level structure of the CRL. The two algorithm identifiers are redundant; however, the digital signature covers one and not the other.

issuer.   The issuer field contains the X.500 distinguished name of the CRL issuer. The Internet Certificate and CRL profile [RFC3280] requires the issuer field to contain a nonempty name. This is generally the identity of the CA; however, some CAs may choose to delegate some or all CRL functions to another authority by including a CRL Distribution Point extension in certificates. Such CRLs are called Indirect CRLs since the certificate issuer and the CRL issuer are different authorities. Additional names, or aliases, for the CRL issuer may also appear in the issuer alternative name extension.

thisUpdate.   The thisUpdate field indicates the issue date of this CRL. There are two forms of date supported: UTC time and generalized time. CRL issuers must encode the this-update field as UTC time for dates through the year 2049, and CRL issuers must encode the this-update field as generalized time for dates in the year 2050 and beyond. This is the same rule as described earlier for the validity period in the certificate.

nextUpdate.   The nextUpdate field indicates the date by which the next CRL will be issued. The same two date forms are supported: UTC time and generalized time. The next CRL could be issued before the indicated date, but it must not be issued any later than the indicated date. As stated previously, CRL issuers ought to include this field, even though it is optional. CRL issuers should include a nextUpdate time equal to or later than all previous CRLs issued for the same distribution point. If this simple rule is not followed, then clients trying to determine when to fetch an updated CRL from the repository may not check when an updated one is available.

revokedCertificates. The revokedCertificates structure lists the revoked certificates. The revokedCertificates structure is optional but should only be absent when none of the unexpired certificates has been revoked. When there are no unexpired revoked certificates, the revoked-Certificates structure is absent; otherwise, the revokedCertificates structure contains one entry for each revoked certificate. The structure contains the certificate serial numbers, time of revocation, and optional CRL entry extensions.

userCertificate. The userCertificate field within the revoked-Certificate structure specifies the serial number of the revoked certificate. Certificates are uniquely identified by the combination of their certificate issuer name and their certificate serial number. Generally, the certificate issuer and the CRL issuer are the same authority, so the CRL structure is optimized for this case. That is, the issuer name is carried once in the issuer field, and it applies to the entire list of serial numbers. When the CRL issuer and the certificate issuer are different, the certificate issuer must be paired with each serial number. The certificate issuer CRL entry extension provides the certificate issuer name. This CRL entry extension, as well as the others, is described later in the chapter.

revocationDate. The revocationDate field specifies the date on which the revocation occurred. The same two date forms are supported: UTC time and generalized time.

crlEntryExtensions. The crlEntryExtensions field is used to provide additional information about CRL entries. This field may only appear if the version is v2. The certificate issuer described previously is one example. This CRL entry extension and others are discussed later.

crlExtensions. The crlExtensions field is used to provide additional information about the whole CRL. Again, this field may only appear if the version is v2. CRL extensions are discussed in the next section.

CRL Extensions

ITU-T and ANSI X9 have defined several CRL extensions for X.509 v2 CRLs, which are specified in [X50997] and [X955]. Each extension in a CRL may be designated as critical or noncritical. A CRL validation fails if an unrecognized critical extension is encountered. However, unrecognized noncritical extensions may be ignored. The X.509 v2 CRL format allows communities to define private extensions to carry information unique to those communities. Communities are encouraged to define noncritical private extensions so that their CRLs can be readily validated by all implementations.

The following CRL extensions are the ones that should be properly handled by all implementations:

Authority Key Identifier.   The authority key identifier extension provides a means of identifying the public key needed to validate the signature on the CRL. The identification can be based on either the key identifier (the subject key identifier extension from the CRL issuer's certificate) or on the issuer name and serial number (again, from the CRL issuer's certificate). This extension is especially useful where a CRL issuer has more than one signing key. In this case, the CRL issuer should have more than one certificate, one corresponding to each signing key.

Issuer Alternative Name.   The issuer alternative names extension allows additional name forms to be associated with the issuer of the CRL. Defined options include an RFC 822 name (an electronic mail address), a DNS name (an Internet host name), an IP address, and a URI (usually a WWW URL). Multiple instances of a name and multiple name forms may be included.

CRL Number.   The CRL number extension conveys a monotonically increasing sequence number for each CRL issued by a CRL issuer. This extension allows users to easily determine when a particular CRL supersedes another CRL from the same CRL issuer.

Delta CRL Indicator.   The delta CRL indicator extension identifies a CRL as a delta CRL. A delta CRL contains updates to revocation information previously issued and distributed in a complete CRL. This earlier CRL is called the base CRL. In some environments, using delta CRLs can significantly reduce network load and processing time. A delta CRL will generally be smaller than the base CRL that it updates, so applications that obtain a delta CRL consume less network bandwidth than applications that obtain the corresponding complete CRL. Applications that store revocation information in a format other than the CRL structure can add new revocation information to such a local database without reprocessing the older information that is already in the database.

Issuing Distribution Point.   The issuing distribution point extension identifies the CRL distribution point for a particular CRL, and it indicates whether the CRL covers revocation for end entity certificates only, CA certificates only, or a limited set of reason codes.

Freshest CRL.   The freshest CRL extension identifies how to obtain delta CRL information for the base CRL that contains the extension. Given the base CRL, the delta CRL can be fetched and processed. This extension has exactly the same syntax as the CRL distribution point certificate extension and the freshest CRL certificate extension. All of the conventions discussed in the previous chapter apply.

CRL Entry Extensions

ITU-T and ANSI X9 have defined several CRL entry extensions for X.509 v2 CRLs. They are specified in [X50997] and [X955], and they associate additional attributes with CRL entries. Each entry extension in a CRL entry may be designated as critical or noncritical. A CRL validation fails if an unrecognized critical entry extension is encountered. However, unrecognized noncritical entry extensions may be ignored. The X.509 v2 CRL format allows communities to define private extensions to carry information unique to those communities. Communities are encouraged to define noncritical private extensions so that their CRLs can be readily validated by all implementations.

The following CRL entry extensions are the ones that should be properly handled by all implementations.

Reason Code.   The reason code entry extension identifies the reason for certificate revocation. We strongly encourage CRL issuers to include meaningful reason codes in CRL entries; however, the reason code entry extension should be absent instead of using unspecified (enumerated value of zero) as the reason code value.

Hold Instruction Code.   The hold instruction code entry extension provides a registered instruction identifier that indicates the action to be taken after encountering a certificate that has been placed on hold.

Invalidity Date.   The invalidity date entry extension provides the date on which it is known or suspected that the private key was compromised or that the certificate otherwise became invalid. This date may be earlier than the revocation date in the CRL entry, which is the date on which the CRL issuer processed the revocation. When a revocation is first posted in a CRL, the invalidity date may precede the date of issue of earlier CRLs, but the revocation date should not precede the date of issue of earlier CRLs. Whenever this information is available, we strongly encourage CRL issuers to share it.

Certificate Issuer.   The certificate issuer entry extension allows a CRL to include entries from more than one certificate issuer. As stated earlier, such CRLs are called indirect CRLs, and they have the indirect CRL flag set in the issuing distribution point extension. The certificate issuer entry extension identifies the certificate issuer associated with an entry in an indirect CRL. If this entry extension is not present in the first entry in an indirect CRL, the certificate issuer for that entry defaults to the CRL issuer. On subsequent CRL entries where the entry extension is not present, the certificate issuer for the entry is the same as that for the preceding entry.

PKI Components and Users

It is difficult to build a single component that can securely create and distribute certificates and CRLs. PKIs are built from a variety of components, each designed to perform a few tasks particularly well. This section reviews the tasks facing an issuer, groups similar tasks, and assigns these groups to the four basic functional components of a PKI:

- The certification authority
- The registration authority
- The repository
- The archive

So far, Alice and Bob played various user roles. At the simplest level, there are always two distinct users in any PKI-enabled transaction. The first user has a private key and is the subject of a certificate containing the corresponding public key. This user is called the *subscriber* or *certificate holder* and will participate in the transaction using the private key. The second user obtains the certificate and uses the corresponding public key to participate in the transaction. The second user is called the *relying party* or *certificate user*.

Infrastructure Users

In this section we introduce the two types of users supported by a PKI and then describe their functionality. The two types of PKI users are subscribers and relying parties. Subscribers are the subject of a certificate and hold the corresponding private key. Relying parties use the public key in a certificate to verify signatures, encrypt data (key transport), or perform key agreement.

In email security solutions, most entities hold both subscriber and relying party roles. In addition, the CA and RA are generally PKI users themselves. They generate and verify signatures and perform key agreement or key transport between themselves and with users.

SUBSCRIBER AND RELYING PARTY AGREEMENTS

When the CA spent all that time writing a CP, he wasn't just thinking about himself. The CP also relates to Alice and Bob as subscriber and relying party. The CA makes Alice sign agreements about how she can legitimately use her certificate; this is a subscriber agreement. Also, the CP tells Bob what to expect if he chooses to rely on Alice's certificate. In some cases, the CA will even ask Bob to sign a Relying Party Agreement.

Subscribers

Subscribers obtain certificates from the infrastructure and use their private keys to implement security services. They generate digital signatures, decrypt data (for example, they might recover symmetric keys encrypted with their public key), and use their private key to establish symmetric keys through key agreement.

To meet these goals, a subscriber must perform the following tasks:

- Identify a CA to issue the certificate(s).
- Request a certificate directly from the CA or through the RA.
- Include the certificate in transactions as appropriate.

Subscribers may need to interact with the repository to obtain their own certificate but do not need to regularly interact with the repository.

Replying Parties

Relying parties use the PKI to implement security services by employing the public key in another user's certificate. They can verify digital signatures, encrypt data (for example, they might encrypt a symmetric key), and use the public key in another party's certificate to establish a symmetric key through key agreement. Relying parties may include CAs, RAs, persons, and computing systems such as routers and firewalls.

To implement these security services, a relying party must perform the following:

- Identifying a CA as its initial trust point
- Verifying signatures on certificates and CRLs
- Obtaining certificates and CRLs from a repository
- Constructing and validating certification paths

A relying party interacts with the repositories on a day-to-day basis. Its interactions with CAs are limited to selection of an initial trust point. Relying parties have no interactions with RAs.

Infrastructure Components

In this section, we introduce the four components of the PKI and describe their functionality. The functionality described for these components is present in any PKI. However, specific implementations may divide this functionality differently. Functions may be combined into a single component or may be assigned to multiple components. For example, the certification authority and registration authority are sometimes combined into a single component. This does not affect what functions must be performed, just where those functions are performed.

Certification Authorities

The certification authority (CA) is the basic building block of the PKI. The CA is a collection of computer hardware, software, and the people who operate it. The CA is known by two attributes: its name and its public key. The CA performs four basic PKI functions:

- Issuing certificates (that is, creating and signing them)
- Maintaining certificate status information and issuing CRLs
- Publishing its current (unexpired) certificates and CRLs, so that users can obtain the information they need to implement security services
- Maintaining archives of status information about the expired or revoked certificates that it issued

We examine each of these functions and identify responsibilities and requirements they impose on the CA. These requirements may be difficult to satisfy simultaneously. To fulfill these requirements, the CA may delegate certain functions to the other components of the infrastructure.

Issuing Certificates

A CA may issue certificates to subscribers, to other CAs, or both. When a CA issues a certificate, it is asserting that the subject (the entity named in the certificate) has the private key that corresponds to the public key contained in the certificate. If the CA includes additional information in the certificate, the CA is asserting that information corresponds to the subject as well. This additional information might be an email address or policy information. When the subject of the certificate is another CA, the issuer is asserting that the certificates issued by the other CA are trustworthy.

The CA inserts its name in every certificate and CRL it generates, and signs them with its private key. Once users establish that they trust a CA (directly or through a certification path), they can trust certificates issued by that CA. Users can easily identify certificates issued by that CA by comparing its name. To ensure that the certificate is genuine, they verify the signature using the CA's public key.

The CA's name is generally public information, and the CA's signature is the actual basis of trust for these certificates. If an attacker obtains the CA's private key, users will trust the certificates the attacker generates as if the CA itself generated them. *The CA must take significant measures to protect its private key from disclosure.*

To protect the private key, a CA must protect the private key when in use and in storage. To meet this requirement, the CA relies on a cryptographic module. Cryptographic modules generate keys, protect private keys, and implement cryptographic algorithms. They may be implemented in hardware, software, or a combination of hardware and software. Software cryptographic modules are programs that run on the computer system. Hardware cryptographic modules, are peripheral devices that perform cryptographic operations on an external processor. Hardware cryptographic modules keep the private key out of the host system memory, so their security is less dependent on the operating system.

Cryptographic modules may also offer varying levels of protection due to flaws in their design or implementation. The National Institute of Standards and Technology (NIST) developed FIPS 140, ''Security Requirements for Cryptographic Modules,'' which specifies four increasing security levels [FIPS140]. NIST and the Canadian Communications Security Establishment (CSE) accredit third-party laboratories to perform validation testing of cryptographic modules against the FIPS 140 standard.

A CA's private key is at risk when stored in host memory or on a hardware device that has not been validated. A CA should always use a validated hardware cryptographic module to generate its signing key and to protect it at all times. At a minimum, the module must be validated as meeting FIPS 140 Level 2. Higher levels of assurance may be required if the CA is located on a site where physical security is weak.

Of course, the contents of the certificates must be correct to be useful. The information in the certificate must all correspond to the subject named in the certificate. *The CA follows specific procedures to verify the information in a certificate before it is issued.*

Verifying a user's identity, personal information, and policy information are quite different from protecting the CA's private key. Performing this verification is inherently an external matter; it relies on information provided by parties outside the CA operational staff.

The CA can verify some of the certificate contents based on technical mechanisms, though. In particular, the CA can use the digital signature mechanism to ensure that a user actually has the private key corresponding to the public key in the certificate. This verification process is often called *proof of possession*. Proof of possession may be achieved by examining the request itself, rather than examining external data.

In addition to correctness, the contents of the certificates and CRLs must also reflect the CA's certificate profile. A CA specifies the types of information that it will include in certificates. Assume the Little Shop of Certificates CA has stated that it will only issue certificates for email. It cannot issue Bob a certificate for contract signing, even if Bob has that authority. *The CA must ensure that all certificates and CRLs it issues conform to its profile.*

To ensure that a CA issues certificates and CRLs that conform to its profile, a CA has to perform two actions: it must protect the integrity of the profile, and it must verify that each and every certificate and CRL it generates conforms to the profile.

To protect the integrity of the profile, the CA restricts access to the CA components. These restrictions may be physical restrictions (for example, locked and guarded rooms or keycard access), logical restrictions (such as network firewalls), or procedural restrictions. Procedural restrictions might require two CA staff members to modify the system or prevent system operators from approving the audit logs.

Maintaining Status Information and Issuing CRLs

As with certificates, the contents of the CRLs must be complete and correct to be useful. Errors of omission may cause a user to accept an untrustworthy certificate, resulting in a loss of security. Listing trustworthy certificates or incorrect revocation dates may cause a user to reject a trustworthy certificate, resulting in denial of service. *The CA must accurately maintain the list of certificates that should no longer be trusted.*

Protecting the certificate status information is similar to protecting the profile. However, the decision to modify the status of a certificate relies on information provided by parties outside the CA operational staff. This is similar to verifying identity and other attributes of the certificate subject.

Publishing Certificates and CRLs

A CA is only useful if the certificates and CRLs that it generates are available to the users. If Alice and Bob cannot obtain the certificates and CRLs they need, they will not be able to implement the security services they want. Of course, Alice and Bob can always exchange their own personal certificates and their CRLs. However, each may need additional CA certificates to establish a certification path. *The CA must distribute its certificates and CRLs.*

When a CA serves an unrestricted user community, distribution of certificates and CRLs is all about availability and performance, not security. There is no requirement to restrict access to certificates and CRLs, since they need not be secret. An attacker could deny service to Alice and Bob by deleting or modifying information, but the attacker cannot make them trust the altered information without obtaining the CA's private key.

A CA may restrict its services to a closed community, though. In this case, the CA may wish to deny the attacker access to the certificates. To achieve these goals, the CA may wish to secure the distribution of certificates and CRLs. The integrity of the certificates and CRLs is not at risk, but the CA may not wish to disclose the information they contain. For example, if a company's certificates implicitly identify its R&D personnel, this information could be exploited by a competitor. The competitor could determine the types of R&D by their backgrounds or simply try to hire the personnel.

Maintaining Archives

Finally, the CA needs to maintain information to identify the signer of an old document based on an expired certificate. To support this goal, the archive must identify the actual subject named in a certificate, establish that they requested the certificate, and show that the certificate was valid at the time the document was signed.* The archive must also include any information regarding the revocation of this certificate. *The CA must maintain sufficient archival information to establish the validity of certificates after they have expired.*

CAs are well suited to the generation of archive information but not to its maintenance. A CA can create a detailed audit trail, with sufficient information to describe why it generated a certificate or revoked it. This is a common attribute of computer systems. However, maintaining that information for long periods of time is not a common function.

Delegating Responsibility

The CA sometimes delegates some of its responsibilities. An entity that verifies certificate contents (especially identifying the user) is called a *registration authority* (RA). An RA may also assume some of the responsibility for certificate revocation decisions. An entity that distributes certificates and CRLs is called a repository. A repository may be designed to maximize performance and availability. The entity that provides long-term secure storage for the archival information is called an archive. An archive does not require the performance of a repository but must be designed for secure storage.

A CA is not restricted to a single RA, repository, or archive. In practice, a CA is likely to have multiple RAs; different entities may be needed for different groups of users. Repositories are often duplicated to maximize availability, increase performance, and add redundancy. There is no requirement for multiple archives.

Registration Authority

As stated previously, an RA is designed to verify certificate contents for the CA. Certificate contents may reflect information presented by the entity requesting the certificate, such as a driver's license or recent pay stub. They may also reflect information provided by a third party. A certificate may reflect data from the company's Human Resources department or a letter from a designated company official. For example, Bob's certificate could indicate

---

*This may require additional information, such as a cryptographic timestamp. Additional information on cryptographic timestamps may be found in [TSP].

that he has signature authority for small contracts. The RA aggregates these inputs and provides this information to the CA.

Like the CA, the RA is a collection of computer hardware, software, and the person or people who operate it. Unlike a CA, a single person often operates an RA. Each CA will maintain a list of accredited RAs; that is, a list of RAs determined to be trustworthy. Each RA is known to the CA by a name and a public key. By verifying the RA's signature on a message, the CA can be sure that an accredited RA provided the information, and it can be trusted. Therefore, it is important that the RA provide adequate protection for its own private key. RAs should always use hardware cryptographic modules that have been validated against FIPS 140.

Repository

A *repository* distributes certificates and CRLs. A repository accepts certificates and CRLs from one or more CAs and makes them available to parties that need them to implement security services.

A repository is a system, and is known by its address and access protocol. It provides certificates and CRLs upon request. Requests could be based on the name of a user or CA or other information. Repositories are not trusted entities; the user accepts the certificates and CRLs because the CA signed them. The source of the information does not affect its trustworthiness. Since the data itself establishes its integrity, a repository may be designed to maximize availability and performance.

Of course, repositories need to restrict the set of users who can update the information. If an attacker replaces the correct certificates with garbage, or simply inserts an expired CRL, he or she can achieve a denial of service (DoS) attack. Users of the PKI would not be fooled into accepting the out-of-date information but may be denied the security services they need.

Archive

An archive accepts the responsibility for long-term storage of archival information on behalf of the CA. An archive asserts that the information was good at the time it was received and has not been modified while in the archive. The information provided by the CA to the repository must be sufficient to determine if a certificate was actually issued by the CA as specified in the certificate and was valid at that time. The archive protects that information through technical mechanisms and appropriate procedures while in its care. If a dispute arises at a later date, the information can be used to verify that the private key associated with the certificate was used to sign a document. This permits the verification of signatures on old documents (such as wills) at a later date.

Secure Email

Protecting Email Message Contents

While email has been around since the 1960s, it wasn't until the late 1980s that email security protocols appeared. Of course, instead of one mechanism, numerous competing protocols showed up. You might expect competition to lead to the ultimate adoption of the strongest protocol, but unfortunately the various alternatives did not work with each other. Too many choices hampered adoption of any of them. Luckily one de facto standard emerged, and this chapter will focus on it. But first we are going to describe the various alternatives, because many of the features supported by today's widespread email security solutions have been cherry-picked, taking important features from their predecessors and competitors.

Interoperability of the security protocol is important. Alice may use security protocol A to secure the message content of an email that she sends to Bob, but if Bob doesn't support the same content security protocol, then Bob can't process the contents. The same is true of the algorithms Alice uses when she's securing the contents. If she picks an algorithm that Bob doesn't support, then Bob is going to be out of luck when he receives the message.

As explained in Chapter 2, email has two parts: the commands and the content. This chapter will focus on securing the content, and Chapter 7 will address securing the commands.

Evolution

There have been six notable solutions to secure email contents: *Privacy Enhanced Mail* (PEM), *Pretty Good Privacy* (PGP), *MIME Object Security Services* (MOSS), *Message Security Protocol* (MSP), *Public-Key Cryptography Standard #7* (PKCS#7), and *Secure Multiple Purpose Internet Mail Extensions* (S/MIME). All provide confidentiality, data origin authentication, message integrity, and non-repudiation of origin, but they all do it differently. Most emerged at around the same time and (some say) competed against each another for supremacy, but really they all evolved and adopted features from one another [HOUS1].

Privacy Enhanced Mail

PEM is the granddaddy of secure Internet email standards. Originally, PEM was developed by the Privacy and Security Research Group (PSRG), but it was transitioned to the IETF to make a standards track document. The IETF first published it in 1987, and it was updated three times, finally resulting in a four part standard in 1993:

RFC 1421 Part I: Message Encryption and Authentication Procedures. This defines the message encryption and authentication procedures. Three message structures are defined:

- MIC-CLEAR, where MIC is message integrity check, provides authentication and integrity, but without confidentiality. The message is said to be *clear-signed* because the message contents are not encoded (i.e., the message contents are human-readable).

- MIC-ONLY provides authentication and integrity, but without confidentiality. MIC-ONLY is different from MIC-CLEAR because it encodes the contents similar to MIME (i.e., the message contents are not human-readable).

- ENCRYPTED supports authentication, integrity, and confidentiality services.

RFC 1422 Part II: Certificate-Based Key Management.   This defines the key management architecture and infrastructure. It supports both asymmetric and symmetric key management techniques.

RFC 1423 Part III: Algorithms, Modes, and Identifiers.   This provides definitions, formats, references, and citations for cryptographic algorithms, usage modes, and associated identifiers and parameters. The hash algorithms are MD2 or MD5, the signature algorithm is RSA, and the confidentiality algorithm is DES in either ECB or CBC mode.

RFC 1424 Part IV, Key Certification and Related Services.   This describes three services that support PEM: key certification, CRL storage, and CRL retrieval.

PEM never really took off, primarily because it was invented before MIME was invented. PEM did introduce numerous ideas that have survived:

Choice of Security Services.   By defining multiple message formats, PEM allowed users to select which services they needed. Accepting that one size doesn't fit all was a really good idea, but PEM did require that encrypted messages be signed first. In this way, authentication was always provided.

Transfer Encoding.   PEM was the first to describe the encoding for arbitrary data in plaintext, which is sometimes referred to as ASCII Armor. This technique is the basis for MIME. PEM invented Base64 encoding.

PKI enrollment request/response.   While X.509 may have defined the public key certificate format in 1988, PEM introduced the idea of client requests and responses to obtain a certificate.

Certificate Profile.   X.509 describes the certificate structure, but it doesn't say what must be included for a particular environment. PEM was the first to describe which of the fields in an X.509 certificate are required and values that must be supported. This idea was not lost and the IETF published [RFC3280] as its profile for X.509 certificates.

There were two main reasons why PEM did not take off:

▪ PEM's PKI called for single hierarchical root CA. First, the cost of implementing one root CA for all of the Internet that would be liable for all of the actions of its users was daunting. Second, privacy pundits, most notably Zimmerman and Gilmore, objected to the concept of a single root because it placed too much power in one entity's hands. Gilmore insisted on support for persona identities for pseudo-anonymous communications. Think about what could happen if the uber-root CA decided it didn't like you, your company, or, heck, your country. It could just revoke the certificate, and you'd be unable to send secure email.

▪ PEM only supported text messages and didn't support MIME attachments.

Pretty Good Privacy

Phil Zimmerman didn't like PEM so much that he went out and wrote his own program called PGP. It was first available in 1991 but not standardized until 1996 in [RFC1991]. PGP defines message formats for digitally signed messages and encrypted messages. It also defines its own public key certificate format and format for storing them. Eventually, support for X.509 certificates was added to PGP, and it was renamed *OpenPGP* [RFC4880].

PGP introduced the following concepts:

Decentralized trust.   The main goal of PGP was to decentralize trust, and it did just that with its *web-of-trust*. The premise is based on introductions and how much you trust the person doing the introduction, which could be completely, partially, or not at all. If Alice knows and completely trusts Bob, and Bob introduces Matt to Alice, then Alice trusts Matt.

Partial trust is a configuration setting that allows Alice to indicate how many people must trust the new person before she will completely trust them. Untrusted keys can be used, but PGP will warn you when it happens.

Key generation.   PGP allowed users to choose how strong their keys were and then to generate the key themselves. This exposed to the user that there were different grades of encryption. The user's choice was based either on some thought or paranoia.

Internet names.   X.509 is part of the X.500 Directory Service series of standards, and it obviously named its subject with X.500 names. PGP was developed without that burden. Various Internet-related name forms are now supported in certificates in the issuer and subject alternative name extensions.

Key fingerprints.   Users needed to determine whether a key was unaltered, so PGP gave the users a tool to make a key fingerprint. It's really just a hash of the key. When Alice wants to know that she got Bob's key, she calls him and reads out his key fingerprint. If it matches, then Alice knows she's got Bob's key. Key fingerprint is now in the certificate. It's in the authority key identifier and subject key identifier certificate extensions.

Compression.   PGP optionally provides for the compression of messages, which shrinks the message size. The standard indicates that compression is always applied after the signature but before encryption to reduce the quantity of known plaintext to an attacker; more importantly the other order would not work well because ciphertext does not compress.

There were two main reasons why PGP wasn't embraced more widely:

Late to standardize.   Security folks like to scrutinize everything and the more time they have to scrutinize things the better. While PGP was first available in 1991, no one got around to standardizing it for many years. Development of secure email standards in open fora leads to peer review, which in turn leads to greater confidence that the promised security is really being provided.

User involvement.   PGP put trust management in the hands of everyday users. Many technology-inclined people (a.k.a. geeks and nerds) embraced PGP and still use it today, but for the common user the number of actions required for trust management was too great.

MIME Object Security Services

MIME Object Security Services (MOSS) was based on PEM but was specifically aimed at supporting Multipurpose Internet Mail Extensions (MIME) and the `multipart/signed` MIME type. Both were published in 1995, with MOSS published as [RFC1848] and `multipart/signed` MIME type was published as [RFC1847]. The designers embraced MIME, which had not been invented when PEM was created. MOSS also included better support for Internet names and completely separating security services, which allowed unsigned but encrypted messages. It was never widely implemented because of S/MIME.

Message Security Protocol

Message Security Protocol (MSP) was the U.S. military's standard for securing email. Development of MSP began at about the same time as PEM. It was originally developed by contractors working for NSA and published by NIST [NISTMSPR]. It was designed to secure X.400 electronic mail, a failed competitor of Internet email, but it also included rudimentary support for Internet email. It used military grade cryptographic algorithms, and it had features like signed receipts, security labels, and encryption for mail lists. Numerous vendors offer MSP, primarily aimed at the government market, but MSP ultimately failed to capture any significant market share.

Public-Key Cryptography Standard #7

Public-Key Cryptography Standard #7 (PKCS#7) was developed by RSA Data Security Inc. as a general syntax for cryptographically protected data; it was not developed specifically for email. It was published in 1991 as part of the Public-Key Cryptography Standards (PKCS) series. RSA Data Security started the effort to address some concerns with PEM, especially creating an encapsulation layer for each security service and the ability to use different keys for signature and encryption. At the time export control was a big concern, so a strong signature key used with a weaker encryption key was an important feature.* PKCS#7 was widely deployed, and a consortium was formed to bring PKCS#7 to the IETF. PKCS#7 version 1.5 was published as [RFC2315], which is an information track document, and then RSA Data Security ceded change control to the IETF.

Secure Multipurpose Internet Mail Extensions

Secure Multipurpose Internet Mail Extensions (S/MIME) makes use of PKCS#7 and MIME to create a security solution for Internet email. RSA Data Security lead the effort, starting in 1995. S/MIME version 2 was published as [RFC2311], which is an information track document, and then RSA Data Security ceded change control to the IETF.

*Actually, export control was a concern for all of the efforts. Many vendors addressed export control concern by offering support for weak encryption algorithms in "exportable" versions of their products or embedding a key escrow capability.

S/MIME version 3 was developed in the IETF. It includes an update to PKCS#7 (referred to as the Cryptographic Message Syntax, or CMS), and it addresses the biggest shortcomings in PKCS#7 version 1.5 and S/MIME version 2; they were designed for the RSA algorithm, and there was no consideration for the Diffie-Hellman key agreement algorithm or the DSA signature algorithm. Additionally, the RSA algorithm, at the time, was patent protected, so the IETF publishing a standards track document with patented technology was not desired. In addition to the CMS specification [RFC2630], the IETF published two documents that specified S/MIME: MSG [RFC2633] and CERT [RFC2632], and both have since been updated. MSG is the message specification, and it indicates which parts of PKCS #7 need to be supported. CERT specifies the certificate-handling procedures. CMS, as an update to PKCS#7, added support for additional key management techniques and digital signature algorithms.

CRYPTOGRAPHIC MESSAGE SYTNAX

CMS [RFC3852] is the star of the S/MIME show. CMS defines the syntax for the secure messages in a transport-agnostic way. In fact, it can be used to protect files on your hard disk, too. CMS doesn't care whether the content is a binary file, the body of an email, a web page, or anything else for that matter. S/MIME makes use of MIME to encode CMS-protected content.

Since S/MIME and CMS are supported by almost every email client software package, we will focus on S/MIME and CMS as the mechanism to protect email's contents.

Protecting Email Content

The first part of protecting email is protecting the message content. CMS defines a number of mechanisms to do this, but before we get in to the nitty-gritty of those mechanisms we need to cover some basic concepts.

WARNING We assume that you have some familiarity with ASN.1. If you need a primer, we suggest starting with Appendix B. Additionally, RFCs are in the process of moving from the 1988 version of ASN.1 to the 2002 version. This document uses the work-in-progress 2002 ASN.1 syntax. This transition is being done to make use of the new constraints mechanism and because the 1988 version of ASN.1 is now no longer supported by the ITU-T.

Concepts

A number of foundational concepts are needed. Content types, encapsulation, version numbers, attributes, and MIME layers are important to understand the design principles.

CMS Content Types

CMS defines a number of content types. This term was taken from MIME and referred to media types; for example, message, audio, and video. The same can be said of CMS content types; it's just that sometimes the media is encrypted, signed, or compressed. We'll divide the CMS content types in to two categories: *protecting CMS content types* and *non-protecting CMS content types*. The difference being that the protecting CMS content types provide one or more of the security services described in Chapter 3 — remember, access control, authentication, integrity, confidentiality, and non-repudiation. The protecting content types are: signed-data, enveloped-data, encrypted-data, digested-data, authenticated-data, and authenticated-enveloped-data. The non-protecting content types on the other hand provide no security services. The non-protecting content types are: data, compressed-data, receipt, content-collection, and content-with-attributes.

The ASN.1 structure below provides an example definition for a content type. It uses TYPE-IDENTIFIER from X.681, where the content type is simply the name of the content type (e.g., ct-ContentTypeName), the definition links the syntax associated with the content type (e.g., ContentTypeSyntax), and the object identifier that names the content type (e.g., id-ContentTypeObjectIdentifier). All of the content type definitions use a similar syntax.

```
CONTENT-TYPE ::= TYPE-IDENTIFIER

ct-ContentTypeName CONTENT-TYPE  ::=
   { ContentTypeSyntax IDENTIFIED BY id-ContentTypeObjectIdentifier }
```

Encapsulating

CMS makes extensive use of the concept of *encapsulating*, which is also referred to as *enveloping*, *layering*, or *wrapping*. The idea is simple: put one content type inside of another content type. (It's akin to putting an envelope in another envelope.) This concept is not unique to CMS and is used in many communications protocols. Figure 6-1 shows an example of this technique and a special case called *triple-wrapping*. Triple-wrapped refers to a content being encapsulated in a signed-data, which is in turn encapsulated in an enveloped-

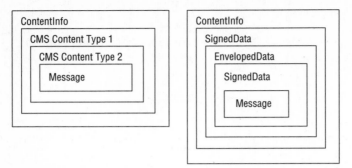

Figure 6-1 Encapsulating content types and triple wrapping

data, which is in turn encapsulated in signed-data, and finally encapsulated in a content info. The signed-data encapsulated in the enveloped-data is said to the inner layer, and the signed-data that encapsulates the enveloped-data is said to be the outer layer.

The very first layer in CMS is always the `ContentInfo` layer. It simply carries the object identifier for the content type that it encapsulates. It uses the following ASN.1, which looks more complicated, but it is really pretty straightforward:

```
ContentInfo ::= SEQUENCE {
   contentType     CONTENT-TYPE.&id({ContentSet}),
   content     [0] EXPLICIT CONTENT-TYPE.&Type
                   ({ContentSet}{@contentType}) }
```

`ContentInfo` is a sequence of the object identifier for the content type followed by the content itself.

The protecting content types use two special encapsulation syntaxes. Signed-data, digested-data, and authenticated-data use the `Encapsulated-ContentInfo` syntax, while enveloped-data, encrypted-data, and authenticated-enveloped-data use the `EncryptedContentInfo`. Both `Encapsulated-ContentInfo` and `EncryptedContentInfo` indicate the syntax of the content type with an object identifier and both have a syntax of *OCTET STRING*. If you're wondering why they don't just use `ContentInfo` it's because cryptographic algorithms work best with octet strings as inputs. There are two differences between the `EncryptedContentInfo` and `EncryptedContentInfo` syntaxes. First, `EncryptedContentInfo` needs to indicate which algorithm was used to encrypt the content; otherwise, we'd have to guess. Second, `EncryptedContentInfo` carries an encrypted content. The ASN.1 syntaxes for both are listed next:

```
EncapsulatedContentInfo ::= SEQUENCE {
   eContentType     CONTENT-TYPE.&id({ContentSet}),
   eContent     [0] EXPLICIT OCTET STRING (CONTAINING CONTENT-TYPE.&Type
                   ({ContentSet}{@eContentType}) OPTIONAL }
```

```
EncryptedContentInfo ::= SEQUENCE {
  contentType                    CONTENT-TYPE.&id({ContentSet}),
  contentEncryptionAlgorithm     ContentEncryptionAlgorithmIdentifier,
  encryptedContent           [0] IMPLICIT OCTET STRING OPTIONAL }
```

Version Numbers

A version number is included at the beginning of many of the ASN.1 structures. This allows for evolution of the protocol and allows implementations to know what version of the syntax they're handling. You might note that not all of version numbers are sequential. This is so because of an update to PKCS#7 that was never formally published.* Because of this, some version numbers were skipped as CMS evolved to ensure that anyone who implemented the unpublished version would not run into trouble. The original authors of PKCS#7 had the foresight to include version numbers from the beginning, which has been very helpful as the protocol has been revised.

Attributes

All of the protecting content types, except digested-data, support the inclusion of attributes with the encapsulated content type (see Table 6-1). Signed and authenticated attributes are cryptographically bound to the content, so that verifiers will be able to detect their removal. Unsigned, unprotected, and unauthenticated attributes are not cryptographically bound or encrypted; therefore, intermediaries can add or remove attributes without affecting the protecting content type.

   Some attributes are limited to the content type and the place in the content type in which they can appear. Also, some attributes are limited as to where they can appear in the encapsulation layers because some attributes require protection themselves. With triple-wrapped messages, some attributes are restricted to the inner layer or the outer layer, while others have no restrictions. We'll return to the subject of attributes later in this chapter, and we'll explain which attributes can in which layer.

MIME Layer

CMS doesn't require a MIME layer between for each content type, but S/MIME does. This adds overhead, and if there are many layers, it can add up to a lot of overhead. We'll return to this subject later in the chapter.

---

*An unpublished version was used for the Secure Electronic Transaction (SET) specification generated by MasterCard and VISA. SET was designed to secure bankcard transactions over open networks like the Internet.

Table 6-1 Protecting Content Types That Allow Attributes

CONTENT TYPE	ATTRIBUTES ALLOWED
signed-data	Signed attributes Unsigned attributes
enveloped-data	Unprotected attributes
encrypted-data	Unprotected attributes
digested-data	N/A
authentication-data	Authenticated attributes Unauthenticated attributes
authenticated-enveloped-data	Authenticated-attributes Unauthenticated attributes

Protecting CMS Content Types

There are six CMS protecting content types defined. This section addresses them all: signed-data, enveloped-data, encrypted-data, digest-data, authenticated-data, and authenticated-enveloped-data. Note however, that S/MIME only makes use of signed-data and enveloped-data.

Signed Data

Signed-data is the workhorse content type. The signed-data content type provides data origin authentication and integrity. It also supports access control, peer-entity authentication, non-repudiation with proof of origin, and non-repudiation with proof of delivery. It does everything but clean the kitchen sink and provide confidentiality. Things to note about signed-data:

Digest Algorithms.   The requirement for the `digestAlgorithms` field says that it may be empty, but in practice each digest algorithm used by a signer is normally included.

Certificates.   Technically the *cert-bag*, which is a grab bag of certificates for the signer or signers, certificates are optional, but the originator normally includes all of them in the certification path up to but not including the trust anchor.

CRLs.   It seems like a good idea to include revocation information in-message so that the relying party doesn't need to go and get it. Well, if you were an attacker, wouldn't you make sure that you put a revocation information in that said your certificate was valid? On a less sinister note, email is store-and-forward, which means that it can take some amount

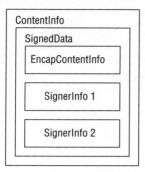

Figure 6-2 Parallel signatures

of time for delivery to occur, and during this delay new revocation information might become available. So practically, even if revocation information is included, it's ignored. For these reasons, most leave it out, because it just makes the message unnecessarily larger.

The signed data content type is identified by the `id-signedData` object identifier, and it has the following syntax:

```
ct-SignedData CONTENT-TYPE  ::=
  { SignedData IDENTIFIED BY id-signedData }

id-signedData OBJECT IDENTIFIER ::=
  { iso(1) member-body(2) us(840) rsadsi(113549) pkcs(1) pkcs7(7) 2 }

SignedData ::= SEQUENCE {
  version              CMSVersion,
  digestAlgorithms     SET OF DigestAlgorithmIdentifier,
  encapContentInfo     EncapsulatedContentInfo,
  certificates     [0] IMPLICIT CertificateSet OPTIONAL,
  crls             [1] IMPLICIT RevocationInfoChoices OPTIONAL,
  signerInfos          SignerInfos }

SignerInfos ::= SET OF SignerInfo
```

One of the more interesting things to note is the `SET OF SignerInfo`. This translates, in layman's terms, to the supporting of signatures over the same content from multiple signers, or *parallel signatures*. Figure 6-2 shows an example of one message with two `SignerInfo` structures, each generated by a different signer. Different signed and unsigned attributes can be conveyed by each signer. Different algorithms can be used by each signer. The signatures do not need to be applied at the same time either, as addition of a new `SignerInfo` does not affect the previous `SignerInfo`.

`SignerInfo` has the following syntax:

```
SignerInfo ::= SEQUENCE {
  version                CMSVersion,
  sid                    SignerIdentifier,
  digestAlgorithm        DigestAlgorithmIdentifier,
  signedAttrs       [0]  IMPLICIT SignedAttributes OPTIONAL,
  signatureAlgorithm     SignatureAlgorithmIdentifer,
  signature              SignatureValue,
  unsignedAttrs     [1]  IMPLICIT UnsignedAttributes OPTIONAL }

SignerIdentifier ::= CHOICE {
  issuerAndSerialNumber       IssuerAndSerialNumber,
  subjectKeyIdentifier   [0]  SubjectKeyIdentifier }

SignatureValue ::= OCTET STRING
```

NOTE There is a link back to the signer's certificate, which must contain the key usage extension with at least the `digitalSignature` or the `nonRepudiation` bit set.

Enveloped Data

The thing to note about the enveloped-data content type is key management. Five different key management techniques are defined to get the content encryption key to the recipient. Key transport recipient info, key agreement recipient info, key encryption key recipient info, password recipient info, and other recipient info are described later in the chapter.

The encrypted-data content type is identified by the `id-envelopedData` object identifier, and it has the following syntax:

```
ct-EnvelopedData CONTENT-TYPE   ::=
   { EnvelopedData IDENTIFIED BY id-envelopedData }

id-envelopedData OBJECT IDENTIFIER ::=
   { iso(1) member-body(2) us(840) rsadsi(113549) pkcs(1) pkcs7(7) 3 }

EnvelopedData ::= SEQUENCE {
  version                CMSVersion,
  originatorInfo    [0]  IMPLICIT OriginatorInfo OPTIONAL,
  recipientInfos         RecipientInfos,
  encryptedContentInfo   EncryptedContentInfo,
  unprotectedAttrs  [1]  IMPLICIT Attributes
                            {{UnprotectedAttribute}} OPTIONAL }
```

```
OriginatorInfo ::= SEQUENCE {
  certs  [0] IMPLICIT CertificateSet OPTIONAL,
  crls   [1] IMPLICIT RevocationInfoChoices OPTIONAL }

RecipientInfos ::= SET SIZE (1..MAX) OF RecipientInfo

EncryptedContent ::= OCTET STRING

RecipientInfo ::= CHOICE {
  ktri       KeyTransRecipientInfo,
  kari   [1] KeyAgreeRecipientInfo,
  kekri  [2] KEKRecipientInfo,
  pwri   [3] PasswordRecipientinfo,
  ori    [4] OtherRecipientInfo }
```

Key Transport Recipient Info

The `KeyTransportRecipientInfo` is used, as its name implies, to support key transport algorithms, namely RSA. If you remember our discussion of RSA from Chapter 4, Alice creates a symmetric key and encrypts it with Bob's public key, and then Bob uses his own private key to decrypt the value and recover the symmetric key. That's why there's no need to include the originator's certificate. The recipient figures out which `KeyTransportRecipientInfo` is theirs with the `rid` field. The `encryptedKey` contains the encrypted content encryption key. A separate `KeyTransportRecipientInfo` is needed for each recipient. The `KeyTransportRecipientInfo` uses the following syntax:

```
KeyTransRecipientInfo ::= SEQUENCE {
  version               CMSVersion,  -- always set to 0 or 2
  rid                   RecipientIdentifier,
  keyEncryptionAlgorithm AlgorithmIdentifier
                             {{KeyTransportAlgorithmList}},
  encryptedKey          EncryptedKey }

RecipientIdentifier ::= CHOICE {
  issuerAndSerialNumber     IssuerAndSerialNumber,
  subjectKeyIdentifier  [0] SubjectKeyIdentifier }
```

NOTE There is a link to the recipient's certificate; it must contain the key usage extension with the `keyEncipherment` bit set.

Key Agreement Recipient Info

The `KeyAgreeRecipientInfo` is used to support key agreement algorithms; for example, DH, ECDH, and ECMQV. If you remember our discussion of DH from Chapter 4, Alice fetches Bob's certificate to obtain his public key and then Alice generates a public/private key pair in the same group as Bob's key pair. Alice combines her private key with Bob's public key to obtain a pairwise symmetric key. Bob needs Alice's public key to combine with his private key to obtain the same pairwise symmetric key. That's why you need to include either Alice's certificate or just her public key. The `ukm` field is used by some key management schemes that make use of additional private keying material. Unlike the `KeyTransportRecipientInfo`, one `KeyAgreeRecipientInfo` can be used by all recipients, assuming that the same algorithm and originator public key are used. Inside, there is a sequence of `RecipientEncryptedKey` values, one for each intended recipient. Recipients figure out which `KeyAgreeRecipientInfo` is theirs by examining the `rid` field. The `KeyAgreeRecipientInfo` uses the following syntax:

```
KeyAgreeRecipientInfo ::= SEQUENCE {
   version                   CMSVersion,  -- always set to 3
   originator            [0] EXPLICIT OriginatorIdentifierOrKey,
   ukm                   [1] EXPLICIT UserKeyingMaterial OPTIONAL,
   keyEncryptionAlgorithm    AlgorithmIdentifier
                               {{KeyEncryptionAlgorithmList}},
   recipientEncryptedKeys    RecipientEncryptedKeys }

OriginatorIdentifierOrKey ::= CHOICE {
   issuerAndSerialNumber     IssuerAndSerialNumber,
   subjectKeyIdentifier  [0] SubjectKeyIdentifier,
   originatorKey         [1] OriginatorPublicKey }

OriginatorPublicKey ::= SEQUENCE {
   algorithm  AlgorithmIdentifier {{AlgorithmList}},
   publicKey  BIT STRING }

RecipientEncryptedKeys ::= SEQUENCE OF RecipientEncryptedKey

RecipientEncryptedKey ::= SEQUENCE {
   rid           KeyAgreeRecipientIdentifier,
   encryptedKey  EncryptedKey }

KeyAgreeRecipientIdentifier ::= CHOICE {
   issuerAndSerialNumber     IssuerAndSerialNumber,
   rKeyId                [0] IMPLICIT RecipientKeyIdentifier }
```

```
RecipientKeyIdentifier ::= SEQUENCE {
  subjectKeyIdentifier  SubjectKeyIdentifier,
  date                  GeneralizedTime OPTIONAL,
  other                 OtherKeyAttribute OPTIONAL }

SubjectKeyIdentifier ::= OCTET STRING
```

NOTE There is a link back to the recipient's certificate; it must contain the key usage extension with the `keyAgreement` bit set.

Key Encryption Key Recipient Info

The `KEKRecipientInfo` is used when the originator and recipient support previously distributed key-encryption keys. The originator indicates which key was used with `kekid` field, and the `encryptedKey` is the content-encryption key encrypted with the previously distributed key-encryption key. The `KEKRecipientInfo` uses the following syntax:

```
KEKRecipientInfo ::= SEQUENCE {
  version                CMSVersion,  -- always set to 4
  kekid                  KEKIdentifier,
  keyEncryptionAlgorithm KeyEncryptionAlgorithmIdentifier,
  encryptedKey           EncryptedKey }

KEKIdentifier ::= SEQUENCE {
  keyIdentifier  OCTET STRING,
  date           GeneralizedTime OPTIONAL,
  other          OtherKeyAttribute OPTIONAL }
```

Password Recipient Info

The `PasswordRecipientInfo` is used when the originator and recipient support a previously distributed shared password or secret as the key-encryption key. The originator indicates how the key is derived and the key encryption algorithm that is used. The `encryptedKey` is the encrypted content-encryption key. The `PasswordRecipientInfo` uses the following syntax:

```
PasswordRecipientInfo ::= SEQUENCE {
  version                   CMSVersion,   -- Always set to 0
  keyDerivationAlgorithm [0] KeyDerivationAlgorithmIdentifier OPTIONAL,
  keyEncryptionAlgorithm    KeyEncryptionAlgorithmIdentifiers,
  encryptedKey              EncryptedKey }
```

Other Recipient Info

The `OtherRecipientInfo` permits the definition of additional key management techniques. It identifies them with an object identifier, which also indicates the syntax of the key management fields. The `OtherRecipientInfo` uses the following syntax:

```
OTHER-RECIPIENT ::= TYPE-IDENTIFIER

OtherRecipientInfo ::= SEQUENCE {
  oriType   OTHER-RECIPIENT.&id({SupportedOtherRecipInfo}),
  oriValue  OTHER-RECIPIENT.&Type({SupportedOtherRecipInfo}{@oriType})}

SupportedOtherRecipInfo OTHER-RECIPIENT ::= { ... }
```

Encrypted Data

The encrypted data content type provides content confidentiality. Unlike enveloped-data, it provides for no key management information for originator or recipients. The keys must be managed via other means. It is often used for when keying material is available from other sources. The encrypted-data content type is identified by the `id-encryptedData` object identifier, and it has the following syntax:

```
ct-EncryptedData CONTENT-TYPE  ::=
  { EncryptedData IDENTIFIED BY id-encryptedData }

id-encryptedData OBJECT IDENTIFIER ::=
  { iso(1) member-body(2) us(840) rsadsi(113549) pkcs(1) pkcs7(7) 6 }

EncryptedData ::= SEQUENCE {
  version                  CMSVersion,
  encryptedContentInfo     EncryptedContentInfo,
  unprotectedAttrs    [1] IMPLICIT Attributes
                              {{UnprotectedAttributes}} OPTIONAL }
```

Digest Data

The digested-data content type provides content integrity. Used by itself, this content type has dubious value because both the hash value and the contents are available; this is why it's normally used an input to enveloped-data. The digested data content type is identified by the `id-digestedData` object identifier, and it has the following syntax:

```
ct-DigestedData CONTENT-TYPE  ::=
  { DigestedData IDENTIFIED BY id-digestedData }

id-digestedData OBJECT IDENTIFIER ::=
  { iso(1) member-body(2) us(840) rsadsi(113549) pkcs(1) pkcs7(7) 5 }
```

```
DigestedData ::= SEQUENCE {
  Version           CMSVersion,
  digestAlgorithm   DigestAlgorithmIdentifier,
  encapContentInfo  EncapsulatedContentInfo,
  digest            Digest }

Digest ::= OCTET STRING
```

Authenticated Data

The authenticated-data content type provides content integrity. The difference between this content type and the digested-data content type is that an authentication-key is also provided for each recipient for verifying the integrity of the content. Things to note include the following:

Content.   Arbitrary content types are supported, but it is unencrypted.

Key management.   This uses the same `OriginatorInfo` and `RecipientInfo` structures as the enveloped-data content type. It supports key transport, key agreement, password, and other key management techniques.

Attributes.   Both authenticated and unauthenticated attributes are supported, but only the authenticated attributes are cryptographically bound to the content. Neither set of attributes is encrypted.

The authenticated-data content type is identified by the `id-authenticatedData` object identifier, and it has the following syntax:

```
ct-AuthenticatedData CONTENT-TYPE  ::=
  { AuthenticatedData IDENTIFIED BY id-authenticatedData }

id-ct-authData OBJECT IDENTIFIER ::=
  { iso(1) member-body(2) us(840) rsadsi(113549) pkcs(1) pkcs-9(9)
    smime(16) ct(1) 2 }

AuthenticatedData ::= SEQUENCE {
  version            CMSVersion,
  originatorInfo  [0] IMPLICIT OriginatorInfo OPTIONAL,
  recipientInfos     RecipientInfos,
  macAlgorithm       MessageAuthenticationCodeAlgorithm,
  digestAlgorithm [1] DigestAlgorithmIdentifier OPTIONAL,
  encapContentInfo   EncapsulatedContentInfo,
  authAttrs       [2] IMPLICIT AuthAttributes OPTIONAL,
  mac                MessageAuthenticationCode,
  unauthAttrs     [3] IMPLICIT UnauthAttributes OPTIONAL }

MessageAuthenticationCode ::= OCTET STRING
```

Authenticated-Enveloped Data

The authenticated-enveloped-data content type provides content integrity and confidentiality. It's similar to authenticated-data except the content is encrypted as well as authenticated. Things to note include:

Content.   Arbitrary content types are supported, and it is encrypted.

Key Management.   This uses the same `OriginatorInfo` and `Recipient-info` structures as the enveloped-data content type. It supports key transport, key agreement, password, and other key management techniques.

Attributes.   Both authenticated and unauthenticated attributes are supported, but only the authenticated attributes are cryptographically bound to the content. Neither set of attributes is encrypted. The `message-digest` attribute is not included in authenticated attributes because it exposes plaintext.

The authenticated-enveloped-data content type is identified by the `id-auth envelopedData` object identifier, and it has the following syntax:

```
ct-AuthEnvelopedData CONTENT-TYPE   ::=
   { AuthEnvelopedData IDENTIFIED BY id-authEnvelopedData }

id-ct-authEnvelopedData OBJECT IDENTIFIER ::=
   { iso(1) member-body(2) us(840) rsadsi(113549) pkcs(1) pkcs-9(9)
     smime(16) ct(1) 23 }

AuthEnvelopedData ::= SEQUENCE {
   version                        CMSVersion,
   originatorInfo             [0] IMPLICIT OriginatorInfo OPTIONAL,
   recipientInfos                 RecipientInfos,
   authEncryptedContentInfo       EncryptedContentInfo,
   authAttrs                  [1] IMPLICIT AuthAttributes OPTIONAL,
   mac                            MessageAuthenticationCode,
   unauthAttrs                [2] IMPLICIT UnauthAttributes OPTIONAL }
```

Non-Protecting Content Types

A number of non-protecting content types have been defined in various RFCs. This section addresses the following content types: data, receipt, compressed-data, content-collection, and content-with-attributes. S/MIME only makes use of data and compressed-data.

WARNING None of these content types provides a security service by itself; they all must be encapsulated by one of the protecting CMS content types described earlier.

Data

The data content type, as defined in [RFC3852], is used to convey arbitrary octet strings. It can carry whatever you want, including text files, video, audio, and so on; however, S/MIME uses the data content type to identify MIME encoded content. The data content type is identified by the `id-data` object identifier, and it has the following syntax:

```
ct-Data CONTENT-TYPE  ::=
  { OCTET STRING IDENTIFIED BY id-data }

id-data OBJECT IDENTIFIER  ::=
  { iso(1) member-body(2) us(840) rsadsi(113549) pkcs(1) pkcs7(7) 1 }
```

Compressed Data

PGP-supported compression and so does CMS. The compressed-data content type, defined in [RFC3274], consists of a version number, the compression algorithm identifier, and the compressed contents. Compressed data can be used, as it was in PGP, after the signature, but before encryption to reduce the quantity of known plaintext available to an attacker. The compressed-data content type is identified by the `id-ct-compressedData` object identifier, and it has the following syntax:

```
ct-CompressedData CONTENT-TYPE  ::=
  { CompressedData IDENTIFIED BY id-ct-compressedData }

id-ct-compressedData OBJECT IDENTIFIER  ::=
  { iso(1) member-body(2) us(840) rsadsi(113549) pkcs(1) pkcs-9(9)
    smime(16) ct(1) 9 }

CompressedData ::= SEQUENCE {
  version               CMSVersion,
  compressionAlgorithm  CompressionAlgorithmIdentifier,
  encapContentInfo      EncapsulatedContentInfo }
```

Receipt Syntax

Recipients use the receipt content-type, defined in [RFC2634], when generating a signed receipt. The receipt is cryptographically bound to the original message providing proof of delivery. The original value from the `content-identifier` attribute, explained later, in the original message is copied to the receipt content. The receipt content type is always included in a signed-data content type. The receipt content type is identified by the `id-ct-receipt` object identifier, and it has the following syntax:

```
ct-Receipt CONTENT-TYPE  ::=
  { Receipt IDENTIFIED BY id-ct-receipt }
```

```
id-ct-receipt OBJECT IDENTIFIER  ::=
  { iso(1) member-body(2) us(840) rsadsi(113549) pkcs(1) pkcs-9(9)
    smime(16) id-ct(1) 1 }

Receipt ::= SEQUENCE {
  version                 ESSVersion,
  contentType             ContentType,
  signedContentIdentifier ContentIdentifier,
  originatorSignatureValue OCTET STRING }

ESSVersion ::= INTEGER  { v1(1) }
```

Content Collection

The CMS encapsulation technique allows you to include one layer in another. It's perfect for when you need to attach one thing to another, but what would you do if you wanted to attach more that just one thing? The content-collection content type, from [RFC4073], was defined for exactly this purpose. Figure 6-3 shows an example where the originator has included three contents, an offer to sell their car, an image of their car, and a signed appraisal letter, gathered together in a content collection and then signed. With this content type you can group things and apply one signature instead of signing three separate contents.

The content collection content type is identified by the `id-ct-content Collection` object identifier, and it has the following syntax:

```
ct-ContentCollection CONTENT-TYPE  ::=
  { ContentCollection IDENTIFIED BY id-ct-contentCollection }

id-ct-contentCollection OBJECT IDENTIFIER  ::=
  { iso(1) member-body(2) us(840) rsadsi(113549) pkcs(1) pkcs9(9)
    smime(16) ct(1) 19 }

ContentCollection ::= SEQUENCE SIZE (1..MAX) OF ContentInfo
```

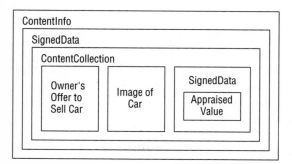

Figure 6-3 Content Collection content type

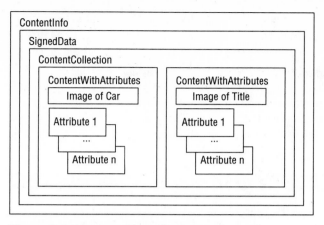

Figure 6-4 Content with attribute content type

Content with Attributes

Not all content types are defined to allow the addition of arbitrary attributes, and the content-with-attributes allows the addition of arbitrary attributes to any content before applying a protecting content type. Figure 6-4 shows an example where the originator has two images, each with some attributes. Both of these images are wrapped in separate content with attribute contents, further encapsulated with a content collection, and then finally signed. Again, only one signature is needed over the two different images and the associated attributes.

The content with attributes content type is identified by the `id-ct-content WithAttrs` object identifier, and it has the following syntax:

```
ct-ContentWithAttrs CONTENT-TYPE   ::=
  { ContentWithAttributes IDENTIFIED BY id-ct-contentWithAttrs }

  id-ct-contentWithAttrs OBJECT IDENTIFIER  ::=
  { iso(1) member-body(2) us(840) rsadsi(113549) pkcs(1)pkcs9(9)
    smime(16) ct(1) 20 }

ContentWithAttributes ::= SEQUENCE {
  content  ContentInfo,
  attrs    SEQUENCE SIZE (1..MAX) OF Attribute }
```

Attributes

CMS uses attributes to add additional services. Fifteen attributes are defined in RFCs that support CMS and S/MIME. Of these, content-type, message-digest, signing-time, and counter-signature are defined in [RFC3852] because they are used by multiple content types in the base document. [RFC2634] defines nine attributes: content-identifier, receipt-request, message-signature-digest, content-hints, content-reference, signing-certificates, security-label, equivalent-label, and ml-expansion-history (see the "Enhanced security services" sidebar). The content-identifier, receipt-request, and message-signature-digest attributes are discussed under the heading Receipt Request because they all work together to support signed receipts. [RFC3851] defines two attributes: S/MIME-capabilities and encryption-key-preference, and these attributes relate directly to S/MIME.

ENHANCED SECURITY SERVICES

To avoid a monolithic RFC, the S/MIME optional enhanced security services were published as [RFC2634]. It specifies four services: signed receipts, security labels, secure mail lists, and signing certificates. Three of these are derived directly from MSP. As you will see, the services from MSP were appropriate for the business and finance communities as well as the government community. Adoption of these services in S/MIME essentially put the final nail in MSP's coffin, with the authors of MSP swinging the hammer.

All CMS attributes use the same syntax. Each attribute has an object identifier that uniquely identifies the syntax. The attribute syntax was adopted from the X.500 Directory environment, and it can technically have more than one value. That is, it can be multi-valued. However, in CMS these attributes constrain the `attrValues` field to one and only one value. Likewise, attributes may only appear once in the attributes field for the content types. The following syntax is used to define an attribute:

```
ATTRIBUTE ::= TYPE-IDENTIFIER

Attribute { ATTRIBUTE:AttrList } ::= SEQUENCE {
   attrType    ATTRIBUTE.&id({AttrList}),
   attrValues  SET OF ATTRIBUTE.&Type({AttrList}{@attrType}) }

Attributes ::= SET SIZE OF (1..MAX) Attribute
```

As mentioned earlier, attributes are sometimes restricted for use with a particular content type and location within that content type.

Content Type

The way they are computed results in the content-type object identifier not being part of the signature. The content-type attribute is used to provide protection for the object identifier for the encapsulated content-type. The content-type attribute is identified by the `id-aa-contentType` object identifier, and it has the following syntax:

```
attr-contentType ATTRIBUTE  ::=
  { ContentType IDENTIFIED BY id-contentType }

id-contentType OBJECT IDENTIFIER  ::=
  { iso(1) member-body(2) us(840) rsadsi(113549) pkcs(1) pkcs9(9) 3 }

ContentType ::= OBJECT IDENTIFIER
```

The recipient must confirm that the protected content-type object identifier in the attribute matches the content-type object identifier carried in the CMS protecting content type itself.

If the content-type attribute is included in a signed-data or authenticated-data, then it must be signed or authenticated attribute. If any signed or authenticated attributes are present, then the content-type attribute must be included. It may appear in either an inner or outer layer.

NOTE Interoperability with PKCS#7 is the reason for the special case logic for including the content-type attribute.

Message Digest

When a content type provides integrity, it uses the message-digest attribute to include the output of the integrity algorithm. The message-digest attribute is identified by the `id-aa-messageDigest` object identifier, and it has the following syntax:

```
attr-messageDigest ATTRIBUTE  ::=
  { MessageDigest IDENTIFIED BY id-messageDigest}

id-messageDigest OBJECT IDENTIFIER  ::=
  { iso(1) member-body(2) us(840) rsadsi(113549) pkcs(1) pkcs9(9) 4 }

MessageDigest ::= OCTET STRING
```

If the content-type attribute is included in a signed-data or authenticated-data, then it must be a signed or authenticated attribute. If any signed or authenticated attributes are present, then the content-type attribute must be included. It may appear in either an inner or outer layer. The message-digest attribute is not included in the authenticated-enveloped data content type because it would disclose the unencrypted digest of the contents. This information could be used by an attacker to determine if the plaintext matches one or more candidate contents.

NOTE Interoperability with PKCS#7 is the reason that the special case logic includes the message-digest attribute.

Signing Time

One obvious attribute that originators of signed-data, authenticated-data, and authenticated-enveloped-data want is an indication of the time the message was originated. Email messages already have this feature as part of a `Submission Time:` but it's not cryptographically protected. The signing-time attribute conveys a cryptographically protected time. It is either `UTCTime` or `GeneralizedTime`, just like `Time` in the certificate. For times before 2049, use `UTCTime`; for times after 2049 use `GeneralizedTime`. The time that is included by the originator is not usually from a trusted time source, so it's up to the recipient to determine the appropriate use of the purported time as the signing time. The signing-time attribute is identified by the `id-aa-signingTime` object identifier, and it has the following syntax:

```
attr-signingTime ATTRIBUTE  ::=
   { SigningTime IDENTIFIED BY id-signingTime }

id-signingTime OBJECT IDENTIFIER  ::=
   { iso(1) member-body(2) us(840) rsadsi(113549) pkcs(1) pkcs9(9) 5 }

SigningTime  ::= Time

Time  ::= CHOICE {
   utcTime          UTCTime,
   generalizedTime  GeneralizedTime }
```

If the signing-time attribute is included in a signed-data, authenticated-data, or authenticated-enveloped-data, then it must be a signed or authenticated attribute. It may appear in either an inner or outer layer.

Counter Signatures

CMS supports parallel signatures, so it should come as no surprise that CMS supports a *serial signature*, which is a signature placed over another signature. A serial signature authenticates only the digital signature, not the contents. In fact, this service is targeted at notary services, where the service doesn't really care about the contents of the message, but it does care that the signature value hasn't been altered. The counter-signature attribute is identified by the `id-aa-countersignature` object identifier, and it has the following syntax:

```
attr-countersignature ATTRIBUTE ::=
   { SignerInfo IDENTIFIED BY id-countersignature }
```

```
id-countersignature OBJECT IDENTIFIER  ::=
  { iso(1) member-body(2) us(840) rsadsi(113549) pkcs(1) pkcs9(9) 6 }
```

The same syntax is used for the original signature: `SignerInfo` from signed-data. It follows the same rules with two minor changes. First, the content-type attribute is not included because there's not a content type. Second, the input to the signature process is the `SignatureValue` (the `OCTET STRING` minus the tag and length octets).

If the counter-signature attribute is included in a signed-data, then it must be an unsigned attribute. It may appear in either an inner or outer layer.

S/MIME Capabilities

Originators often need to indicate to recipients the capabilities that they support, mostly notably the cryptographic algorithms that they support. This information is obviously most helpful before the originator and recipient start communicating, so it can be placed in a repository or it can be exchanged in a signed or authenticated attribute during the communications. The capabilities are indicated by an object identifier. The S/MIME-capabilities attribute is identified by the `id-aa-smimeCapabilities` object identifier, and it has the following syntax:

```
attr-smimeCapabilities ATTRIBUTE  ::=
  { SMIMECapabilities IDENTIFIED BY id-smimeCapabilities }

smimeCapabilities OBJECT IDENTIFIER  ::=
  { iso(1) member-body(2) us(840) rsadsi(113549) pkcs(1) pkcs-9(9) 15 }

SMIMECapabilities ::= SEQUENCE OF SMIMECapability

SMIME-CAPS ::= TYPE-IDENTIFIER

SMIMECapability ::= SEQUENCE {
  capabilityID   SMIME-CAPS.&id({SMimeCapsSet}),
  parameters   SMIME-CAPS.&Type({SMimeCapsSet}{@capabilityID}) OPTIONAL }

SMimeCapsSet SMIME-CAPS ::= { ... }
```

If the S/MIME-capabilities attribute is included in a signed-data, authenticated-data, or authenticated-enveloped-data, then it must be signed or authenticated attribute. It may appear in either an inner or outer layer. The smime-capabilities attribute is also a certificate extension, as documented in [RFC4262].

Encryption Key Preference

If an originator uses the same public/private key pair for both digital signatures and key management, then it's easy to figure out which key to use when replying or generating a receipt, but nowadays many originators use separate key pairs for digital signatures and encryption. Recipients can use the S/MIME-encryption-key-preference attribute to locate the public key that the signer would like others to use for key management operations. Now you might be thinking, "Isn't that what the key usage certificate extension is intended to do?" and you'd be right; however, if the signer has more than one, then additional clues are needed. The S/MIME-encryption-key-preference attribute is identified by the `id-aa-encrypKeyPref` object identifier, and it has the following syntax:

```
attr-encryptKeyPref CMS-ATTRIBUTE  ::=
  { SMIMEEncryptionKeyPreference IDENTIFIED BY id-aa-encrypKeyPref }

id-aa-encrypKeyPref OBJECT IDENTIFIER  ::=
  { iso(1) member-body(2) us(840) rsadsi(113549) pkcs(1) pkcs-9(9)
    smime(16) id-aa(2) 11 }

SMIMEEncryptionKeyPreference ::= CHOICE {
  issuerAndSerialNumber     [0] IssuerAndSerialNumber,
  receipentKeyId            [1] RecipientKeyIdentifier,
  subjectAltKeyIdentifier   [2] SubjectKeyIdentifier }
```

If the S/MIME-capabilities attribute is included in a signed-data, authenticated-data, or authenticated-enveloped-data, then it must be signed or authenticated attribute. It may appear in either an inner or outer layer.

Signed Receipts

Signed receipts allow originators to verify that the message has been delivered to the recipients, which is called *proof of delivery*. Originators can then use the signed receipt to prove to a third party that the recipient was able to verify the signature of the original message.

> **NOTE** Proof of delivery does not indicate that the recipients actually understood the message; it indicates only that they could process the signed message. If the originator wants that kind of assurance, they need to explicitly ask the recipient send a signed reply in the body of the message.

The process works with multiple attributes and the receipt content type. The process is shown in Figure 6-5.

Content Identifier

For receipts to work, messages need to be uniquely identifiable. Email messages already have this feature as part of a `Message ID:` header, but it's not signed and it's assigned after the message signature has been generated. [RFC2634] recommends that the concatenation of username or key identifier, current

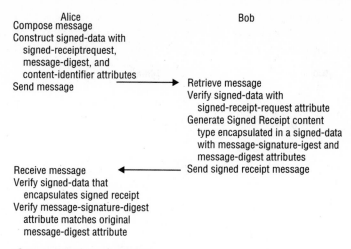

Figure 6-5 Signed receipts

time, and a random number. The content-identifier attribute is identified by the `id-aa-contentIdentifier` object identifier, and it has the following syntax:

```
attr-ContentIdenfier ATTRIBUTE  ::=
   { ContentIdentifier IDENTIFIED BY id-aa-contentIdentifier }

id-aa-contentIdentifier OBJECT IDENTIFIER  ::=
   { iso(1) member-body(2) us(840) rsadsi(113549) pkcs(1) pkcs-9(9)
     smime(16) id-aa(2) 7 }

ContentIdentifier  ::= OCTET STRING
```

The content-identifier may be included in either the inner or outer layer, and it may be a signed attribute. If it's used as part of the signed receipt request process, then it's included as a signed attribute.

Receipt Request

Another primary thing for receipts to work is the actual request for the receipt. There are three parts to the receipt request:

1. Pointing to the message's content-identifier attribute

2. Requesting whom you want receipts from

3. Indicating where receipts should be sent

Pointing to the message's content-identifier attribute is easy because the field is just copied from the attribute and placed in the `signedContentIdentifier` field. You can request receipts from all recipients, non-mail-list recipients, or specific recipients. You can also request where receipts should be sent;

maybe your boss wants to be copied on everything or maybe you want an administrative assistant to track the receipts for you. Either way, you can include your name, someone else's name, or an arbitrary list. The receipt-request attribute is identified by the `id-aa-receiptRequest` object identifier, and it has the following syntax:

```
attr-receiptRequest ATTRIBUTE  ::=
  { ReceiptRequest IDENTIFIED BY id-aa-receiptRequest }

id-aa-receiptRequest OBJECT IDENTIFIER  ::=
  { iso(1) member-body(2) us(840) rsadsi(113549) pkcs(1) pkcs-9(9)
    smime(16) id-aa(2) 1 }

ReceiptRequest  ::=  SEQUENCE {
  signedContentIdentifier  ContentIdentifier,
  receiptsFrom             ReceiptsFrom,
  receiptsTo               SEQUENCE SIZE (1..ub-receiptsTo)
                               OF GeneralNames }

ub-receiptsTo INTEGER  ::=  16

ReceiptsFrom  ::=  CHOICE {
  allOrFirstTier  [0] AllOrFirstTier,
  receiptList     [1] SEQUENCE OF GeneralNames }

AllOrFirstTier  ::=  INTEGER {
  allReceipts (0),
  firstTierRecipients (1) }
```

The receipt-request attribute must be included in an inner layer, and it must be a signed attribute.

Message Signature Digest

The recipient needs to bind the original message that included the receipt to the signed receipt. This is done by placing the message digest of the original message in the message-signature-digest attribute. Recipients do this by including signed attributes from the original message, which was validated when the signature was verified. The message-signature-digest attribute is identified by the `id-aa-msgSigDigest` object identifier, and it has the following syntax:

```
attr-msgSigDigest ATTRIBUTE  ::=
  { MsgSigDigest IDENTIFIED BY id-aa-msgSigDigest }

id-aa-msgSigDigest OBJECT IDENTIFIER  ::=
  { iso(1) member-body(2) us(840) rsadsi(113549) pkcs(1) pkcs-9(9)
    smime(16) id-aa(2) 5 }

MsgSigDigest  ::= OCTET STRING
```

The message-signed-digest attribute must be included in an inner layer, and it must be a signed attribute.

Content Hints

The content-hints attribute is used to peek into encrypted messages that are also signed. By including a content-hints in the outer signed-data content, the originator can provide the content type and a description of the contents of the inner signed data, as shown in Figure 6-6. The content-hints attributes can be used by a recipient with an inbox full of encrypted messages decide which ones to decrypt and read first.

WARNING Any description you put in this attribute will be available to an attacker; it is not encrypted.

The content-hints attribute is identified by the `id-aa-contentHint` object identifier, and it has the following syntax:

```
attr-contentHints ATTRIBUTE  ::=
  { ContentHints IDENTIFIED BY id-aa-contentHint }

id-aa-contentHint OBJECT IDENTIFIER  ::=
  { iso(1) member-body(2) us(840) rsadsi(113549) pkcs(1) pkcs-9(9)
    smime(16) id-aa(2) 4 }

ContentHints  ::=  SEQUENCE {
  contentDescription  UTF8String (SIZE (1..MAX)) OPTIONAL,
  contentType         ContentType }
```

The content-hints may be included in either the inner or outer layer, and it may be a signed attribute.

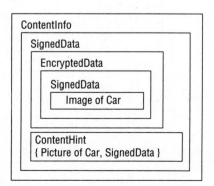

Figure 6-6 Content hints attribute

Content Reference

Like the content-hint attribute, the content-reference attribute isn't necessarily used with signed receipts. It's used by recipients to cryptographically link a reply to a previous signed message, which is much different than a receipt. The content-type, content-identifier, and the original signed attributes are used to link back to original message. The content-reference attribute is identified by the `id-aa-contentReference` object identifier, and it has the following syntax:

```
attr-contentReference ATTRIBUTE  ::=
  { ContentReference IDENTIFIED BY id-aa-contentReference }

id-aa-contentReference  OBJECT IDENTIFIER  ::=
  { iso(1) member-body(2) us(840) rsadsi(113549) pkcs(1) pkcs-9(9)
    smime(16) id-aa(2) 10 }

ContentReference  ::=  SEQUENCE {
  contentType              ContentType,
  signedContentIdentifier  ContentIdentifier,
  originatorSignatureValue  OCTET STRING }
```

The signed-content-reference may be in either an inner or outer layer, and it must be a signed attribute.

Signing Certificates

CMS carries certificates outside of the protecting content types, meaning that they are vulnerable to attackers. Attackers can remove the certificate in a *denial of service* attack, or they can substitute a different certificate. Substituting one certificate for another might seem like a silly attack, but recall the discussion in Chapter 5; if Eve pulls the key out of a certificate and re-signs it, then she can make the relying party look up a different certification path. You can stop this attack by placing a signing-certificate-V2 attribute in signed-data to identify the certificate you expect to be used for validation of your signature. The signing-certificates-V2 attribute is identified by the `id-aa-signingCertificateV2` object identifier, and it has the following syntax:

```
attr-signingCertificateV2 ATTRIBUTE  ::=
  { SigningCertificateV2 IDENTIFIED BY id-aa-signingCertificateV2 }

id-aa-signingCertificateV2 OBJECT IDENTIFIER  ::=
  { iso(1) member-body(2) us(840) rsadsi(113549) pkcs(1) pkcs9(9)
    smime(16) id-aa(2) 47 }
```

```
SigningCertificateV2  ::=  SEQUENCE {
  certs      SEQUENCE OF ESSCertIDv2,
  policies   SEQUENCE OF PolicyInformation OPTIONAL }

ESSCertIDv2 ::=  SEQUENCE {
  hashAlgorithm  AlgorithmIdentifier DEFAULT {algorithm id-sha256},
  certHash    .  Hash,
  issuerSerial   IssuerSerial OPTIONAL }

Hash ::= OCTET STRING

IssuerSerial ::= SEQUENCE {
  issuer        GeneralNames,
  serialNumber  CertificateSerialNumber }
```

WARNING ESS was updated by [RFC5035] to add one-way hash algorithm agility. Previously, the hash algorithm used to generate the reference to the certificate used to sign the message was fixed to SHA-1. `ESSCertIDv2` allows the signer to indicate any hash algorithm.

The signed-content-reference may be in either an inner or outer layer, and it must be a signed attribute.

Security Labels

Large enterprises have security policies that address both physical and electronic security requirements. One requirement that has manifested itself electronically is the marking of documents with information like company confidential, highly confidential, or legal department use only. The security label provides a mechanism to indicate these markings. The security policy, like the certificate policy, is indicated with an object identifier, and it provides the syntax and semantics for the remaining fields. The `security-classification` indicates the classification of the message, say as highly confidential, via an integer. The `privacy-mark` includes information not used in an access control decision. The `security-categories` are a little more complicated and only necessary for complex security policies, but they are a way to provide arbitrary categories, compartments, and caveats. [RFC3114] provides three example company security policies. The security-label attribute is identified by the `id-aa-securityLabel` object identifier, and it has the following syntax:

```
attr-securityLabel ATTRIBUTE  ::=
  { SecurityLabel IDENTIFIED BY id-aa-securityLabel }

id-aa-securityLabel OBJECT IDENTIFIER  ::=
  { iso(1) member-body(2) us(840) rsadsi(113549) pkcs(1) pkcs-9(9)
    smime(16) id-aa(2) 2 }
```

```
ESSSecurityLabel  ::=  SET {
  security-policy-identifier  SecurityPolicyIdentifier,
  security-classification     SecurityClassification OPTIONAL,
  privacy-mark                ESSPrivacyMark OPTIONAL,
  security-categories         SecurityCategories OPTIONAL }
```

The security-label attribute may be in either an inner or outer layer, and it must be a signed or authenticated attribute.

Equivalent Labels

Obviously, there are many security policies. Enterprises are allowed to define their own. When two enterprises communicate a lot, they may wish to define equivalencies between their security policies. The equivalent-labels attribute allows enterprises to do just that. The equivalent-labels attribute is identified by the id-aa-equivalentLabels object identifier, and it has the following syntax:

```
attr-equivalentLabels ATTRIBUTE  ::=
  { EquivalentLabels IDENTIFIED BY id-aa-equivalentLabels }

id-aa-equivalentLabels OBJECT IDENTIFIER  ::=
  { iso(1) member-body(2) us(840) rsadsi(113549) pkcs(1) pkcs-9(9)
    smime(16) id-aa(2) 9 }

EquivalentLabels  ::= SEQUENCE OF ESSSecurityLabel
```

The equivalent-labels attribute may be in either an inner or outer layer, and it must be a signed attribute.

Secure Mail Lists

The concept of a secure mail lists comes from the Mail List Agent (MLA) defined by MSP and heavily used in the US DoD Defense Message System. In that system, messages are signed and encrypted, and sometimes there are many, many recipients. The processing power to generate thousands of recipient tokens is quite significant, and it takes a very long time. To eliminate this burden from the user's email client, the MSP authors invented the MLA. The originator sends one message to the MLA, and then the MLA generates all the recipient tokens for the recipients, as shown in Figure 6-7.

Mail lists get interesting when there's more than one MLA involved. These are called *nested mail lists*. Since you want to avoid the case where the mail lists end up sending messages in an endless loop, you also need to uniquely identify the mail lists, indicate which MLAs have handled the message, and set

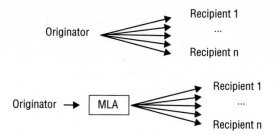

Figure 6-7 Mail List Agent

receipt policies. When a MLA is about to expand the message for its recipients, it adds the ml-expansion-history attribute to provide this information. When the next MLA gets the message, it examines the ml-expansion-history attribute to detect and break loops. The ml-expansion-history attribute is identified by the `id-aa-mlExpansionHistory` object identifier, and it has the following syntax:

```
attr-mlExpansionHistory ATTRIBUTE   ::=
  { MLExpansionHistory IDENTIFIED BY id-aa-mlExpansionHistory }

id-aa-mlExpandHistory OBJECT IDENTIFIER   ::=
  { iso(1) member-body(2) us(840) rsadsi(113549) pkcs(1) pkcs-9(9)
    smime(16) id-aa(2) 3}

MLExpansionHistory ::= SEQUENCE
  SIZE (1..ub-ml-expansion-history) OF MLData

MLData ::= SEQUENCE {
  mailListIdentifier   EntityIdentifier,
  expansionTime        GeneralizedTime,
  mlReceiptPolicy      MLReceiptPolicy OPTIONAL }

EntityIdentifier ::= CHOICE {
  issuerAndSerialNumber  IssuerAndSerialNumber,
  subjectKeyIdentifier   SubjectKeyIdentifier }

MLReceiptPolicy ::= CHOICE {
  none          [0] NULL,
  insteadOf     [1] SEQUENCE SIZE (1..MAX) OF GeneralNames,
  inAdditionTo  [2] SEQUENCE SIZE (1..MAX) OF GeneralNames }

ub-ml-expansion-history INTEGER ::= 64
```

The ml-expansion-history attribute may be in either an inner or outer layer, and it must be a signed attribute.

Algorithms

Algorithms supported by S/MIME have changed over time. Tables 6-2 through 6-5 provide a history of the hash, signature, key-encryption, and content-encryption algorithms from S/MIME version 2 (v2) through the latest proposed (soon to be approved) S/MIME documents. CMS, when it was originally published, also included algorithms, and they matched those in S/MIME v3 specification. The algorithms were removed from CMS and placed in their own RFC, [RFC3370], so that every time an algorithm was changed it wasn't necessary to perturb the baseline protocol document, which is much more stable.

Table 6-2 Hash Algorithms

DOCUMENT	SENDING	ALGORITHM RECEIVING
S/MIME v2	SHA-1 SHOULD	SHA-1 MUST MD5 MUST
S/MIME v3	SHA-1 MUST	SHA-1 MUST MD5 SHOULD
S/MIME v3.1	SHA-1 MUST	SHA-1 MUST MD5 SHOULD
S/MIME v3.2	SHA-256 MUST SHA-1 SHOULD-	SHA-256 MUST SHA-1 SHOULD- MD5 SHOULD-

Table 6-3 Signature Algorithms

DOCUMENT	SENDING	ALGORITHM RECEIVING
S/MIME v2	RSA MUST	Same as sending
S/MIME v3	DSA MUST RSA SHOULD	Same as Sending
S/MIME v3.1	RSA with SHA-1 or DSA with SHA-1 MUST	DSA MUST RSA MUST
S/MIME v3.2	RSA with SHA-256 MUST RSA with SHA-1 SHOULD- RSA-PSS with SHA-256 SHOULD+ DSA with SHA-1 SHOULD- RSA with MD5 SHOULD-	Same as Sending

Table 6-4 Key Management

DOCUMENT	ALGORITHM SENDING	RECEIVING
S/MIME v2	RSA MUST	Same as sending
S/MIME v3	E-S D-H[1] MUST RSA SHOULD	Same as Sending
S/MIME v3.1	RSA MUST E-S D-H[1] SHOULD	Same as Sending
S/MIME v3.2	RSA MUST RSA-OAEP SHOULD+ E-S D-H[1] SHOULD-	Same as Sending

[1]There are two popular modes of Diffie-Hellman: Ephemeral-Static (E-S D-H) and Static-Static (S-S D-H). When S-S D-H is used, both the originator and recipient have a static and certified key pair. When E-S D-H is used, the recipient has a static certified key pair, but the originator generates a new key pair for each message. It's called ephemeral because it's only used for that one message.

Table 6-5 Content Encryption and Key Wrap

DOCUMENT	ALGORITHM SENDING	RECEIVING
S/MIME v2	RC2 MUST	Same as Sending
S/MIME v3	Triple-DES MUST RC2 SHOULD	Same as Sending
S/MIME v3.1	Triple-DES MUST RC2 SHOULD AES 128 CBC SHOULD AES 192 CBC SHOULD AES 256 CBC SHOULD	Same as Sending
S/MIME v3.2	AES 128 CBC MUST AES 192 CBC SHOULD+, AES 256 CBC SHOULD+ Triple-DES SHOULD-	Same as Sending

The switch from S/MIME v2 to v3 was done primarily because RSA Data Security held patents on the signature algorithm. Patented technology in a standard isn't unheard of, but there were other unencumbered solutions available, namely DSA. Almost immediately after these patents expired, S/MIME v3.1 was produced to return to the de facto standard algorithm. The proposed update will move to a new hash algorithm.

REQUIREMENTS TERMINOLOGY

[RFC2119] defines the terms that are used to indicate whether a protocol element or algorithm needs to be implemented. The terms, which are capitalized in Internet Drafts and RFCs, are:

MUST, SHALL, and REQUIRED.   Implementation of this protocol element, algorithm, and so on is an absolute requirement.

MUST NOT and SHALL NOT.   Implementation of this protocol element, algorithm, and so on is prohibited.

SHOULD and RECOMMENDED.   Implementation of this protocol element, algorithm, and so on can be ignored in certain scenarios. However, the full consequences of not implementing it must be understood and carefully weighed before choosing to not implement it.

SHOULD NOT and NOT RECOMMEND.   Implementation of this protocol element, algorithm, and so on can be carried out in certain scenarios; however, the full consequences of not implementing it must be understood and carefully weighed before choosing to not implement it.

MAY and OPTIONAL.   Implementation of this protocol element, algorithm, and so on is up to individual implementors.

Protocol specifications are living documents. You may have deduced that algorithms in the security protocol specifications get updated relatively often. To provide additional information to implementers many RFCs have started to use:

SHOULD+.   This means the same things as SHOULD, but in the next version of the RFC it will likely be changed to a MUST.

SHOULD-.   This means the same things as SHOULD, but in the next version of the RFC it will likely be changed to a MAY or removed.

MUST-.   This means the same this as MUST, but in the next version of the RFC it will likely not be a MUST.

All of this is very necessary so that implementors know what it is they need to implement to achieve interoperable products from many different vendors.

Generating an S/MIME Message

The previous sections describe CMS and S/MIME. To recap, here's S/MIME v3.1 requirements for content types and attributes:

Content types.   Compressed-data, data, enveloped-data, and signed-data MUST be supported.

Attributes.   Content-type, message-digest, signing-time, signing-certificate, smime-capabilities, and smime-key-encryption-preference

SHOULD be supported. However, content-type and message-digest MUST be supported if any others are supported because the others are signed attributes.

The process to create an S/MIME message is defined in [RFC3851]:

- **MIME type is prepared:**   Examples of MIME types include text, audio, and video.

- **MIME leaf parts are canonicalized:**   You might be asking yourself: what's canonicalization? It's the process of making sure that there is one and only one representation of data. This is very important in security because we want to compare two copies of the data to make sure that they use the same representation; the desired representation is the canonical one.

- **Transfer encoding is applied to MIME leaf parts:**   If you're wondering, a *transfer encoding* is a reversible transformation applied so that 8-bit or binary data may be sent via a channel that only handles 7-bit data. More information on transfer encodings can be found in Appendix C.

The next stage depends really on the selected services. In most cases, service selection involves clicking on either a pen/lock button or ticking some boxes in security settings. Many applications allow you to set defaults so you only have to check the boxes once.

WARNING Very few webmail providers support S/MIME. Many times they advertise secure email, but they are probably referring to the security solutions described in the next chapter. This is because the webmail server would need access to the private key, so you would need significant confidence in the serer and its operators. Most people would be very uncomfortable with the server holding their private key. A few do support encrypted email, but it is password based and both originator and recipients must use the same service provider.

Signed only.   If an originator wishes to invoke authentication and integrity services, then he or she has two choices (see Figure 6-8):

`multipart/signed; application/pkcs7-signature`. This option allows the signer to include a signature and the cleartext so that those that do not support digital signatures can still read the message; this is a clear-signed message. This uses the same concept as the PEM MIC-CLEAR message.

`application/pkcs7-mime; smime-type=signedData`. This option is MIME encoded and does not include the cleartext. Usually recipients can tell this was chosen because you need to click on a View Message button to read the message. This uses the same concept as the PEM MIC-ONLY message.

Encrypted only.   If an originator wishes to invoke confidentiality services, then he or she should choose this option. It uses enveloped-data.

Signed and encrypted.   If an originator wishes to invoke authentication, integrity, and confidentiality, then he or she should choose this option. An enveloped-data wraps either one of the two signature options.

Certificates only.   If an originator wishes to convey just the certificates or CRLs, then they choose this option. The signed-data content type includes the certificate and CRLs fields they wish to send to the recipient, but they omit the `SignerInfos` field. The `application/pkcs7-mime; smime-type=certsOnly` is used.

Clear-signing

```
Content-Type: multipart/signed;
    protocol="application/pkcs7-signature";
    micalg=sha256; boundary=boundary42

    --boundary42
    Content-Type: text/plain

    This format is preferred. Recipients that cannot verify signatures or
    decode PKCS#7 ASN.1 objects can still read the message content.

    --boundary42
    Content-Type: application/pkcs7-signature; name=smime.p7s
    Content-Transfer-Encoding: base64
    Content-Disposition: attachment; filename=smime.p7s

    ghyHhHUujhJhjH77n8HHGTrfvbnj756tbB9HG4VQpfyF467GhIGfHfYT6
    4VQpfyF467GhIGfHfYT6jH77n8HHGghyHhHUujhJh756tbB9HGTrfvbnj
    n8HHGTrfvhJhjH776tbB9HG4VQbnj7567GhIGfHfYT6ghyHhHUujpfyF4
    7GhIGfHfYT64VQbnj756
    --boundary42--
```

Unclear-signing

```
Content-Type: application/pkcs7-mime; smime-type=signed-data;
    name=smime.p7m
Content-Transfer-Encoding: base64
Content-Disposition: attachment; filename=smime.p7m

 567GhIGfHfYT6ghyHhHUujpfyF4f8HHGTrfvhJhjH776tbB9HG4VQbnj7
 77n8HHGT9HG4VQpfyF467GhIGfHfYT6rfvbnj756tbBghyHhHUujhJhjH
 HUujhJh4VQpfyF467GhIGfHfYGTrfvbnjT6jH7756tbB9H7n8HHGghyHh
 6YT64V0GhIGfHfQbnj75
```

Figure 6-8 Clear- and unclear-signed messages

CHAPTER 7

Protecting Email Passwords, Headers, and Commands

In Chapter 6, you learned how to secure an email message that is sent from the originator to a list of recipients. This chapter explains security for the other parts of the email system — namely protecting the network. If you're using S/MIME to protect the content, then there are two network security issues:

1. Making sure the password that you use to access your mail server is not disclosed. If you don't protect it, then you may be sending secure email, but some spammer could also be using your account to blast out Viagra emails or worse.

2. Protecting the headers from disclosure. You can protect your email headers from originator to recipients (called *end-to-end*) only if you control the entire network and you run encryption between all the servers as well as client-server connections. However, you probably don't control the entire network, so you should protect your communication with your server, and then hope the recipients of your email do the same.

There are two popular techniques for performing these functions: scrambling your password and encrypting the link between you and your mail server. This chapter will explain both of these possible solutions.

Unlike securing email contents, interoperability between Alice and Bob is not required on an end-to-end basis. Say that Alice secures the SMTP commands sent to her server with protocol X, but Bob protects the SMTP commands sent to his server with security protocol Y. Since each interacts with their own server, each can use different protocols without any interoperability concerns. If they're using the same server, the server could support both protocol X and protocol Y, and Alice and Bob could still have client software that supports only one of the protocols.

Password Scramble

Scrambling your password is something you can do to thwart attackers, but if you don't support encryption, how do you do it? There are two popular methods, while neither method requires encryption, both methods require that the client and server share a secret. Neither method sends the password *in the clear* over the connection. Both methods use the concept of a server challenge followed by a client response, which is referred to as a *challenge-response* authentication mechanism:

AUTH Command. The SMTP Service Extension for Authentication [RFC 2554] defines an SMTP command called "AUTH". It starts with the server indicating that it supports one both of these mechanisms. The two versions supported are:

CRAM-MD5. Listing 7-1 shows the same interaction in Listing 2-1, but extended with server's AUTH CRAM-MD5 command. This new server command indicates that it supports CRAM-MD5, where CRAM stands for Challenge-Response Authentication Mechanism. The client takes the server up on its offer and returns an AUTH CRAM-MD5 command. The server returns a challenge, which is random data. The client then responds with its username, a space, and a digest value, all of which is *base64* encoded. The digest is the output of the HMAC with the MD5 hash function [RFC2104] using the shared secret and the server's random data as inputs. When the server receives the client's response, it matches the digest value presented to the one it computes over the same data. If the two match, then access is granted.

```
S: 220 pleasantville.ca.us
C: EHLO washington.dc.us
S: 250-pleasantville.ca.us greets washington.dc.us
S: 250-8BITMIME
S: 250-SIZE
S: 250-DSN
S: 250 HELP
S: 250 AUTH CRAM-MD5
C: AUTH CRAM-MD5
S: 334 PENCeUxFREJoU0NnbmhNWitOMjNGNndAZWx3b29kLmlubm9zb2Z0LmNvbT4=
C: ZnJlZCA5ZTk1YWVlMDljNDBhZzJJiODRhMGMyYjNiYmFlNzg2ZQ==
S: 235 Authentication successful
C: MAIL FROM: <aadams@washington.dc.us>
S: 250 sender <aadams@washington.dc.us> OK
C: RCPT TO:<bburton@pleasantville.ca.us>
```

Listing 7-1 AUTH SMTP service extension interaction

```
S: 250 recipient <bburton@pleasantville.ca.us> OK
C: RCPT TO:<mrogers@pleasantville.ca.us>
S: 250 recipient <mrogers@pleasantville.ca.us> OK
C: DATA
S: 354 Start mail input; end with <CRLF>.<CRLF>
C: Date: Mon, 11 Feb 2008 09:55:06 -0400
C: From: Alice <aadams@washington.dc.us>
C: Subject: Meeting Date and Time
C: To: Bob <bburton@pleasantville.ca.us>
C: Cc: Matt <mrogers@pleasantville.ca.us>
C: Message-ID: <1234@washington.dc.us>
C:
C: Bob,
C:
C: Can we meet on Tuesday 1 April 2008?
C:
C: Alice
C: .
S: OK
C: QUIT
S: 221 pleasantville.ca.us closing transmission channel
```

Listing 7-1 (*continued*)

DIGEST-MD5.   This signaling mechanism for DIGEST-MD5 [RFC2831] is basically the same as the CRAM-MD5 mechanism except that the server indicates AUTH DIGEST-MD5. The real difference is the information passed in the challenge. The information passed is much richer and allows for authentication at a later time using a previous challenge-response result.

IMAP AUTHENTICATE.   IMAP uses the AUTHENTICATE command [RFC 2195] in much the same way as AUTH CRAM-MD5 command; obviously, the connection is to an IMAP server and not an SMTP server. The only real difference is the random data returned is a timestamp.

Connection Security

Protecting the link between your MUA and MTA is a better choice than scrambling your password because it not only protects your password from unauthorized disclosure but also protects the email header, at least on submission, from unauthorized disclosure. If you don't control the network (i.e., own and operate the MTAs) and you can't force the recipient to use these same mechanisms (perhaps because he or she doesn't work for the same enterprise), then your headers are going to be exposed to someone at some point. This section addresses two of the most popular choices for providing connection security.

Transport Layer Security

The most readily available solution is to use the *Transport Layer Security* (TLS), or the *Secure Sockets Layer* (SSL), protocol. Many ISPs support this solution, and using it simply becomes a matter of you checking some boxes and changing some port settings in your email application. As always, the devil is in the details, as you'll see. For complete coverage of SSL and TLS, we recommend Eric Rescorla's *SSL and TLS: Designing and Building Secure Systems* [RESC].

Netscape originally published the SSL [SSL] specification. Attempting to gain broader acceptance, Netscape released the specifications to the IETF. The IETF process does not simply publish specifications developed elsewhere, so the IETF made several improvements. The results are the TLS Version 1.0 [RFC2246, RFC3546] specification, and later, the TLS Version 1.1 [RFC4346, RFC4366] specification.* The IETF also published [RFC3207] to indicate how to use TLS with SMTP and [RFC2595] to indicate how to use TLS with IMAP and POP.

The goal of both SSL and TLS is to provide authentication, integrity, and confidentiality between two communicating applications. The protocols are composed of two layers: the Handshake Protocol and the Record Protocol. The Handshake Protocol authenticates the server and the client, negotiates an encryption algorithm, and establishes cryptographic keys before any application protocol data is transferred. The Record Protocol encapsulates and protects higher-level protocols, including the Handshake Protocol. The Record Protocol depends on a reliable, stream-oriented transport protocol such as TCP [RFC793]. For this reason, SSL and TLS cannot easily provide protection for UDP [RFC768] or connectionless application protocols.* SSL and TLS are application-protocol independent, so any stream-oriented application protocol can transparently operate on top of SSL or TLS. Both SSL and TLS provide stream-oriented security with the following three properties:

Authentication.   The identity of the peer is confirmed. The Handshake Protocol uses certificates and digital signature verification to confirm the identity of the remote application.

---

*Some differences between SSL and TLS are to be expected, such as changing version numbers and removing nonpublic algorithms; others are more fundamental, such as changing the message authentication procedure, adding additional message types, and changing key material generation procedures. Both result in noninteroperable solutions. Although they don't interoperate, the TLS 1.1, TLS 1.0, and SSL 3.0 implementations support negotiation to the highest version supported by both parties. The IETF is currently developing TLS 1.2 [TLS12].

*The Datagram Transport Layer Security (DTLS) protocol [RFC4347] was developed to handle these situations.

Integrity.   The application protocol data is protected from undetected modification. The Record Protocol employs an integrity check value, computed by using HMAC, to confirm that the data stream is unaltered.

Confidentiality.   The connection is private. After the Handshake Protocol establishes a symmetric encryption key, the Record Protocol encrypts the remainder of the session.

Both SSL and TLS can provide mutual authentication. However, this is not the way that they are most commonly used. Usually, SSL and TLS provide certificate-based authentication of the server to the client, then some other means of authenticating the client is employed over the encrypted session. For example, the server may ask the client to provide a username and password or a valid credit card number and expiration date.

Handshake Protocol

The Handshake Protocol is composed of three subprotocols that allow peers to agree upon security parameters for the Record Protocol, authenticate themselves, instantiate negotiated security parameters, and report error conditions to each other.

The Handshake Protocol is responsible for negotiating a session for the Record Protocol, which consists of the following items:

Session identifier.   This is an arbitrary byte sequence chosen by the server to identify a session.

Peer certificate.   This is an X.509 certificate of the peer. This element may be absent if authentication is not performed.

Compression method.   This is the algorithm used to compress data prior to encryption.

Cipher spec.   This specifies the bulk data encryption algorithm (such as Triple DES) and the HMAC one-way hash algorithm (such as SHA-1). It also defines cryptographic attributes (such as hash size).

Master secret.   This is a large secret value shared between the client and server.

Is resumable.   This is a flag indicating whether the master secret for this session can be used to initiate new sessions.

These items are then used to set Record Protocol security parameters. The resumption feature allows many protected connections to be established from the single handshake. This feature is used to reduce the overhead and is especially important when a client and server have several short connections.

The cryptographic parameters are produced by the Handshake Protocol. When a client and server first start communicating, they agree on a protocol version, select cryptographic algorithms, optionally authenticate each other, and use public key cryptography to establish shared secret values. The Handshake Protocol involves the following six steps. Figure 13-7 illustrates the protocol messages that implement these six steps.

1. Exchange *hello messages* to negotiate algorithms and exchange random values.

2. Exchange cryptographic parameters to agree on the *premaster secret*.

3. Optionally exchange certificates and cryptographic information to authenticate the client and server to each other.

4. Generate a *master secret* from the premaster secret and exchanged random values.

5. Provide security parameters to the Record Protocol layer.

6. Confirm that the peer has calculated the same security parameters and that the handshake occurred without tampering.

To improve performance by avoiding pipeline stalls, the change cipher spec message is an independent TLS Protocol content type, and it is not actually a TLS Handshake Protocol message. Figure 7-1 includes the change cipher spec message to show the logical flow.

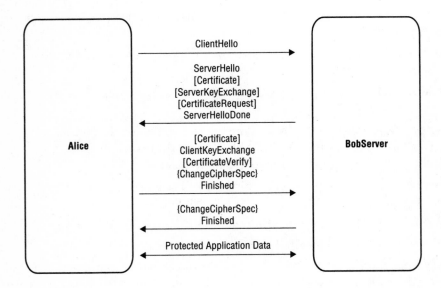

Legend:
[ ] Optional Handshake Protocol message
{ } Not really part of the Handshake Protocol

Figure 7-1 TLS Handshake Protocol

When the client wants to resume a previous session or duplicate an existing session, the client sends a client hello message that includes the Session ID of the session to be resumed. If the server still has the session parameters in its cache and the server is willing to reestablish the connection, the server sends a server hello message with the same Session ID value. At this point, both the client and server send change cipher spec messages and finished messages.

One should not rely on the Handshake Protocol to always negotiate the strongest possible protection for a connection between two peers. Eve, employing a man-in-the-middle attack, may be able to convince two peers to select an insecure set of parameters. For example, Eve might cause the peers to negotiate an unauthenticated connection. To avoid man-in-the-middle attacks, the application protocol must be cognizant of its security requirements and not transmit on the protected stream unless those requirements are met. Of course, this is in conflict with transparently layering applications on SSL and TLS. To preserve transparency, all of the offered alternatives in the negotiation should meet the application protocol security requirements. The SSL and TLS protocols are secure to the level of the cipher suite that is selected. If an AES-128 symmetric key is transferred using a 2048-bit RSA key from a validated certificate, then one can expect very reasonable cryptographic security.

The certificate and key exchange messages convey the data necessary to establish the premaster secret. When RSA is employed, the client generates the random premaster secret value and encrypts it in the server's RSA public key. When Diffie-Hellman is employed, the client and server exchange public keys, then the result of the classic Diffie-Hellman key agreement computation is used as the premaster secret.

In TLS 1.0 and TLS 1.1, a *pseudorandom function* (PRF) built from SHA-1 [FIPS180] and MD5 [RFC1321] is used to generate the master secret and symmetric keying material. Two different one-way hash functions are used to ensure security even if one of the algorithms is found to have a flaw. The problem is that both of them have been shown to weaker than expected. It is not a catastrophic failure by any mean, and this concern is being addressed by the IETF in the TLS 1.2 specification. The first use of the PRF generates the master secret from the premaster secret and the random values from the client hello message and the server hello message. The second use of the PRF generates two symmetric keys, two initialization vectors (IVs), and two Message Authentication Code (MAC) secret values from the master secret and the random values from the client hello message and the server hello message. In a resumed session, the master secret from the parent session is used, but new random values are employed, resulting in different keying material.

The Record Protocol uses one symmetric key, one IV, and one MAC secret value to protect the traffic flowing from the client to the server. The Record Protocol uses the other symmetric key, the other IV, and the other MAC secret value to protect the traffic flowing from the server to the client. Obviously, both client and server need all six secret values for correct operation of the Record Protocol.

Record Protocol

The Record Protocol is composed of several sublayers. It processes application protocol data by fragmenting the data into manageable blocks, optionally compressing the data, computing the integrity check value, encrypting the output from the previous sublayer, and finally transmitting the result. Received data is processed in the opposite order. It is decrypted, integrity checked, optionally decompressed, reassembled, and then delivered to the application.

The Fragmentation sublayer breaks information into records. A record is 16,384 bytes or less. Application protocol message boundaries may not be preserved. Multiple application protocol messages of the same content type may be aggregated into a single record; also, a single application protocol message may be fragmented into several records.

The Compression sublayer performs compression and decompression on all fragments. Initially, the compression method is *null*, but a real compression algorithm can be negotiated. Compression must not lose data.

The Payload Protection sublayer computes an integrity check value on the compressed record and then encrypts the compressed record and the integrity check value. The integrity check value is referred to as a MAC, even though a keyed hash (HMAC) is used. On reception, decryption recovers the plaintext, and the MAC is recomputed to ensure the integrity of the plaintext. The MAC computation also includes an implicit sequence number to detect missing, extra, or repeated compressed records.

When encryption employs a block cipher with a mode that requires an IV, such as Cipher Block Chaining (CBC) mode, the IV for the first record is generated when the security parameters are set by the Handshake Protocol. The IV for subsequent records is the last ciphertext block from the previous record. This technique avoids the transmission of explicit IVs.

Figure 7-2 shows a TLS Record Protocol data unit with all of the sublayer protocol control information. The Payload Protection sublayer includes a header and a trailer; the pad and pad length fields are only present when a block cipher is used for encryption. There is no need for padding when a stream cipher, such as RC4, is used.

Protection Head: ContentType ProtocolVersion Length	Compression: ContentType ProtocolVersion Length	Fragmentation: ContentType ProtocolVersion Length	Application Protocol Data	Protection Tail: MAC Pad (Optional) Pad Length (Optional)

Figure 7-2 TLS Record Protocol

IPsec

While TLS provides a publicly and readily available connection security protocol, the other common approach to solve connection security is IPsec. Currently though, IPsec is really only available to those who own and control their network because it is not offered by most ISPs yet.

IPsec provides security for individual IP (Layer 3) datagrams; all Internet traffic is carried by IP datagrams. IPsec protects communication from one machine to another, or it protects communications from one border of an organizational enclave to another. IPsec is the security protocol used to implement *virtual private networks* (VPNs). There were many proprietary solutions developed before the IETF began development of the IPsec specification. Many of these proprietary solutions were studied in the development of IPsec, but none was selected. Rather, IPsec is a hybrid of the many proprietary solutions. The result is a comprehensive, but complex, IP security architecture.

IPsec is described in a series of eight documents. The series begins with an overview of the IPsec architecture [RFC4301]. *Security associations* (SAs) form the foundation of the cryptographic security services provided by IPsec. A security association is shared symmetric keying material and attributes that govern its use. Next, the *Authentication Header* (AH) is specified [RFC4302, RFC4304, RFC4305]. The AH protocol provides IP datagram authentication and integrity, and AH optionally provides anti-replay protection. Next, the *Encapsulating Security Payload* (ESP) is specified [RFC4303, RFC4304, RFC4305]. The ESP protocol may provide IP datagram confidentiality, authentication, and integrity, and ESP optionally provides limited address hiding and/or anti-replay protection. Finally, the *Internet Key Exchange* (IKE) is specified [RFC4306, RFC4307]. The IKE protocol provides security associations for AH and ESP. Basically, IKE establishes symmetric keying material and negotiates the attributes that will govern the use of that keying material.

It makes it easy to configure IPsec, some shorthand conventions to select the most commonly used cryptographic algorithms were defined in [RFC4308].

There are several ways to implement IPsec in a host, router, or firewall. An IPsec-enabled router or firewall is called a *security gateway*. Common implementation alternatives include:

Integration into the native stack.   Many operating system vendors will integrate IPsec capabilities directly into their IP stack. Access to the IP source code is needed, so third-party vendors cannot use this approach. In many popular operating systems, this code resides in the kernel.

Replacement stack.   A third-party vendor may write a complete replacement for the original stack that includes IPsec capabilities in addition to the original communication capabilities. Significant effort is needed to recreate the native IP capabilities, and the operating system architecture may make the installation quite difficult.

Bump-in-the-stack implementations.   A third-party vendor may insert an IPsec implementation into the native IP stack. IPsec is inserted between the native IP and the local network drivers. Source code access for the IP stack is not required, making this implementation approach especially appropriate for legacy systems. Using APIs can make this approach much more straightforward and avoids the tedious task of reverse engineering module interfaces.

Bump-in-the-wire implementations.   Outboard cryptographic processors are commonly used in military and financial industry network security systems. Bump-in-the-wire implementations are usually dual-port devices with high-quality IPsec capabilities and minimal communications capabilities. The bump-in-the-wire device usually has an IP address of its own. When providing security services for a single host, the bump-in-the-wire device may be quite analogous to a bump-in-the-stack implementation. However, when providing security services for a router or firewall, the bump-in-the-wire device must operate as a security gateway.

Security Associations

Security associations are simplex — they apply to communication in a single direction. Two security associations are needed to secure normal bidirectional communications: one for incoming datagrams and one for outgoing datagrams. The security association attributes vary for each protected connection. The security association can name the security protocol (AH or ESP), specify symmetric algorithms and their mode of operation, include authentication keys and encryption keys, define key validity periods, and identify peer IP addresses. These security association attributes direct the processing of incoming security protocol packets, and they direct the security protocol processing for outgoing packets.

A security association is uniquely identified by three items: a *security parameter index* (SPI), a destination IP address, and a security protocol identifier (identifying either AH or ESP). The SPI is an identifier that is carried in AH and ESP to identify the security association. The destination IP address identifies the IPsec peer. In principle, the destination IP address may be a unicast address, a broadcast address, or a multicast group address. However, IKE is currently defined only for unicast addresses. Support for broadcast addresses and multicast group addresses presently requires manual key distribution to all destinations.

Two types of security associations are defined for both AH and ESP: *transport mode* and *tunnel mode*. Table 7-1 shows when each type of security association must be employed. Figure 7-3 shows two protocol stacks, one employing transport mode and the other employing tunnel mode.

Table 7-1 Security Association Type Used for Different Communicating Peers

	HOST	**ROUTER OR FIREWALL**
Host	Transport mode or tunnel mode	Tunnel mode
Router or Firewall	Tunnel mode	Tunnel mode

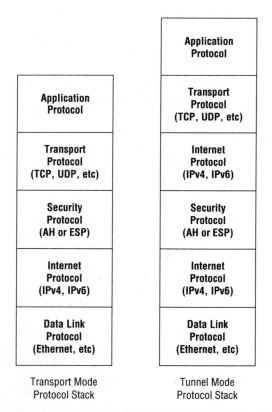

Transport Mode
Protocol Stack

Tunnel Mode
Protocol Stack

Figure 7-3 Transport mode and tunnel mode protocol stacks

A transport mode security association provides protection between two hosts. In transport mode, the AH or ESP security protocol header appears between the IP header and the higher-layer protocol such as TCP or UDP. Transport mode ESP protects only the higher-layer protocol; it does not protect any part of the IP header. Transport mode AH protects the higher-layer protocol and also protects selected portions of the IP header.

A tunnel mode security association provides protection to an IP tunnel. If either end of a security association is a router or firewall, a tunnel mode security association must be employed. Tunnel mode security associations avoid potential problems with fragmentation and reassembly of AH and ESP packets and problems when multiple paths exist to the same destination behind the IPsec-aware router or firewall. In tunnel mode, the AH or ESP security protocol header appears between two IP headers. The outer IP header specifies the IPsec processing destination, and the inner IP header specifies the ultimate destination for the unprotected datagram. Tunnel mode ESP protects the inner IP header and higher-layer protocol; it does not protect any part of the outer IP header. Tunnel mode AH protects the inner IP header, the higher-layer protocol, and selected portions of the outer IP header.

Authentication Header

The Authentication Header (AH) security protocol provides integrity for an individual IP datagram, and it authenticates the datagram source, either by the source's IP address or by the end-system's domain name. AH provides integrity for selected portions of the IP header in addition to the higher-layer protocol. AH also offers anti-replay service (really a partial sequence integrity service) to the receiver. This service helps counter denial of service attacks. AH does not provide confidentiality.

Originally, the AH integrity check value was computed using either a MD5 or a SHA-1 one-way hash value combined with a symmetric shared secret (i.e., HMAC MD5 or HMAC SHA-1). It's been updated and now HMAC MD5 is downgraded to MAY, HMAC SHA-1 remains MUST, and AES-XCBC-MAC [RFC3566] has been added as SHOULD+. This AES variation includes extensions to protect variable length messages.

Figure 7-4 illustrates a typical AH protocol data unit. AH contains the following five fields:

Next Header.   The next header field tells which higher-layer protocol is encapsulated by AH. In tunnel mode, the next header field will always indicate IP (either IPv4 or IPv6). In transport mode, the next header field will usually indicate TCP, UDP, or ICMP.

Length.   The length field tells the size of the AH protocol header. The size depends on the one-way hash function employed since the integrity check value is contained in the only variable length field.

SPI.   The security parameter index (SPI) field contains a 32-bit arbitrary value that identifies the security association. The SPI and the destination IP address uniquely identify the AH security association for this datagram.

Sequence Number.   The sequence number field contains the anti-replay sequence number. It contains an unsigned 32-bit monotonically increasing counter value. The sender must include this value; the receiver may either process it or ignore it.

Authentication Data.   The authentication data field contains the integrity check value for this datagram. The field is variable length, but it must be a multiple of 32 bits in length.

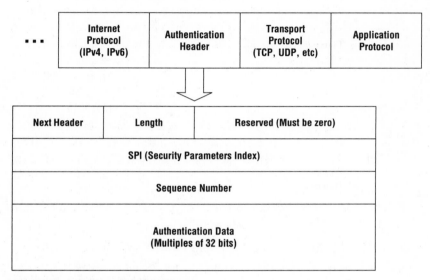

Figure 7-4 AH protocol header

On transmission, the sequence number is incremented, and then portions of the IP header and the higher-layer protocol are hashed along with the symmetric shared secret to create the integrity check value. On reception, the same calculation is performed. If the calculated integrity check value does not match the one received in the AH protocol, the datagram is discarded. Also, if the security association indicates that the anti-replay facility is in use, then the sequence number must fall within the expected range and it must not duplicate any prior value. If either check fails, the datagram is discarded.

Encapsulating Security Payload

The Encapsulating Security Payload (ESP) protocol can provide confidentiality, authentication, and integrity. ESP provides confidentiality by encrypting the payload (and part of the ESP Header and ESP Trailer). The strength of the confidentiality service depends primarily on the encryption algorithm employed. ESP provides authentication and integrity using an integrity check value (just like AH). Although both confidentiality and authentication (which encompasses integrity) are optional, at least one of them must be provided in each ESP security association. If authentication is used, an anti-replay service with the same features as the AH anti-replay service is available. ESP provides narrower authentication and integrity protection than does AH. The IP header that carries the ESP header is not covered by the integrity check value.

If tunnel mode ESP using encryption is active between two security gateways, then partial traffic flow confidentiality is provided. The use of tunnel mode encrypts the inner IP headers, concealing the identities of the ultimate traffic source and destination. However, the addresses of the security gateways are clearly available. Further, the truly paranoid can employ ESP payload padding to hide the size of the datagrams, somewhat concealing the external characteristics of the traffic.

Originally, either DES or Triple DES could be used for encryption. ESP has been updated since, so that DES is SHOULD NOT, Triple DES is SHOULD-, AES-CBC with 128 bit keys is SHOULD+, and AES-CTR is SHOULD.

Originally, the ESP integrity check value was computed using either a MD5 or a SHA-1 one-way hash value combined with a symmetric shared secret (i.e., HMAC MD5 or HMAC SHA-1). It's been updated, and HMAC MD5 has been downgraded to MAY, HMAC SHA-1 remains MUST, and AES-XCBC-MAC [RFC3566] was added as SHOULD+.

Figure 7-5 illustrates a typical ESP protocol data unit. ESP includes a header and a trailer. The ESP Header contains two fields:

SPI.   The security parameter index (SPI) field contains a 32-bit arbitrary value that identifies the security association. The SPI and the destination IP address uniquely identify the ESP security association for this datagram.

Sequence Number.   The sequence number field contains the anti-replay sequence number. It contains an unsigned 32-bit monotonically increasing counter value. The sender must include this value; the receiver may either process it or ignore it.

The ESP Trailer contains four fields:

Padding.   The padding field ensures that the size of the data to be encrypted is a multiple of the cryptographic block size and that the next header field ends on a 32-bit boundary.

Pad Length.   The length field tells the size of the padding. The size depends on the encryption algorithm employed and the extent of traffic flow confidentiality that is desired.

Next Header.   The next header field tells which higher-layer protocol is encapsulated by ESP. In tunnel mode, the next header field will always indicate IP (either IPv4 or IPv6). In transport mode, the next header field will usually indicate TCP, UDP, or ICMP.

Authentication Data.   The authentication data field contains the integrity check value for this datagram. The field is a variable length, but it must be a multiple of 32 bits in length. If authentication and integrity are not desired, then the authentication data field is absent (or zero bits long).

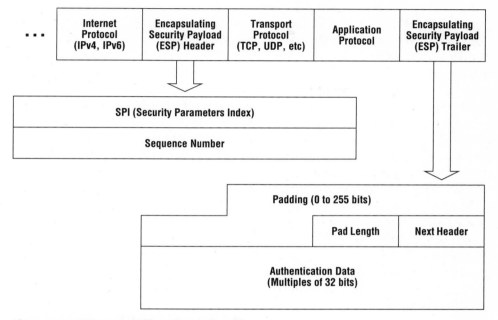

Figure 7-5 ESP protocol header and trailer

On transmission, the sequence number is incremented, and then the ESP Header, the higher-layer protocol, and the ESP Trailer, with the exception of the authentication data, are hashed along with the symmetric shared secret to create the integrity check value. Next, the higher-layer protocol and ESP Trailer, except the authentication data, are encrypted. If an IV is needed, it is carried as a prefix to the ciphertext. On reception, decryption is performed, and then the same integrity check value calculation is performed. If the calculated integrity check value does not match the one received in the ESP trailer, then the datagram is discarded. Also, if the security association indicates that the anti-replay facility is in use, then the sequence number must fall within the expected range and it must not duplicate any prior value. If either check fails, then the datagram is discarded.

Internet Key Exchange (IKE)

Widespread use of IPsec requires scalable, automated security association management. The on-demand creation of security associations and the anti-replay features of AH and ESP require an automated solution. The Internet Key Exchange (IKE) protocol is the automated solution. IKEv1 [RFC2407, RFC2409] is a subset of ISAKMP [RFC2408] and OAKLEY [RFC2412].

The Internet Security Association and Key Management Protocol (ISAKMP) is a complex and comprehensive key management protocol. ISAKMP provides a cryptographic, mechanism-independent authentication and key exchange framework. IKEv1 selects a core set of features from ISAKMP and selects OAKLEY as the means for symmetric key establishment.

IKEv1 uses OAKLEY to establish a shared symmetric key between two IPsec implementations. OAKLEY includes a variant of Diffie-Hellman key agreement. OAKLEY key determination establishes an initial security association, and then allows a more lightweight exchange to establish subsequent security associations.

IKEv1 operates in two phases. The first phase establishes an authenticated and encrypted channel. This creates two IKEv1 security associations, one for communication in each direction. DSA is usually used to provide authentication in the first phase. In both cases, certificates are needed to bind the identity of the remote IPsec implementation to the public key. The second phase establishes one or more security associations for AH and ESP.

The idea of IKE was well liked by the IETF IPsec Working Group and the people developing security solutions relying on IPsec, but IKEv1 was considered too complicated. IKEv1 was described in four documents. Developers wanted a protocol that was as simple and straightforward as possible, and the result is IKEv2, which is defined in one document for the protocol [RFC4036] and one for the algorithms [RFC4307]. This split was done so that the algorithms could be changed over time without touching the protocol specification at all. The biggest change was to reduce the complexity; with IKEv2 only four messages are needed to establish the SA, whereas IKEv1 took eight messages to set up the SA. There were many changes, but the most significant ones are:

- Changed the IKEv2 protecting cryptographic syntax be similar to that used in ESP

- Removed domain of interpretation (DOI), situation (SIT), and label domain identifier fields

- Added support for *Network Address Translation* (NAT) and the *Extensible Authentication Protocol* (EAP)

- Reduced the number of error states

- Fixed cryptographic weakness

Tokens

Tokens and Hardware
Security Modules

One of the main themes of this book is the protection of your symmetric keys and private keys, as well as the reliance on infrastructure components to do this as well. We're not putting the discussion off any further.

The term *token* (and in some situations the term *credential*) describes a wide variety of devices that aid authentication in one way or another. Some tokens are hardware devices, while some are software programs. Some tokens support PKI operations, while others merely store PKI information, especially private keys. Some tokens provide tamper resistance, while others do not. We're going to limit our discussion to tokens that support cryptographic operations either by storing cryptographic information such as keys and certificates or by performing cryptographic operations. As a result, we're not discussing tokens such as RSA Security's SecureID that rely on a time-based authentication mechanism to authenticate the token holder. Likewise, we're not discussing tokens such as VeriSign's Unified Authentication tokens, which rely on a shared secret and a challenge-response authentication protocol to authenticate the token holder. These authentication tokens have an important role in network security, but they do not support the protection of PKI-related secrets needed to secure email.

Technically, a token can be used to protect both user and infrastructure keys, but the term *hardware security module* (HSM) is very often used when talking about a device that stores and protects infrastructure private keys. The main difference between tokens and HSMs is portability. A token is a small device that is easily portable, whereas an HSM shouldn't be. Why? Important infrastructure keys should be intentionally less portable, making them much harder to steal.

A second difference is that HSMs need to be faster. Infrastructure components need to perform many, many more cryptographic operations compared to a single user, so it follows that the infrastructure operations need to be accelerated. Think of the CA that needs to support a million users: The number of hash and signature operations per day that the CA performs will greatly outnumber the operations per day of even the most advanced single power user. HSMs aren't restricted to infrastructure components, but their cost makes them impractical for deployment for most single users.

This chapter will explain the evaluation criteria for selecting tokens and HSMs. We're not going to explain the microprocessor design of either the tokens or the HSMs in great detail; instead, we're going to try to arm you with the knowledge to ask the right questions when you're evaluating products. This chapter also discussions popular application programming interfaces (APIs) that are required to make use of the keys stored in tokens and HSMs.

Evaluation Criteria

Before we get in to the details of tokens and HSMs, it's a good idea to explain the jargon associated with them because it will help you understand the marketing literature. There are two sets of jargon that shouldn't be confused.

The first set of jargon comes from the NIST FIPS 140-2 [FIPS140], which we mentioned briefly in Chapter 5. [FIPS140] provides requirements for cryptographic modules and defines "requirements for four security levels for cryptographic modules to provide for a wide spectrum of data sensitivity (e.g., low value administrative data, million dollar funds transfers, and life protecting data) and a diversity of application environments (e.g., a guarded facility, an office, and a completely unprotected location)." There are three important things to note here:

- Conformance to FIPS 140-2 does not ensure the security of the overall system. This is a warning to make sure that you pick the right level for the information you are trying to protect. Picking a Level 1 software module to protect a Fortune 500 company's CA keys is not prudent.

- Using a validated module does not ensure the security of the overall system. That is, the cryptographic module is one component in an overall system. Make sure that you give adequate attention to the other components too. There are any number of secure products that have been deployed in an insecure manner. A good, strong product implemented incorrectly is just a waste of money. And, it provides a false sense of security.

- FIPS 140-2 evaluated products may have features that were not tested in the evaluation. Beware of these features because you may not know how well they actually work.

The requirements address eleven areas of cryptographic module design: module specification; cryptographic module ports and interfaces; roles, services, and authentication; finite state models; physical security; operational environment; cryptographic environment; cryptographic key management; electromagnetic interference (EMI) and electromagnetic compatibility (EMC); self-tests; design assurance; and mitigation of other attacks. In general, the requirements increase as the FIPS 140-2 Level number increases.

The four FIPS 140-2 levels can be quickly summarized as follows and as shown in Figure 8-1:

	Level 1	Level 2	Level 3	Level 4
Cryptographic Module Specification	Specification of cryptographic module, cryptographic boundary, Approved algorithms, and Approved modes of operation. Description of cryptographic module, including all hardware, software, and firmware components. Statement of module security policy.			
Cryptographic Module Ports and Interfaces	Required and optional interfaces. Specification of all interfaces and of all input and output data paths.		Data ports for unprotected critical security parameters logically or physically separated from other data ports.	
Roles, Services, and Authentication	Logical separation of required and optional roles and services.	Role-based or identity-based operator authentication.	Logical separation of required and optional roles and services.	
Finite State Model	Specification of finite state model. Required states and optional states. State transition diagram and specification of state transitions.			
Physical Security	Production grade equipment.	Locks or tamper evidence.	Tamper detection and response for covers and doors.	Tamper detection and response envelope EFP or EFT.
Operational Environment	Single operator. Executable code. Approved integrity technique.	Referenced PPs evaluated at EAL2 with specified discretionary access control mechanisms and auditing.	Referenced PPs plus trusted path evaluated at EAL3 plus security policy modeling.	Referenced PPs plus trusted path evaluated at EAL4.
Cryptographic Key Management	Key management mechanisms: random number and key generation, key establishment, key distribution, key entry/output, key storage, and key zeroization.			
	Secret and private keys established using manual methods may be entered or output in plain text form.		Secret and private keys established using manual methods shall be entered or output encrypted or with split knowledge procedures.	
EMI/EMC	47 CFR FCC Part 15. Subpart B, Class A (Business use). Applicable FCC requirements (for radio).		47 CFR FCC Part 15. Subpart B, Class B (Home use).	
Self-Tests	Power-up tests: cryptographic algorithm tests, software/firmware integrity tests, critical functions tests. Conditional tests.			
Design Assurance	Configuration management (CM). Secure installation and generation. Design and policy correspondence. Guidance documents.	CM system. Secure distribution. Functional specification.	High-level language implementation.	Formal model Detailed explanations (informal proofs). Preconditions and postconditions.
Mitigation of Other Attacks	Specification of mitigation of attacks for which no testable requirements are currently available.			

Figure 8-1 Summary of security requirements

Level 1.   This is the basic level of security requirements. Major characteristics include one approved algorithm and production-grade components. Modules can be implemented in either software or hardware and do not need to be the only software implemented on the computing system.

Level 2.   This level enhances the security requirements of Level 1. Primarily, Level 2 adds *tamper-evidence* requirements and asks that a role (e.g., user and crypto officer) be authenticated prior to performing a service (e.g., self-test and algorithms). The module is allowed to run on a general-purpose computer system only if the computer system must meet a Common Criteria (CC) Protection Profile (PP) evaluation assurance level EAL2. (We'll explain more about CC, PP, and EAL shortly.)

Level 3.   This level further enhances the security requirements of Level 2. The physical protections are beefed up; there must be a high probability of detecting and responding to physical access or modification of the module. That is, opening the module will cause it to be *zeroized*, which is the destruction of the sensitive data that an attacker might want to access. The module must also support identity-based authentication of the operator. This level requires that the input and output ports for the *Critical Security Parameters* (CSPs) are physically separated from other ports. The module is allowed to run on a general-purpose computer system only if a *trusted path* is provided and the computer system must meet a CC PP evaluation assurance level EAL3. A trusted path provides confidence that the human user is communicating with the intended part of the system, ensuring that attackers can't intercept or modify the data is being communicated.

> **NOTE**   A trusted path protects the cryptographic module's plaintext CSPs, the software, and the firmware components from other untrusted software or firmware that may be executing on the system. By ensuring the cryptographic module is not affected by other untrusted components, the security of the cryptographic module is increased. The trusted path should stop Trojan horse software from fooling the user into providing sensitive data to anything other than the legitimate (and trusted) cryptographic module.

Level 4.   This is the highest level, and it builds on the security requirements of Level 3. The physical protections are strengthened even further; there must be a very high probability of detecting and responding to physical access or modification of the module; opening the module must cause it to immediately zeroize. There are also protections against environmental changes outside of the module's normal operating range (e.g., it's too cold or too hot). The module is still allowed to run on a general-purpose computer system only if the trusted path is EAL 4. As part of the design assurance requirements, formal modeling of the module is required.

The second set of jargon comes from the *Common Criteria for Information Technology Security Evaluations*, which is simply called the *Common Criteria* or *CC*. The CC was defined jointly by the International Organization for Standardization (ISO) and International Electrotechnical Committee (IEC) in [ISO15408] and [CC], both of which are three-part standards.* Instead of specifying requirements like FIPS 140-2, CC "specifies a common set of requirements for the security functionality of IT products and for assurance measures applied to these IT products during security evaluation." A user community specifies a *Protection Profile* (PP), which lists the desired security functionality, properties, and behavior. A developer then writes a *Security Target* (ST) to indicate the security properties of the *Target of Evaluation* (TOE), which is the security software, firmware, or hardware. The TOE and ST are inputs to the Common Criteria evaluation against a particular Protection Profile. In practice, what's happened is governments and consortia have developed PPs for commercial product offerings and for internal development projects. One aspect of a commercial operating system PP will address the trusted path. Then, vendors that want to supply to these customers have their product tested against the appropriate PP. This is depicted in Figure 8-2. To make things easier on everyone, the standard defined a set of *Evaluation Assurance Levels* (EAL).

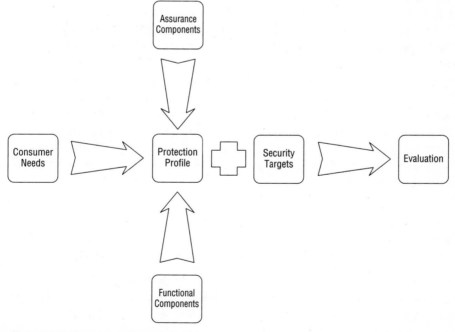

Figure 8-2 Common criteria concepts

*Also see www.commoncriteriaportal.org/public/files/ccintroduction.pdf for additional information.

Seven levels are defined, like the FIPS 140-2 levels, as the number increases so does the depth of the evaluation. The first level gives some confidence that the product will work as advertised, and the seventh level offers an extremely high confidence. This assurance comes from the increase in documentation and much more rigorous testing. The seven EAL levels are:

- EAL1: Functionally Tested
- EAL2: Structurally Tested
- EAL3: Methodically Tested and Checked
- EAL4: Methodically Designed, Tested, and Reviewed
- EAL5: Semi-formally Designed and Tested
- EAL6: Semi-formally Verified Design and Tested
- EAL7: Formally Verified Design and Tested

An assertion by a manufacturer that a product meets a FIPS 140-2, an EAL, or is compliant with standards, is a completely empty statement and possibly fraudulent unless, of course, it was actually tested by a certified, independent evaluator. NIST in conjunction with Canada's Computer Security Establishment (CSE) developed the *Cryptographic Module Verification Program* (CMVP) that accredits third-party *Cryptographic Module Testing* (CMT) laboratories. For CC evaluations, each lab must conform to [ISO17025]. NIST also developed the *National Voluntary Laboratory Accreditation Program* (NVLAP) to accredit the *Common Criteria Testing Laboratories* (CCTL). Of course, testing isn't free, and the price goes up with the level. The testing also takes a significant amount of time. It costs somewhere on the order of $100K for a FIPS certificate and even more for CC. Once a product is tested, a certificate is provided that states the level that was achieved. If a product claims that they're compliant or conformant, then ask for the product's certificate number and also make sure that the product was actually tested, by going to the website and looking it up yourself.*

Tokens

Tokens come in a variety of form factors and connect to desktops, laptops, and PDAs via a number of interfaces. Some tokens are more cryptographically aware than others, but all of them are of some use to us. This section will address various token characteristics.

*See http://csrc.nist.gov/groups/STM/cmvp/documents/140-1/ 140val-all.htm for a complete list of the FIPS 140 certificates.

PC Cards

The first type of card we're going to look at is the PC Card, which is officially called the Personal Computer Memory Card International Association (PCMCIA) card. The PCMCIA was formed in the late 1980s to develop common standards for expansion cards. Prior to the PCMCIA standards, peripherals like additional memory, network interface cards, and modems were designed to work with only one manufacturer's machine. Additionally, when mobile computing evolved, there was often no room in the machine for both Ethernet and modem circuitry. The PCMCIA standards abstracted the interface and allowed the vendors to develop peripherals for multiple manufacturers' machines.

There have been multiple versions of the PCMCIA standard release with the major developments in Releases 1, 2, 5, and 8. Release 1, published in 1990, was the original release, but it only addressed memory cards. Release 2 added I/O support. Release 5 added *CardBus* support, more about this later. Release 8 published in 2001 added *CardBay* support, more about this later too.

> **NOTE** "Plug-and-play" was one of the most important features that the PC Card supported. Normally, adding a peripheral required rebooting for the peripheral to be recognized. With plug-and-play, there's no need to reboot to have the peripheral recognized by Windows.

Physically the PC Cards are 54 mm wide by 85.6 mm long and have a 68-pin connector. The thickness of the PC Card varies; they can be 3.3, 5.0, or 10.5 mm. The thickness signifies the type of PC Card: Type I is 3.3 mm, Type II is 5.0 mm, and Type III is 10.5 mm. The different thickness support different applications; Type I is typically used to support memory devices. Type II is physically larger so that it can support small rotating media, but its big use is for modem cards with the connector extended out beyond the end of the card or via a dongle. Type III is thick enough to support larger rotating media, full-sized phone connectors, and Ethernet connectors. The PC Cards are a combination of plastic and stainless steel, making them relatively rugged.

The throughput on the card varies based on the interface. The 16-bit memory interface supports either a 10 or 20 MB per second, with the speed depending on which transfer mode the card is using; the 16-bit I/O interface supports 3.92 or 7.84 MB per second; the 32-bit interface support 33, 66, and 132 MB per second. The 32-bit interface is referred to as CardBus because it uses a busmastering* technique to achieve the higher speeds. The addition of a grounding strip is a visual confirmation that the PC Card supports CardBus. Type I only supports

---

*Busmastering is a feature that allows a device connected to the bus to communicate with other devices connected to the bus without going through the CPU.

the 16-bit memory interface, while Type II and Type III cards support the 16-bit I/O and 32-bit interfaces. The CardBay interface, defined in Release 8 of the PCMCIA standard, intended to allow the Universal Serial Bus (USB) interface with a PC Card format, but it has not been widely adopted.

PCMCIA is an interface standard, so the internals of the PC Cards are almost always company proprietary. In general, the cryptographic PC Cards have miniature computers that communicate with the host machine through the PCMCIA connector. These miniature computers include a microcontroller or central processing unit (CPU) that runs the PC Card's operating system stored in the read-only memory (ROM). There's also random access memory (RAM) that the CPU uses for temporary storage. Some include coprocessors to speed up the math computations necessary for cryptography, which is why the coprocessor is sometimes called a cryptographic module. The operating system, which manages the hardware resources on the miniature computer, is also proprietary.

There have been many PC Cards developed that support either storing cryptographic keying material or performing cryptographic operations. Most Type I cards are memory-only, so at most they'd be good for storing encrypted private keys and certificates. There is little difference between this and storing them on your local hard drive, except that the PC Card is more portable, allowing it to be kept with the owner. There have been many Type II and Type III PC Cards developed that support storing private keys and certificates as well as performing cryptographic operations.

NOTE Arguably the most famous type of PC Card tokens is the FORTEZZA Crypto Cards developed by the NSA to support the U.S. Defense Message System (DMS). SPYRUS was the primary vendor and they delivered around 500,000 cards.

In addition to the PC Card there needs to be a PC Card reader as well as drivers for the computer to access the card. Initially, no computers had PC Card readers, but eventually all laptops included at least two. The desktops, on the other hand, rarely had a PC Card reader. The DoD tried to combat this by specifying a policy that required all computers including desktops to have two slots, but this never really took off in the commercial world. Now, readers are available that connect via USB and Small Computer System Interface (SCSI).* Regardless, not having the readers built into the computer definitely slowed PC Card deployment for desktop computers.

In addition to the PC Card reader, drivers and middleware also need to be installed on the machine. Both have always proved expensive to develop, challenging to keep updated, and difficult to manage.

The PCMCIA has closed development on PC Card standard and notes that future developers should move to the *ExpressCard* standard. The last

---

*SCSI is another standard for connecting peripherals to computers.

version of the PCMCIA standard was published in 2001. There were many of PC Card implementations, but there are significantly fewer ExpressCard implementations available.

> **NOTE** There are numerous ExpressCard smart card readers. They use the ExpressCard interface to connect to the computer, PDA, or tablet and then insert the smart card in to it. To date there haven't been ExpressCards that support cryptographic operations.

The PC Card has been overtaken by USB as the de facto interface for both laptops and desktops. The widespread support for USB has really dampened support for PC Cards. Other reasons PC Cards are no longer in favor:

- The amount of space required for a PC Card socket is significantly larger than that required for USB connectors.
- The 68-pin connectors are more problematic than the USB connector — bending a pin in the reader can cause all kinds of problems.
- Smart card performance has greatly improved.
- The focus of PC Cards, namely FORTEZZA Crypto Cards, was to do all of the cryptography on the card and support end-to-end security. The focus now has changed to be protecting the private key and allowing some of the cryptography to be performed on the desktop and laptops.

If you're looking to implement tokens, we'd suggest looking at smart cards or USB tokens because that's where all the innovation is taking place.

Smart Cards

The next token we're going to look at is smart cards. They've been around since the mid-1970s when a credit card was first merged with a microprocessor (we refer to the chip on a smart card as an integrated circuit chip, or ICC). Independently, the two have become enormously popular, and coupled they are becoming the runaway favorite choice for tokens. For a complete and much more detailed look at the internals of smart cards we recommend Rankl and Effing's book the *Smart Card Handbook* [WOLFGANG] and Dreifus and Monk's book *Smart Cards: A Guide to Building and Managing Smart Card Applications* [DRIEFUS].

There are four important standards that define a smart card:

ISO/IEC 7810. This defines the dimensions of the credit card, which are 85.60 mm by 53.98 mm and .76 mm thick. The cards can be made of plastic, paper, or another material, but typically the cards are made of plastic, specifically polyvinyl chloride (PVC).

ISO/IEC 7816 Parts 1-13 and 15.   This defines just about everything else about smart cards. The various parts of the standard address properties such as

- The amount of X-rays, UV light, and static electricity they must be able to withstand
- How much the card can bend before it breaks
- The physical location of ICC; the size of the ICC (10.25 mm by 19.23 mm); the number of ICC contacts (there are 8)
- What each contact does; the electrical characteristics of the contacts
- A common syntax and format for cryptographic information
- Mechanisms by which to share this information

ISO/IEC 14443 Parts 1-4.   This defines what is referred to as *Proximity Cards*. This multipart standard specifies contactless smart cards: physical dimensions as specified in ISO/IEC 7810; radiofrequency (13.56 MHz); communication protocols; transmission protocols. It allows for the card be about 10 cm away from the contactless card reader.

ISO 15693 Parts 1-3.   This defines what is referred to as *Vicinity Cards*. This multipart standard is similar to ISO/IEC 1443 except that the card and card reader can be between 1 and 1.5 meters apart. This standard has never really taken off, but it's included in this list for completeness.

> **NOTE** There are other standards that apply to what goes on the physical surface of the card, such as embossed letters and magnetic strips, but we're going to focus on the ICC interface.

There are a number of ways to categorize smart cards, but we'll keep it simple and use just two categories: how the card is read and the type of card.

Readers. Smart cards work with two types of readers: *contact* or *contactless*. With contact card readers, the card needs to be inserted into the reader for it to be read, but with contactless cards the card does not actually need to touch the reader. It needs to be within either 10 cm or 1.5 m of the reader. There are some technical differences between the two readers, of course. The contact reader has more available power, whereas the contactless readers have less wear and tear, but need antennas as well as security protocols for communicating with the card and the reader. There is also one big practical difference: Contact readers are about 10 times cheaper than contactless card readers, with contact readers are currently going for around $20, while contactless ones are going for around $200. Some cards now support both and are referred to as *combi cards*.

Type. With all the marketing hype and brand names in the smart cards retail space it's easy to be confused about the types of cards. Next, you'll find a list of the card types in order of increasing security:

Memory-only.   Because they have the same form factor as an ICC, some advertise this type of card as a smart card, but these are really on the lowest rung of the security ladder and shouldn't be considered smart cards at all. In reality, these read-only memory cards are only a little better than the magnetic strips on the back of credit cards, and even then they're only better because they can store more information than the strip alone can, not because they are more secure.

Serial Protected.   These cards, which are also sometimes referred to as *Segmented Memory Cards* or *Intelligent Memory Cards,* are on the next step up the security ladder, but they shouldn't really be considered smart cards either. (They are sometimes grouped with the memory-only cards.) These cards offer both read and write capability. Manufacturers often claim that these cards support "authentication," but this usually refers to the card identifier that allows the card to be tracked or the fact that some of the memory can be protected with a PIN or symmetric key. What makes them better than the memory-only cards is the built-in logic that controls access to the memory on the card, which allows some or all of the memory to be protected.

Wired Logic.   One more step up the security ladder are Wired Logic cards, sometimes referred to as *ROM-mask* cards. The ROM-mask, which contains the chip's OS, also contains a logic-based state machine supporting encrypted memory and authenticated access to the memory. However, the ROM is burned in when the card is manufactured, so once the card leaves the factory, there's no changing the way the card works. Wired Logic cards really shouldn't be considered smart cards either.

Secure Microcontroller.   These cards are at the top of the smart card ladder, because they really are smart. What puts them above the rest is the addition of a CPU that runs programs, performs calculations, and manages data. These are really the only cards that should be referred to as "smart cards," so beware of the marketing hype!

Looking under the Hood

Without digressing too much into microprocessor design, you should take a quick look at the internals of the four cards and note their similarities and differences.

The previous three card types have address and security logic: EEPROM and ROM, whereas the secure microcontroller removes the address and security logic and adds a CPU, an optional coprocessor, and some RAM.

As mentioned earlier, the ROM holds most of the operating system. EEPROM is the nonvolatile, read/write memory (NVM), which in Secure Microcontroller cards ranges up to 256 KB. The EEPROM is important because it stores information even when the card is not powered; PINs, keys, and certificates are stored here. EEPROM also stores the parts of the operating system that are critical to software patches and updates. RAM also serves as temporary storage for data.

The CPU runs the operating system and applications. CPUs range in processing power from 8 bit to 32 bit; more bits means more processing power for quicker cryptographic operations. Some smart cards also include a coprocessor to accelerate cryptographic operations. These coprocessors are sometimes called a cryptographic module. Obviously, for the types of smart cards discussed in the book, you should be looking for one with a coprocessor; it's important to achieve an acceptable user experience.

Operating Systems and Smart Cards

There are a number of OSs that run on smart cards. Initially, all OSs were proprietary and required their own middleware. Now the Multiple Operating System (MULTOS) and the Java OS have been developed to abstract the card and allow middleware from different vendors. Smart cards that run the Java OS are referred to as *Java Smart Cards*. There are also a variety of application development tools. The lack of a standard in this area has actually been a problem, but the *Global Platform* and *OpenCard* are being filling this void by providing interfaces for both smart cards and applications on the card.

Choosing Smart Cards

We believe the smart card is a prudent token choice, especially in environments where there is a desire to couple a picture identification badge with the token. Smart cards offer the ability to print photos, logos, magnetic strips, and text on the card's surface. The only choice left now is the reader.

Contact readers are available in many places now. They are integrated into keyboards for desktops and directly into laptops, and there are also a number of readers that support PCMCIA and USB connectors. As mentioned previously, contactless readers are also readily available, but they're currently an order of magnitude more expensive. It's not an obvious choice, because the way you want to use the card will influence your choice. For example, in some cases physical access control might be better suited to contactless smart cards because the reader can read the card without requiring that the users remove the badges hanging from their necks — speeding access control decisions for high-flow areas.

OPEN STANDARDS WIN AGAIN

The primary reason that smart cards have taken off is their adherence to open standards (granted they are ISO/IEC standards), which helps ensure interoperability. The ICC, the contacts, the communication protocol, and the readers are all standardized. Vendors offer features and specialized commands outside of these standards, especially in the area of loading cryptographic keying material. Also, the operating system in the ROM and application development tools are often vendor specific. However, there are efforts to develop standards in these areas as well.

This standardization effort, of course, won't actually happen unless developers feel there's a market — and there is. All over the world, governments and businesses are realizing the need for smart cards, and they're investing in them as well as the systems that support them.

USB Tokens

The Universal Serial Bus (USB) has been around since the mid-1990s when Intel, Microsoft, and others wanted to lower the number of peripheral connection standards. Before USB, there were serial ports, parallel ports, keyboard ports, mouse ports, joystick ports, and so on. It was out of hand! As always, there were early adoption issues, but now USB is nearly ubiquitous. Many credit this to the iMAC; from 1998 on it had only USB connectors. There is now a USB Implementors Forum (USB-IF) that oversees development of the USB standards.

There have been three major releases of the USB standard. 1.0, 1.1, and 2.0. USB 1.0 offered speeds up to 1.5 Mbps, whereas USB 1.1 supported 12 Mbps for high-speed devices and 1.5 Mbps for lower bandwidth devices (such as keyboards and joysticks). USB 2.0 offers speeds up to 480 Mbps. USB 3.0 is rumored to be in the works, and it's said to be shooting for 4.8 Gbps.

USB supports seven different connectors: USB A, USB B, Mini-A, Mini-B, Mini-AB, and Micro-A, and Micro-B. The Mini and Micro are normally used for small devices like cameras and cell phones, while the normal sizes are used by devices like printers, keyboards, and joysticks.

There are no standards for USB cryptographic tokens other than the connectors. They come in two flavors. The first are memory-only devices — think of a USB *memory stick*. They are basically little portable hard drives that offer the same amount of security as the other memory-only devices. The second type is characterized by either proprietary chips on a stick or a connection to an ICC that is eerily similar to the ICCs offered on smart cards.

One major advantage that USB tokens have over smart cards is that there is no need for a reader, since just about every computer on the planet has one or more USB connector. They're on monitors, desktops, laptops, and keyboards. USB is the de facto connector choice for the foreseeable future.

USB cryptographic tokens are a prudent choice for environments where integration with a picture identification badge isn't required or where readers difficult to deploy.

Software Tokens

Software tokens are private keys and certificate stored in software. Obviously, storing private keys without somehow associating them with their corresponding certificates would make them difficult to use. Further, storing them in plaintext is insecure. The de facto standard for performing the task of associating a private key with a certificate and encrypting them for storage in a file is PKCS#12 [PKCS12]. It defines an ASN.1 structure for storing encrypted private keys and certificates — and unsurprisingly it makes use of CMS. If the key is encrypted with a password, then it's placed in an `EncryptedData`. If the key is encrypted using public key cryptography, it's placed in an `EnvelopedData`. The contents are called a `SafeBag`, and it contains an unencrypted public key, and an encrypted private key, a certificate bag, a CRL bag, miscellaneous secrets, or another `SafeBag`. Attributes about the bag are also supported, such as friendly names for the `SafeBag`. The file extension is either `.p12` or `.pfx`. Originally, `.p12` was used by Netscape and `.pfx` was used by Microsoft, but they're considered synonymous at this point, and everyone supports both file extensions.

Software tokens can be used to make those not-so-smart memory-only PCMCIA, smart cards, and USB tokens a little more secure. If you can store the encrypted private keys and their associated certificates, or even just the symmetric keys, that's one step more secure than storing unencrypted keys on a memory stick. Software tokens are extremely portable because they can be copied to multiple tokens or to any file system for that matter, allowing easy backup copies to be made, too. This is also their danger. If there are too many copies, it gets difficult to keep track of them.

For some environments, this type of token is a prudent choice. It is best suited for environments where there are strong procedures to make sure that the machines on which the software tokens are used have not been infected with Trojan horses.

iButton Tokens

An iButton isn't a new Apple product or an expansion thingamajig for your iPod — it's a security token developed by Dallas Semiconductor, which was bought by Maxim Integrated Products. The token itself is about the size of a round lithium camera battery; it's a stainless steel "can" that is 17.35 mm in radius and either 3.10 or 5.89 mm thick. A microchip and various types of memory are housed inside, and when the iButton is touched to the reader, the chip communicates with the 1-Wire protocol at either 16 Kbps or 142 Kbps. Both read and write operations are supported. It is, however, company proprietary, so tokens, readers, software development kits (kits are free), and so on all come from the same company.

iButtons can be simple, memory-only devices. They're probably slightly more secure than the other devices because the attacker is going to need some uncommon drivers to access the iButton and a not-so-common reader, but neither of these things will stop a determined attacker.

They also developed a Java-powered cryptographic iButton. The can contained a microcontroller, a clock, a math accelerator, and 64 Kbytes of ROM and NVM. The catch is that there were no keys implemented, and the token only supported SHA-1.

The one advantage iButton has over smart cards is the durability of the "can." Since it's stainless steel, it can take a pounding — literally.

For future token deployments, the iButton falls a little short. If you're just looking for a memory-only token, we suggest a USB device because you don't need to buy a reader. For a cryptographic token, smart cards or USB are better choices.

Embedded Tokens

Up to now we've talked about tokens that are inserted or installed in on your desktop, laptop, or PDA, but what about having them burned directly into the chips that run the desktop, laptop, or PDA? Enter the *Trusted Computer Group* (TCG), which aims to do just that. The TCG was formed in 2003 to develop open standards for trusted computing. There are currently around 170 members, including Intel, Sun, Microsoft, AMD, IBM, Dell, and many more.

One of their standards specifies what's called the *Trusted Platform Module* (TPM). Their website states:

> *The TPM is a microcontroller that stores keys, passwords and digital certificates. It typically is affixed to the motherboard of a PC. It potentially can be used in any computing device that requires these functions. The nature of this silicon ensures that the information stored there is made more secure from external software attack and physical theft. Security processes, such as digital signature and key exchange, are protected through the secure TCG subsystem. Access to data and secrets in a platform could be denied if the boot sequence is not as expected. Critical applications and capabilities such as secure email, secure web access and local protection of data are thereby made much more secure. TPM capabilities also can be integrated into other components in a system.*

The private keys stored on the TPM can be used to authenticate a particular desktop, laptop, or PDA, so it is called a *fixed token*. If lots of people use the same machine, then the only thing that's authenticated is the actual machine, not the users. Add a smart card or USB token though and you can authenticate both the machine and the user. If only one person ever uses the machine, then the keys in the TPM could authenticate both the user and the machine. The TCG knows that their solution needs to support a variety of environments so they say that user tokens are complementary.

The TCG also has developed the *Trusted Computer Group Software Specification* (TSS). This specification defines the API that is used to access the functions of the TPM. Without it, the TPM wouldn't be very useful.

TCG took machine authentication one step further when they developed the *Trust Network Connect* (TNC) protocol. The TNC collects endpoint configuration and user data, transmits the data to the organization, and then compares it to an organization for comparison against a predefined set of criteria. Access is granted based on an appropriate level. For example, if you logged in using your work machine that's got your organization's standard software load, you'd get complete access, but if you access from a machine you tweaked you might get none at all. This way the organization is in control of who accesses their networks and what they do it with. The whole process uses the keys resident in the TPM.

Currently, TPM v1.2 requires support for SHA-1 and RSA. It also includes a random number generator that, along with the TSS API, other applications can use. 3DES is the symmetric algorithm, and this version doesn't support AES, but we'll bet a version in the not to distant future will.

As for speed — well it's on the chip, so it's fast. There are claims of 1024-bit RSA claim signatures in 100 ms and 2048-bit RSA signatures in 500 ms. This is good because most of the keys are required to be 2048-bit.

The other added benefit of on TPM is that there's absolutely positively no need for a reader.

Hardware Security Modules

If you had to pick a place to put your most important set of valuables, then you'd probably pick a well-established bank with a safe deposit box that's got 24-hour guards, a sophisticated alarm system, and multiple keys for the box. Well the same should be true of infrastructure keys because they are the basis of trust for the whole PKI. Now, though the HSM vendors won't provide the guards or the room (I bet they know somebody who could), they *will* provide an HSM that's been put through the NIST 140-2 ringer. Obviously, these are a little more costly than what's provided to users because HSMs are designed to be more secure.

You won't be mortgaging the house though because you usually only need a couple of them: one for each key generator, signing engine, high-speed VPN authenticator — and anyway the vendors need to make their money somehow.

HSMs come in two varieties: blades that plug into the Peripheral Component Interconnect (PCI) slots on a computer's motherboard and standalone external devices. In either case, the machine that is connected to an HSM is solely to make keys, sign objects, and validate signatures.

Network-Attached Multi-User Hardware Security Modules

Traditional PKI systems are based on distributing keys to the end users, which, aside from security concerns [Marchesini], creates a high burden in logistics, cost, help-desk support and user acceptance [Whitten] and also introduces training obstacles [Nielsen]. Management of a large distributed system of any kind is extremely hard and PKI systems are no exception.

Network-attached multi-user (NAMU) HSMs may improve the scalability and adoption of PKI-driven applications by offering secure centralized key management for a large community of users with diverse distributed application environments, while alleviating administrative overhead associated with provisioning and managing individual tokens. Other efficiencies offered by this approach include a reduction in revocation management. When users' privileges must be revoked, their private keys can instantly be revoked from a central HSM server. The need for distributing CRLs or OCSP checking may be greatly diminished since the users will no longer have access to their private key. For key management and real-time authentication, denying access to the private key may be sufficient. For signatures, removing access to private key prevents the creation of new signatures, but previously generated ones will still be considered valid. So, the need for revocation must be considered in this light.

The NAMU HSM can be viewed as a virtual, network-attached token. Each user has a profile within the NAMU HSM that maintains their keys while allowing key operations only after successfully using a specified user authentication mechanism. Depending on the assurance needs, the user authentication could make use of simple username/password, Kerberos, biometrics, one-time-password tokens, or strong cryptographic-based challenge-response protocols. User authentication to the NAMU HSM usually runs on top of SSL or TLS.

Some administrators manage the NAMU HSM and the user-directory systems together. In this way, any user listed in the enterprise directory has keying material available to them. This is sometimes called *directory-driven* deployment, and its primary benefit is one user management and authentication policy can administer for all applications, whether PKI-enabled or not.

NAMU HSMs can greatly reduce the cost of ownership and administrative overheard associated with a PKI-enabled application. The NAMU HSM may offer these savings:

1. Eliminate costs associated with acquiring key tokens, their provisioning, and their ongoing management

2. Leverage existing authentication infrastructure and security policies

3. Leverage existing directory systems and user-management policies

4. Reduce the need to distribute CRLs and to subscribe to OCSP responders

Application Program Interfaces

All of the tokens require some kind of *application programming interface* (API). If the cryptographic operations are performed on the token, then the API minimally needs to support passing the data that is going to be encrypted, hashed, or signed on and off the card. Proprietary APIs were the norm for a very long time. If every application that makes use of cryptography needs to write its own code, cryptographic adoption will be slow and bug riddled. With standardized APIs, applications don't need to know about the cryptography; they just need to know about the API. Two APIs have emerged to meet this need: Microsoft's Cryptographic API (CAPI) and RSA's PKCS #11.

If you're going to do cryptography on a Microsoft operating system, then you need to learn how to use Microsoft CAPI. Microsoft CAPI 1.0 has a number of predefined functions to perform operations such as generating keys, hashing data, generating signatures, verifying signatures, encrypting files, and decrypting files. Cryptographic operations are performed by independent modules known as *cryptographic service providers* (CSP). With this architecture, all that is necessary to add a new module is to add a new CSP. So, each hardware device vendor needs to provide a CSP that works with their particular device, handling any functions that are not implemented in the hardware in the CSP software. CAPI 2.0 added a lot of support for PKI, including functions to validate certificates. Windows Vista includes a major upgrade to CAPI, called the Cryptography API Next Generation (CNG). It supports all the algorithms that CAPI 1.0 and 2.0 supports but accesses them a differently. It uses what are referred to as *routers* to access the different algorithms: random number generator router, hash router, symmetric encryption router, asymmetric encryption router, signature router, and secret agreement router. This approach is better for hardware device vendors. CNG adds support for

ECC algorithms, replaceable random number generator, and a *kernel mode* among other things. The kernel mode operation allows the cryptographic functions to be accessed by parts of the operating system kernel, such as the IPsec implementation. CNG is targeted at FIPS Level 2 certification.

If you're going to do cryptography on a UNIX operating system (or one of the many spin-off operating systems such as Linux), then you need to learn PKCS #11 [PKCS11]. PKCS#11 is sometimes referred to as *Cryptoki*, which is short for cryptographic token interface. Cryptoki, like Microsoft CAPI, specifies data types and functions for applications that need to use cryptographic functions. The interface was greatly influenced by token vendors, and it includes features that are important to them, such as separation of user and security office (SO) roles. The SO initializes the token and sets the PIN. Applications access the token in sessions that are either read-only or read-write. Once access is granted different operations can be performed, such as initializing signatures, hashes, encryption, and decryption. As with Microsoft CSPs, a PKCS#11 library provided by a hardware device vendor will often include some functionality in software in order to give a comprehensive solution, not just the functionality that is offered by the hardware.

Case Studies

Signatures and Authentication for Everyone

The Signatures and Authentication for Everyone (SAFE) initiative, previously known as Secure Access for Everyone, evolved out of a Pharmaceuticals Research and Manufacturers of America (PhRMA) strategic project started in 2003 to build a business case for identity management. The business case was successful because it was based on open standards for digital signatures, identities, and PKI that would be used not only for business communications but also for regulatory communications. The business case showed how the biopharmaceutical industry could save money by adopting digital signatures as equivalent to, and therefore as replacements for, traditional wet signatures.

The SAFE-BioPharma Association was formed by a coalition of nine founding biopharmaceutical companies: AstraZeneca, Bristol-Myers Squibb Company, GlaxoSmithKline, Johnson & Johnson, Merck, Pfizer, Procter & Gamble, and Sanofi-Aventis. They developed the SAFE Standard Version 1.0, which included operating policies, legal structure, a business and governance model, technical specifications, and functional processes.

The SAFE-BioPharma Association is a not-for-profit organization, which at first might seem like odd arrangement for a business. The drivers are cost savings and business efficiency for the association's members. The estimates of these members show that they were spending over $1 billion on independent identity management systems, that 40 percent of annual research and development costs (around $9 billion) were a result of paper-based business processes, and that 31 percent of health care costs (around $500 billion) were the result of paperwork. Reducing paper-related costs, time, management, and storage, would be a huge savings for them and their customers, which undoubtedly includes you.

Another major driver of the SAFE-BioPharma Association is regulatory compliance. The members must deal with regulatory bodies, such as the U.S. Food and Drug Administration (FDA) and the European Medicines Agency (EMEA), that want to make sure that there are excellent practices in every process: clinical, lab, safety, trials, and manufacturing. There are also huge privacy protection concerns and data integrity requirements. The Association involved the regulatory bodies early in the process to ensure that they considered the effort worthwhile and invited them to join the association in an advisory role.

In this chapter, we present the architecture for the SAFE-BioPharma Association and discuss the successes and lessons learned by the SAFE effort. We'll focus on the current version of the SAFE Standard, which is currently Version 2.17.

For more information on SAFE see `www.safe-biopharma.org`.

SAFE Architecture

In this section, we provide an overview of the SAFE architecture. The discussion includes cryptographic algorithms; PKI architecture; certificate, CRL, and Online-Certificate Status Protocol (OCSP) profiles; cryptographic tokens and modules; and SAFE-enabled applications.

Cryptographic Algorithms

SAFE uses commercial algorithms to provide authentication, integrity, confidentiality, and to enable non-repudiation services for SAFE-enabled applications. Specifically, SAFE uses

- RSA for digital signatures and key management.
- SHA-1 or SHA-256 for one-way hash functions.
- Triple-DES or AES-128 for symmetric encryption.

Because they're dealing with the FDA, it's no surprise that SAFE follows the NIST guidelines [NISTSP] for key sizes and algorithm migration:

- RSA 1024-bit keys before 2011 and 2048-bit keys beyond 2010.
- SHA-1 before 2011 and SHA-256 beyond 2010.
- 80 bits of strength through 2010 and 112 bits thereafter. Triple-DES provides 112 bits, and AES-128 provides 128 bits.

PKI Architecture

Making a number of independent and heterogeneous PKIs from different companies interoperable is a challenge. Realistically, there are two approaches: everyone cross-certifies with each other or a bridge is used. SAFE chose to implement a bridge CA, which is called the SAFE Bridge CA (SBCA). The bridge is the least labor-intensive approach to achieve cross-certification.

The SBCA was designed by SAFE, but it outsourced the day-to-day operations to Cybertrust/Verizon Business. The SBCA was tested in mid-2005 and has been in operation since late 2005. It is in the process of being cross-certification with U.S. Federal Bridge Certificate Authority (FBCA) to enable trust paths between SAFE certificate issuers and U.S. Government CAs. Figure 9-1 shows the SAFE architectural vision, but note that not all of the cross-certified domains are shown. The Federal Bridge Certification Authority is shown because it is the route to interoperate with the FDA and DEA.

Member PKIs may be either hierarchical or mesh PKIs. Member PKIs are also free to establish other bilateral cross-certification relationships amongst each other. The SBCA can cross-certify with a Principal CA or a sub-CA. The Principal CA may be a self-signed CA or it may utilize an existing trust anchor.

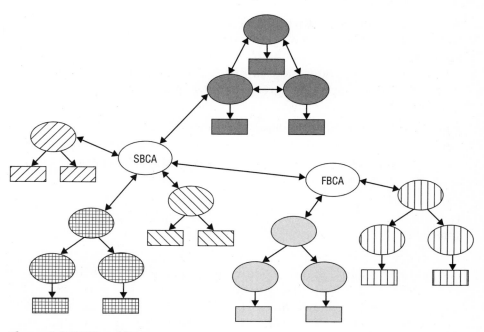

Figure 9-1 SBCA architecture

The SBCA also provides a repository for cross-certificates; access by HTTP is supported.

The SAFE architecture also supports a *Certificate Status Authority* (CSA). Status response via either OCSP or SCVP may be supported. OCSP provides status information on one or more certificates. SCVP provides a full path validation service. The SBCA currently implements an OCSP responder.

The cross-certification process can be daunting to those with PKIs who want to join SAFE, SAFE produced a document to describe the cross-certification process and to provide a checklist to make sure all the i's are dotted and t's are crossed. They divided the cross-certification process into six phases:

1. **Initiation:**   In the first phase, the applicant applies for cross-certification. There's a form to fill out and agreements to sign. The idea is that major differences will be documented and used as input to the second stage.

2. **Policy review:**   In the second phase, both parties review the application to determine suitability and resolve any policy differences. The outcome of this step could be to stop the entire process, get a waiver, or proceed. Theoretically, this is a give-and-take process, but in reality it's almost always the applicant that has to change their policy to avoid the need to revisit existing cross-certifications.

3. **Technical interoperability testing:**   In the third phase, assuming that the outcome of phase two was successful or a waiver was obtained, tests are performed to ensure that both cross-certificates can be verified, that repositories interoperate, and that the right OCSP responders can be accessed. Depending on the agreement, there may be fees associated with this testing.

4. **Agreement:**   In the fourth phase, lawyers get involved to review the agreements that dictate the actions of the applicant as they pertain to the cross-certification. Once everything is agreed on, the applicant signs the agreement.

5. **Cross-certification:**   In the fifth phase, the SBCA signs the CA's digital certificate and vice versa. The public portion of each is published on the Internet.

6. **Maintenance:**   In the sixth phase, the SBCA needs to perform compliance audits to ensure that the cross-certification agreements are implemented properly and any uncovered problems are addressed. If any changes are planned that affect the trust of the cross-certificate, then these changes must be discussed by both parties. Cross-certification agreements indicate the duration of the agreement, and it's normal that the agreements need to be reviewed and in some cases terminated.

Certificate Policies

SAFE does not support encrypted email and does not have key archive. We know that any large-scale PKI will be used with many applications beyond email. The primary focus for the use of SAFE certificates is strong authentication and digital signatures. The certificate policies needed to support this situation can be application specific or can be assigned according to assurance level. The former approach, while prudent for a small, fixed set of applications, is not prudent for a PKI intended to support general interoperability. Think of the proliferation of object identifiers and the need to change the cross-certificate every time a new application is developed. For this reason, SAFE followed the FBCA lead and defines two categories, or classes, that group the applications based on assurance level. Table 9-1 lists them in decreasing levels of assurance. The assurance levels are:

Medium Hardware. With the medium hardware, the private key is generated in and protected by a hardware device or hardware security module (HSM). The maximum lifetime of the private key is five years.

Medium Software. With the medium software policy, the private key is generated in and protected by software. The maximum lifetime of the private key is five years.

When the SBCA cross-certifies with a member's principle CA or another bridge CA, it is expected to use the policy-mapping extension to indicate which subject domain policies may be accepted as equivalent to the SBCA policies. Principal CAs are likewise expected to use the policy-mapping extension to indicate which SBCA policies may be accepted by its users as equivalent to the local policy. Members that have not already deployed a PKI can use the SBCA policies in their own PKI.

Certificate, CRL, and OCSP Profiles

The SBCA CP includes profiles for certificates issued by the SBCA to Principal CAs, certificates issued by the Principal CA to the SBCA, Issuer CA certificates, and subscriber signature certificates. There is a profile for encryption certificates, but it's only for reference purposes. All of the certificates are

Table 9-1 SBCA Certificate Policy Object Identifiers

LEVEL OF ASSURANCE	OID NAME	OBJECT IDENTIFIERS
Medium Hardware	mediumHardware	1.3.6.1.4.1.23165.1.3
Medium Software	mediumSoftware	1.3.6.1.4.1.23165.1.2

version 3 certificates, as they include extensions, and all of the certificates use X.500 distinguished names. The SBCA uses the X.500-style (e.g., c=, o=, ou=, cn=) for its subject name, but Principle CAs are free to use either the X.500-style or DNS-style (e.g., dc=, dc=, ou=, cn=) in their names and the names they issue. We're going to focus on the certificates issued by and to the SBCA.

Table 9-2 lists the extensions included in certificates issued by the SBCA to Principal CAs. Only four critical extensions are required in these certificates:

- The basic constraints extension to identify the subject as a CA.

- The key usage extension to identify the subject public key as appropriate for signing certificate and CRLs.

- The name constraints extension to protect against transitive trust relationships between a member PKI and an external CA by restricting the names to the agency name space.

- The policy constraints extension to indicate that a certificate policy must be present in every certificate and that policy mapping may only be performed by the SBCA and Principal CA.

Table 9-2 Extensions in Certificate Issued to Principal CAs

EXTENSION	CRITICALITY	CONTENTS
Basic constraints	Critical	`cA=True`; path length constraints is optional.
Key usage	Critical	The `keyCertSign` and `cRLSign` bits are asserted.
Name constraints	Critical	Permitted subtrees for X.500 distinguished names is set to the Principal CA's name up to the organization level (e.g., dc=com, dc=Pfizer).
Policy Constraints	Critical	All certificates must include a certificate policy. All certificates, except those issued to another BCA, must inhibit policy mapping.
Policy mapping	Non-critical	SBCA `mediumHardware` and/or `mediumSoftware` policy may appear as issuer domain policies mapping to member policies. This extension may also be omitted.

(continued)

Table 9-2 (*continued*)

EXTENSION	CRITICALITY	CONTENTS
Certificate policies	Non-critical	The SBCA `mediumHardware` and/or `mediumSoftware` policy asserted in policy mapping must be asserted in this extension.
Inhibit any-policy	Non-critical	The `any-policy` object identifier is not considered equivalent to SCBA policies.
CRL distribution points	Non-critical	Identifies the HTTP and LDAP directory entry that contains the CRL.
Authority information access	Non-critical	Two access methods are included one for the CA (both HTTP and LDAP) and one for the OCSP responder. The CA access method points to a .p7c file contain certificates issued to the SBCA.
Authority key identifier	Non-critical	Bit string identifying the key used to sign the certificate.
Subject key identifier	Non-critical	Bit string identifying the public key in the certificate.

The path length constraints in basic constraints may also be included if the member PKI uses a hierarchical PKI. The other extensions are non-critical. Certificate policies and policy-mapping extensions are used to translate locally relevant policy information into SBCA policies. Inhibit any-policy indicates that the special any-policy is not considered equivalent. The remaining four extensions provide hints for certificate path and construction validation.

NOTE The word "everyone" in SAFE ought to be a dead give-away that it's an inclusive group. For that reason, certificate policies and policy mapping are non-critical to allow those that don't support the policy to still be able to generate and validate signatures.

The certificates issued to the SBCA are similar to the certificates issued by the SBCA to the Principal CA, as shown in Table 9-3. The same critical extensions are included. The differences are that the member's name is excluded in name constraints, the policies in policy mapping are swapped from the certificate issued to the Principal CA, the revocation information points to the Principal CA's CRL location, and the AIA points to its OCSP responder.

Table 9-3 Extensions in Certificate Issued by Principal CAs to SBCA

EXTENSION	CRITICALITY	CONTENTS
Basic constraints	Critical	`cA=True`; path length constraints is omitted (recommended).
Key usage	Critical	The `keyCertSign` and `cRLSign` bits are asserted.
Name constraints	Critical	Excluded subtrees for X.500 distinguished names is set to the Principal CA's name up to the o level (e.g., c=US, o=Pfizer).
Policy Constraints	Critical	All certificates must include a certificate policy. Inhibit policy mapping is omitted.
Policy mapping	Non-critical	SBCA policy may appear as subject domain policies mapping to member policies. This extension may also be omitted.
Certificate policies	Non-critical	SBCA equivalent policies asserted in policy mapping must be asserted in this extension.
CRL distribution points	Non-critical	Identifies the X.500 and LDAP directory entry that contains the CRL (optional).
Authority information access	Non-critical	Two access methods may be included one for the CA (HTTP and/or LDAP) and one for the OCSP responder. If the PCA is a trust anchor the CA access method is omitted.
Inhibit any-policy	Non-critical	The any-policy object identifier is not considered equivalent to SCBA policies.
Authority key identifier	Non-critical	Bit string identifying the key used to sign the certificate.
Subject key identifier	Non-critical	Bit string identifying the public key in the certificate.

CRLs issued by the SBCA are always version 2 CRLs, since they include two non-critical CRL extensions: the CRL number and authority key identifier. The invalidity date and reason code non-critical CRL entry extensions may also be included but normally won't be.

OCSP requests and responses are also profiled in the CP; we'll describe why in the "Applications" section later in this chapter. The OCSP requests and responses are version 1 and optionally allow the use of a nonce request extension to protect against replay attacks. The OCSP request must include the Distinguished Name (DN) of the requestor and the OCSP responder is identified by their subject key identifier. Requestors can ask for the status of one or more certificates. Likewise, responses can include information about more than one certificate.

Tokens and Cryptographic Modules

All of the components in the SAFE architecture must use FIPS 140–evaluated cryptographic modules, as listed in Table 9-4.

Within the SAFE infrastructure, all entities must use hardware cryptographic modules to generate private keys and to perform any operation that requires the use of the private key. CAs and CSAs must use hardware modules evaluated to FIPS 140 Level 3 or higher. The SBCA uses the nCipher cryptographic module, and the SBCA's CSA use the nCipher cryptographic module. RAs and LRAs must use hardware modules evaluated to FIPS 140 Level 2 or higher.

SAFE subscribers asserting the medium hardware policy must use hardware cryptographic modules to generate private keys, and subscribers asserting the medium software policy may use either hardware or software to generate private keys. SAFE also supports networked hardware credentials, which is a virtual token in a network-attached HSM. Private keys can be generated either on the user's tokens or by a key generator. In the later case, the private key must be securely transferred to the subscriber's token or software.

Table 9-4 FIPS 140 Levels

PKI ENTITY	TYPE	FIPS 140 LEVEL
CAs	Hardware	Level 3 (or higher)
CSAs	Hardware	Level 3 (or higher)
RAs	Hardware	Level 2 (or higher)
LRAs	Hardware	Level 2 (or higher)
EE: Medium Hardware	Hardware	Level 2 (or higher)
EE: Medium Software	Software	Level 1 (or higher)*

*Generated in an environment that provides private key protections comparable to FIPS 140 Level 2 (or higher).

Applications

As mentioned earlier, SAFE supports strong authentication, digital signatures, and web-based applications, as well as applications that support regulatory filings and other business-related processes. An application that enforces the SAFE rules is said to be SAFE-enabled. The signature process is similar to the normal process:

- Signer selects data to sign; signer acknowledges SAFE signature.
- Signer acknowledges the reason for signing.
- Signer provides strong authentication to use the private key, such as entering a token PIN or pass phrase.

The explicit acknowledgement of the signature's purpose is the additional part. On the relying party side, the signature verification process is automated by the application as it validates the entire certification path. This process is supported by CRLs as well as OCSP. Figure 9-2 depicts the actions of a SAFE-enabled application.

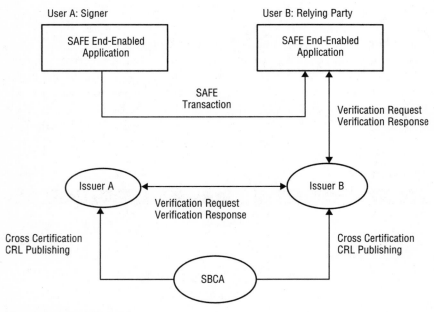

Figure 9-2 SBCA in action

Portable signatures are a tantalizing prospect, made possible by the Portable Document Format (PDF) from Adobe. Adobe Acrobat allows anyone to apply signatures to PDFs (as well as encrypt PDFs). When applying signatures, signers can indicate the reason for signing:

- I have reviewed this document.
- I am the author of this document.
- I am approving this document.
- I attest to the accuracy and integrity of this document.
- I agree to the terms defined by the placement of my signature on this document.
- I agree to specified portions of this document.

The signature is added to the document as an RSA PKCS#7 (the earlier version of CMS as described in Chapter 6) block stored in a PDF dictionary object reference by a PDF for field. Relying parties can click on the signature to verify the signature and determine why the signer applied the signature.

Successes and Shortcomings

SAFE has seen the greatest adoption with applications and business processes that are under the control of an organization. Two successful implementations were Pfizer's Chemistry electronic Notebook (CeN) application and AstraZeneca's implementation of the FDA Electronic Submission Gateway (ESG):

CeN. CeN was developed to replace the paper-based process used during the discovery phase for a new drug. Before CeN, scientists recorded their experiments in a paper lab notebook, signed the experiments, and then met with another scientist who witnessed the experiment. After the experiments were completed and witnessed, the notebook was provided to a records management organization for archiving. The signature, witness, and date and time provide non-repudiation for the discovery of a new compound. This process is important when defending a patent for the drug many years later. With CeN, the scientists complete their experiment and digitally sign in to CeN, using their SAFE credential. After submission of the experiment, an email is automatically sent to a witness, who reviews it and digitally signs it. A PDF of the signed and witnessed experiment is automatically sent to the records management database for archival. Scientists have found the application nonintrusive; it fits in with their daily work, and it is faster than the paper process because they spend less time managing paper (and more time in the lab). Also, the process is timely and speedy, resulting in greater compliance with internal policies.

FDA ESG.   The FDA has accepted submission of Advanced Evidence Reporting System (AERS) reports, which are drug safety reports, since 2000, but the FDA only supports one type of report, and the FDA Electronic Standards for the Transfer of Regulatory Information (ESTRI) gateway was in need of an update. The FDA ESG web-based submission service is the single point of entry for the transfer and processing of electronic submissions. For AstraZeneca to support these submissions, they needed to have digital signatures that conform to Title 21 Code of Federal Regulations Part 11 (21 CFR Part 11) and the Health Insurance Portability and Accountability Act (HIPAA). Fortunately, SAFE meets, and in many cases exceeds. these requirements. SAFE signatures on the FDA forms (a PDF) and the validation report, which shows the digital signature was valid at the time it was applied, can be verified by the FDA through the FBCA and SAFE cross-certification. The certificates are also used to provide confidentiality for the submission by using a TLS protected channel. In September of 2006, AstraZeneca submitted the first digitally signed submission to the FDA that had no paper copies. AstraZeneca sees great cost savings as they eliminate activities to create, sign, store, and maintain paper copies.

Trust can be a hard thing to establish between competing companies. SAFE solved this problem by setting up an independent third party to run the SBCA. With this arrangement, there are many fewer issues with trust.

Users lose all kinds of things, especially if the item isn't used very often. Storing the credential on the integrated badge helps minimize the chance of it being lost. People use their badge everyday for building access and are, therefore, more likely to have it with them. Additionally, users will always have their badge with them when performing cryptographic operations such as singing a document.

Lessons Learned

The lessons learned listed next are drawn from SBCA lessons learned as well as individual SAFE member experiences. Many of the individual member lessons learned are taken from white papers produced by the SAFE members [ASAFE, PSAFE]. Some of the most important lessons learned during SAFE are:

Build business case for all players.   The SBCA was realized because the competing businesses came together and built industry-wide business cases to support lower costs for information technology, especially by eliminating costs associated with paperwork and document storage. Going paperless can save everyone money and increase productivity.

Involve regulators early in the process.   SAFE involved the FDA early in the process. By gaining FDA support early in the process, it saved time in the long run, as the FDA saw the benefit to both the industry and themselves. The FDA continues in an advisory role as new efforts are being developed to ensure that course corrections, when necessary, are received as early as possible in the design process.

Desktop setup can be a challenge.   Drivers for tokens and smart cards are a major challenge. These Drivers are not under the control of SAFE, but the members need to make sure that these are loaded on user's machines. Additional issues relating to the desktop included the following:

- Often there were conflicts with existing drivers and software.

- Users did not have administrative control of the desktop and could not install drivers themselves.

- Due to HIPPA considerations, some users did not have access to USB ports.

- Desktop challenges are the primary reason that SAFE ultimately accepted the use of software-based credentials and credentials hosted on network-attached devices in the SAFE policy framework.

Streamline initial identification and authentication process.   The identification and authentication can require several steps and may involve a paper notary service. Often users wouldn't complete all of the steps. A streamlined process will increase the likelihood that users will complete the process in a timely manner.

Start small.   The Pfizer team learned that small pilots are adequate to test business and information technology concepts. The scale makes it easier to isolate and fix any problems that arise; however, one should never ignore the issue of scale, particularly when it comes to provisioning and ease of use. For example, Pfizer choose to centralize signing with an application environment based on a product called MySignatureBook from TriCipher. This solution removed much of the complexity from of the desktop, putting it into a centralized, more manageable environment that was easily accessible by all Pfizer's users.

Stay focused.   Instead of trying to solve the entire company's identity management problem, stay within the scope of the pilot. AstraZeneca found that the FDA ESG application could easily have been late and over budget if they had tried to expand beyond SAFE signatures. By expanding the scope of an application, more systems and business areas are affected, resulting in the need for credentials for many more users.

By staying focused on their FDA ESG application, they avoided these pitfalls and delivered on time and on budget.

Test firewall access.   The SAFE architecture requires the exchange of information between the user and SAFE CA both for certification request/ response and for certificate status checks. Both Pfizer and AstraZeneca found this required access through their firewalls, but the solution to the problem was different for each company. Adequate time for testing and problem resolution must be built into the project timeline.

Application configurations might need to be updated.   Interfacing with the tokens requires token drivers, middleware, and the application itself. AstraZeneca found that its standard desktop configuration had an earlier version of Adobe Acrobat than the one required by SAFE, which is Acrobat 6 or above. Installing new applications on user machines does cause some disruption, but the benefits outweighed the risks, and they decided to install Acrobat 7 Professional for their FDA ESG users.

Rely on existing infrastructure.   Wherever possible rely on existing infrastructure. Users are generally comfortable with existing infrastructure, which eliminates human anxiety and the need for training in something new.

Build strong partnership with the internal legal organization.   Affixing a wet signature to a document has legal ramifications and this is also true for digital signatures. Information technology people need to work hand in hand with legal professionals to resolve issues in this area. Information technologists usually delve into too much technical detail, and let's face it, they're not lawyers. The best approach is to engage with the attorneys from the beginning. Make sure that the attorneys understand the issue, and then work with the attorneys to answer the business questions regarding non-repudiation and other legal issues. Attorneys are a great help when it comes to formalizing internal policies, explaining records management, and determining risk management approaches.

Involve all potential business colleagues from the beginning.   Moving from wet signatures to digital signatures requires business process change. For a smooth and successful transition to the new digital business process, everyone involved in the wet signatures process should be involved in design of the new business process, preferably from the start. Primarily, this allows everyone to understand the new process, but it also allows everyone to provide input so that process actually works. What Pfizer found was that changing the business process actually had more impact than the technology, and introducing digital signatures required many hours of education and process review with the people concerned with business and quality assurance.

Determine dispute resolution policy.   Cross-organization systems involve more than one IT group. It is helpful if there's one IT sponsor to resolve priorities and solve resourcing issues. If you're going across multiple companies, it's helpful to have a dispute resolution process that is acceptable to all of the stakeholders.

Make use and installation painless.   User uptake is based almost entirely on ease of use. Application installation is the first step that is visible to the users. If the application is complicated to install, users won't accept it and use it. Not everyone has enough computer savvy (it's actually often patience) to wade through a complicated installation. Further, providing the training to make everyone computer savvy would be too expensive. The key to successful application deployment and acceptance is ease of use.

CHAPTER 10

Department of Defense Public Key Infrastructure, Medium Grade Service, and Common Access Card

The U. S. Department of Defense (DoD) has three well-known programs that work together to provide security for their email (and some other things, too): the DoD Public Key Infrastructure (PKI), the Medium Grade Service (MGS), and the Common Access Card (CAC).

The DoD PKI was started as a pilot program in 1997 by the DoD Defense Information Systems Agency (DISA). It was started as part of the effort to transition to a paperless DoD environment, but a more compelling reason was to support the vast majority of DoD users who didn't need and couldn't afford the high-assurance Multi-level Information Systems Security Initiative (MISSI) PKI, which was a major part of the Defense Message System (DMS). DMS provides formal messaging between organizations and uses X.400 in combination with the Message Security Protocol (MSP). It is official record traffic, such as military orders. By contrast, MGS provides an informal messaging capability to satisfy the messaging needs of individuals, which are vital for making any large organization function. It uses SMTP and S/MIME.

The first application targeted to use the DoD PKI was the Defense Travel System (DTS) that resides on the NIPRNet, or the DoD Unclassified but Sensitive Internet Protocol Router Network. In 1999, the DoD PKI Program Management Office (PMO) was formed to oversee the DoD PKI pilot program and bring it to Initial Operational Capability (IOC). The program manager comes from the National Security Agency (NSA), an organization that recognizes the importance of security. The deputy program manager comes from the DISA, which recognizes the large impact the PKI will have on many DoD information systems. The DoD PKI has been wildly successful, issuing over 23 million certificates for people and devices. It has also been instrumental in evolving PKI-enabled products and arguably speeding their availability in commercial markets.

In 1998, DISA also launched the Medium Grade Service (MGS), which has also been called Medium Assurance Messaging and Medium Grade Messaging (MGM). The DMS program uses cryptographic algorithms that are rarely used outside governmental circles, but MGS uses commercial cryptographic algorithms — more on the distinction later in the chapter.

In 1999, the DoD Defense Manpower Data Center (DMDC) was tasked to deliver a smart-card-based identity management card for each person on active duty military, as well as most National Guard, Reserve, DoD civilian employees, and DoD on-site contractor personnel. The DoD Common Access Card office and the DoD PKI PMO were tasked to work together to deliver the CAC with DoD PKI certificates in 1999. (That's right; delivery was expected the same year that they were asked to do it.) The DoD CAC process would serve as the enrollment front end for subscribers. The Real-Time Automated Personnel Identification System (RAPIDS) interacts with the Defense Enrollment Eligibility Reporting System (DEERS) to determine eligibility for a CAC. The end result was a set of CAC requirements that is met by more than one vendor. The CAC hasn't fully replaced the Uniformed Services Identification and Privilege Cards because, while the roll out has been very fast and extensive, not all National Guard, Reserves, DoD civilian employees, contractors, retirees, and family members have them yet. DoD has issued around 12 million CACs, and there are around 3.5 million active CACs. With numbers like that they are getting closer every day.

In this chapter, we present the architecture that supports the DoD PKI, MGS, and CAC programs and discuss the successes and the lessons learned.

Architectures

This section provides an overview of the different system components that make the whole system work. This is really a system of systems. The discussion includes the cryptographic algorithms, PKI architecture, DEERS/RAPIDS architecture, certificate and CRL profiles, CAC and other cryptographic modules, and, finally, applications.

Cryptographic Algorithms

The DoD PKI supports both military and commercial algorithms for providing authentication, integrity, confidentiality, and the enabling of non-repudiation services for DoD PKI-enabled applications. The algorithms supported are:

- RSA, DSA, and ECDSA for digital signatures.
- Key Encryption Algorithm (KEA) and RSA for key management.

- SHA-1 for one-way hash functions with DSA and ECDSA.
- SHA-256, SHA-384, and SHA-512 with RSA.
- SKIPJACK, Triple-DES, and AES for symmetric encryption.

The DoD PKI supports a variety of algorithms, but for the DoD MGS and CACs only commercial-grade algorithms are supported. Algorithms are updated as the commercial applications develop support for newer cryptographic algorithms; however, some algorithms that are used in commercial products are simply not acceptable to DoD. These are mostly proprietary algorithms, and support for them is turned off when the products are installed for DoD users. Currently, the MGS supports:

- RSA for digital signatures and key management.
- SHA-1 for one-way hash functions.
- Triple-DES and AES for symmetric encryption.

DoD helps shape policy for the key sizes, but right now they specify only those in the list that follows, but be assured DoD will adopt the NIST guidelines [NISTSP] for key sizes and algorithm migration when the time comes:

- **Digital Signature:**   RSA and DSA 1024-bit keys and ECDSA on curve P256 or P384.
- **Key management:**   KEA and RSA 1024-bit keys.
- **Symmetric encryption:**   At least 80 bits of strength.

Again, the DoD MGS and CAC only support commercial key sizes. For signature and key management a 1024-bit key for RSA is supported. For symmetric algorithms, AES with a 128-bit key is available in many commercial packages, and it is much more efficient in software than Triple-DES. AES is used even though the key management is not up to the same strength. Triple-DES offers 112 bits of strength.

PKI Architecture

The DoD PKI architecture is hierarchical, with two levels of certificate issuers. The root CA issues certificates to subordinate CAs and OCSP responders. The root CA is policy agnostic to allow the different communities to communicate with their users and those outside of the DoD. Subordinate CAs issue certificates to subscribers. A directory is also support for storage of names, email address, encryption certificates, and CRLs. Another component supported is the Key Recovery Agent. Registration Authorities (RAs) and Local Registration Authorities (LRAs) are also supported to ease the CAs job of application processing. Figure 10-1 depicts this hierarchy.

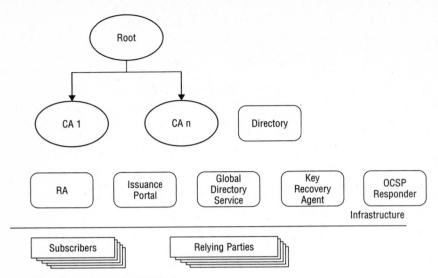

Figure 10-1 DoD PKI architecture

The root CA generates its own key pairs and signs a certificate for itself. This self-signed certificate contains the root's X.500 distinguished name and its public key. The self-signed certificate is installed in the subscriber's certificate store and establishes a trust point. To trust more than one root CA, the subscriber includes additional certificates in the certificate store.

Registration of users relies on the DEERS/RAPIDS system, described below, while the RAs/LRAs are used to generate certificates for devices and some others.

DEERS/RAPIDS Architecture

The DoD PKI wants to give certificates only to those who are eligible. They don't have that kind of information on hand at every enrollment station, but the organization responsible for paying active duty and civilian employees has the information in their database. That's why the RAPIDS system accesses the DEERS database, which is where information on everyone who has served in the U.S military is stored. This is shown in Figure 10-2.

The process of getting a CAC is called CAC Issuance. A person wishing to get a CAC card must present themselves in person to the verification officer (VO). The process involves four components:

RAPIDS workstation.   VOs use the RAPIDS workstation to interact with the DEERS database and the issuance portal. The VO is authenticated before they are allowed to issue CACs to others. The VO must insert their CAC, type in their PIN, and provide a fingerprint scan. The DEERS database is then queried to determine whether the person logging in is authorized to act as a VO, and the issuance portal is queried to determine whether the person logging in is authorized to request certificates. Both of these interactions (and the upcoming interactions) with DEERS database and issuance portal are SSLv3 or TLS protected. The VO's certificate is used to provide client authentication.

DEERS database.   The DEERS database is queried as part of the VO authentication process and as part of the CAC issuance process. It serves as DoD's central repository for personal information. The database is available 24 hours a day 7 days a week because it serves a worldwide audience.

Issuance portal.   The issuance portal is accessed as part of the VO authentication process and as part of the CAC issuance process. During the issuance process, it creates a secure channel between the CAC that is about to be issued and itself. This channel is used to instantiate Java applets on the CAC. Three applet types are installed: PKI applets, a PIN applet, and generic container applets. There are two PKI applets: one for the identity/signer and one for encryption private keys. There's only one PIN applet, because there is only one PIN per card. The number of generic container applets varies by manufacturer, but many support four. The issuance portal also interacts with the CA to request certificates. These interactions with the CA are SSLv3 or TLS protected. The issuance portal also acts with three other components, but these aren't shown in the figures:

Issuance Portal audit system.   This component records every RAPIDS workstation command and its outcome.

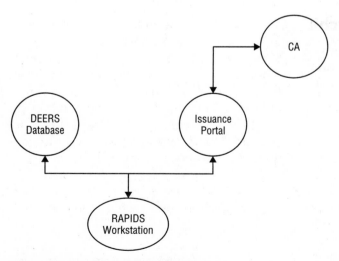

Figure 10-2 DEERS/RAPIDS architecture

Card Repository System (CRS). This component tracks everything about each card, including which applets were loaded and unloaded, the size of the applet, and the applet version.

Inventory Logistics Portal (ILP). This component manages the card inventory, ordering more cards for specific CAC-issuing sites as required.

Certification Authority. The CA processes certification requests and signs certificates. Two types of certificates are issued to subscribers:

Identity/signature.* The public key used for identity/signature verification is provided as part of the identity/signature certification request. The private key is generated on the card. The certificate is returned as part of the certification response.

Encryption. The encryption key is generated by the CA and stored in a key escrow database. This allows authorized individuals to recover data that was encrypted even if the card is lost or damaged.

The CAC issuance process can be summarized as follows:

- Verify VO
- Verify applicant
- Initialize CAC
- Load and initialize Java applets
- Update ILP and DEERS

Certificate Policies

The DoD has a large number of policies and many people working to set policy. DoD's policies affect its entire enterprise, so it's no wonder that they created a group for the DoD PKI called the DoD PKI Certificate Policy Management Working Group (CPMWG) to provide a forum for CP discussions and the final approving authority for their CP [DODCP]. The CPMWG is chaired by the DoD PKI PMO and has members from the Combatant Command, Services, and Agencies (CC/S/As) with both technical and legal focus. The latest approved CP v9.0 is dated February 9, 2005, and it includes information on four certificate policies that apply to the DoD PKI in support of MGS, CAC, and DMS; they are listed in Table 10-1 in increasing level of assurance. The policies are designed in a pragmatic way that identifies the environment in which the policy is used and the level of protection of the network. Information

---

*Initially, the CA issued three certificates: one for identity, one for the digital signature, and one for encryption. The identity certificate was used for Windows smart card logon. Today, one certificate is used for identity and the digital signature.

is categorized as low value, medium value, and high value, and the networks are categorized as minimally, moderately, and highly protected environments.

DoD Basic. Applications that handle unclassified information of low value in a minimally or moderately protected environment assert this policy. Not surprisingly, the DoD doesn't issue certificates under this policy, but it does allow relying parties to use what they consider commercially equivalent certificates for access to information available for unlimited distribution. Things like meeting coordination and website access. This policy level could also be met through cross-certification.

DoD Medium. Applications that handle unclassified medium-value information in moderately protected environments, unclassified high-value information in highly protected environments, and discretionary access control of classified information in highly protected environments assert this policy. This CP is asserted in a software certificate associated with private keys stored in computer files. That is, the private key is not protected by a hardware token.

DoD Medium Hardware. Applications that handle unclassified medium-value information in minimally protected environments, unclassified high-value information in moderately protected environments, and discretionary access control of classified information in highly protected environments assert this policy. This level has a higher degree of assurance and technical non-repudiation. This CP is asserted in certificates associated with private keys stored in a CAC.

DoD Medium High. Applications that handle high-value unclassified information in minimally protected environments assert this policy. This CP is asserted in certificates associated with private keys stored in a FORTEZZA Crypto Card, which is the hardware token used in DMS.

> **NOTE** As we mentioned in Chapter 5, picking a good CP name counts. DoD Basic was Class 2, DoD Medium was Class 3, and DoD High was Class 4.

Table 10-1 DoD PKI Certificate Policy Object Identifiers

LEVEL OF ASSURANCE	OBJECT IDENTIFIER NAME	OBJECT IDENTIFIERS
DoD Basic	id-US-dod-basic	2.16.840.1.101.2.1.11.2
DoD Medium	id-US-dod-medium	2.16.840.1.101.2.1.11.5
DoD Medium Hardware	id-US-dod-mediumhardware	2.16.840.1.101.2.1.11.9
DoD High	id-US-dod-high	2.16.840.1.101.2.1.11.4

Table 10-2 DoD ECA Certificate Policy Object Identifiers

LEVEL OF ASSURANCE	OBJECT IDENTIFIER NAME	OBJECT IDENTIFIERS
ECA Medium	id-eca-medium	2.16.840.1.101.3.2.1.12.1
ECA Medium Hardware	id-eca-medium-hardware	2.16.840.1.101.3.2.1.12.2

The DoD needs to interoperate with other communities beyond their active duty and civilian employee subscribers, especially with their industry suppliers. The idea of issuing certificates to these very different communities from the same PKI is not palatable for a number of reasons. To support interoperability with various external communities, the DoD PKI developed the External Certification Authority (ECA) program. Operational Research Consultants (ORC) was the first vendor in this program, and they were followed by IdenTrust and Verisign. Each vendor is required to conform to the ECA CP, but they are free to offer different services. For example, ORC offers six types of EE certificates, and IdenTrust offers five types of EE certificates. As of this writing IdenTrust doesn't offer code-signing certificates, but they may well do so in the future. We describe the certificate types in more detail in the next section. The latest approved version, v3.1, of the ECA CP is dated August 2006, and it includes information on two policies, which are listed in Table 10-2 in increasing levels of assurance.

> **NOTE** The architecture for the ECA PKI is identical to the DoD PKI, but it is a separate and distinct architecture.

ECA Medium.   Applications handling sensitive medium-value information, with the exception of transactions involving issuance or acceptance of contracts and contract modifications, assert this policy.

ECA Medium Hardware.   Applications operating in environments appropriate for medium assurance but that require a higher degree of assurance and technical non-repudiation assert this policy.

> **NOTE** It's interesting to note that neither one of these CPs conform to [RFC3647], but they do conform to the earlier [RFC2527].

Certificate and CRL Profiles

The ECA CP includes certificate profiles for a number of different certificates. All of the certificates are version 3 certificates, as they include extensions, and all of the certificates use X.500 distinguished names. Tables 10-3–10-7 list the required extensions.

Table 10-3 Extensions in Self-Signed Root CAs

EXTENSION	CRITICALITY	CONTENTS
Basic constraints	Critical	`cA = True`; path length is omitted.
Key usage	Critical	The `digitalSignature`, `keyCertSign`, and `cRLSign` bits are asserted.
Certificate policies	Non-critical	The `id-eca-medium` and `id-eca-medium-hardware` object identifiers are both included.
Authority key identifier	Non-critical	Bit string identifying the key used to sign the certificate.
Subject key identifier	Non-critical	Bit string identifying the public key in the certificate.

Table 10-4 Extensions in Subordinate CAs

EXTENSION	CRITICALITY	CONTENTS
Basic constraints	Critical	`cA = True; path length = 0.`
Key usage	Critical	The `digitialSignature`, `keyCertSign`, and `cRLSign` bits are asserted.
Certificate policies	Non-critical	The `id-eca-medium` and `id-eca-medium-hardware` object identifiers are both included.
Authority information access	Non-critical	Optional — contains `id-ocsp` access methods.
CRL distribution points	Non-critical	Identifies LDAP directory entry that contains the CRL.
Authority key identifier	Non-critical	Bit string identifying the key used to sign the certificate.
Subject key identifier	Non-critical	Bit string identifying the public key in the certificate.

The latest version of the DoD PKI certificate profile is considered sensitive. Although we're not sure why they are considered sensitive because certificates that follow this profile are used on the Internet every day. We are not trying to pick a fight, so we have omitted these profiles from this discussion.

CRLs issued by the SBCA are always version 2 CRLs, since they include two non-critical CRL extensions: CRL number and authority key identifier. The reason-code non-critical CRL entry extension is also always included. The invalidity date non-critical CRL entry extensions may also be included.

Table 10-5 Extensions in Identity/Signature and Encryption Certificates

EXTENSION	CRITICALITY	CONTENTS
Key usage	Critical	Identity: The `digitalSignature` and `nonRepudiation` bits are asserted. Encryption: The `keyEncipherment` bit is asserted.
Certificate policies	Non-critical	Either `id-eca-medium` is asserted or both `id-eca-medium` and `id-eca-medium-hardware` are included.
Subject alternative name	Non-critical	Always present and includes RFC822 email address.
Subject directory attributes	Non-critical	Contains `id-pda-countryOfCitizenship` to include two letter ISO country code for subject's citizenship.
Authority information access	Non-critical	Contains both `id-ocsp` and `id-caIssuers` access methods.
CRL distribution points	Non-critical	Identifies the LDAP directory entry that contains the CRL.
Authority key identifier	Non-critical	Bit string identifying the key used to sign the certificate.
Subject key identifier	Non-critical	Bit string identifying the public key in the certificate.

Certificate Status Responders

It is well known that the DoD PKI has very large CRLs, on the order of tens of megabytes. To speed up certificate path validation, they support OCSP. They support OCSP responders that are:

Enterprise-wide.   A self-signed v3 certificate with no extensions is installed in the client certificate trust store and all OCSP responses from that server are trusted. It's also configured as a well-known location in the relying party application to ensure that all requests are sent to the proper responder.

CA specific.   A v3 certificate issued from a subordinate CA that is similar to an identity/signature certificate with the following differences: subject alternative name includes a URL for the OCSP responder, a critical extended key usage extension is included to indicate `id-kp-OCSPSigning`, and the no check extension is included. The `id-kp-OCSPSigning` extended key usage indicates that the public key can be used to validate OCSP responses. The no check certificate extension indicates that the relying

Table 10-6 Extensions in Code-Signing Certificates

EXTENSION	CRITICALITY	CONTENTS
Key usage	Critical	The `digitalSignature` and `nonRepudiation` bits are asserted.
Extended key usage	Critical	The `id-kp-codeSigning` object identifier is included.
Certificate policies	Non-critical	Both `id-eca-medium` and `id-eca-medium-hardware` are asserted.
Subject alternative name	Non-critical	Always present and includes X.500 DN of private key holder.
Subject directory attributes	Non-critical	Contains `id-pda-countryOfCitizenship` to include two-letter ISO country code for subject's citizenship.
Authority information access	Non-critical	Contains both `id-ocsp` and `id-caIssuers` access methods.
CRL distribution points	Non-critical	Identifies the LDAP directory entry that contains the CRL.
Authority key identifier	Non-critical	Bit string identifying the key used to sign the certificate.
Subject key identifier	Non-critical	Bit string identifying the public key in the certificate.

party does not need to check the status of the OCSP responder's certificate during its validity period, which essentially makes the OCSP responder a trusted certificate until it expires.

OCSP requests and responses are profiled in the CP. The OCSP requests and responses are version 1, and the request may include the DN of the requestor. Requestors can ask for the status of one or more certificates. The request can be unsigned, and no extensions are required. Likewise, responses can include information about more than one certificate.

Repositories

The DoD PKI includes a directory, as shown in Figure 10-1, but it is not the responsibility of the DoD PKI; rather, the DoD PKI is one customer of a directory that was set up to serve the whole DoD. PKIs are responsible for publishing certificates and CRLs, while a general-purpose directory is responsible for a lot more "white pages" information, which includes names, phone numbers, postal address, email address, and other information. That's

Table 10-7 Extensions in Component (Server) Certificates

EXTENSION	CRITICALITY	CONTENTS
Key usage	Critical	The `digitalSignature` and `keyEncipherment` bits are asserted.
Certificate policies	Non-critical	The `id-eca-medium` object identifier is included.
Subject alternative name	Non-critical	Always present and includes host URL, host name, or IP address.
Authority information access	Non-critical	Contains both `id-ocsp` and `id-caIssuers` access methods.
CRL distribution points	Non-critical	Identifies the LDAP directory entry that contains the CRL.
Authority key identifier	Non-critical	Bit string identifying the key used to sign the certificate.
Subject key identifier	Non-critical	Bit string identifying the public key in the certificate.

why the DoD has the Global Directory Service (GDS). The GDS interfaces with the DoD PKI directory and the CC/S/As directories to collect the data and provide a common place for users to retrieve certificates as well as point of contact information, as shown in Figure 10-3. The DoD PKI only supplies names, email addresses, email encryption certificates, and CRLs. There's no need to include the signature certificate, since it is provided by the signer at the time the message is composed and signed.

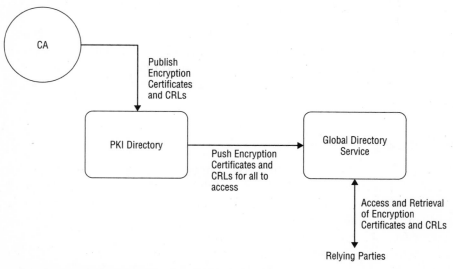

Figure 10-3 DoD PKI repository and GDS interaction

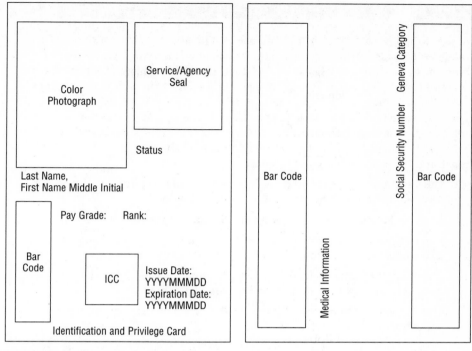

Figure 10-4 CAC layout

CAC and Cryptographic Modules

As noted earlier, the DoD PKI supports issuing certificates for different policy levels in three token formats: software, CAC, and FORTEZZA Crypto Card. We're focusing in this section on the CAC.

The CAC is a multipurpose smart card. The CAC layout was studied, had briefs prepared on it, and was debated. The end result is as shown in Figure 10-4. As noted earlier, the CAC was designed to be multipurpose.

- It provides an integrated circuit chip (ICC) to store the subscriber's private keys and public key certificates. There are two certificates issued: one for identity and authentication and the other for encryption.

- It works as a badge. It provides a picture, an affiliation, a rank, a status, and other identifying information. It also serves as Geneva Convention identification.

- It provides two barcodes that can be used for physical access to buildings, without the use of cryptography.

"CODE BLUE"

Access to the private key requires the use of a personal identification number (PIN). Well guess what — users lose their PINs at an alarming rate. Without a mechanism to reset the PINs, the CAC becomes useless when the PIN is lost. It does still work as a visual identity badge, but it won't help with email security. Initially, there was one option — go back to the DEERS/RAPIDS workstation and get a new one issued. This was not practical for the operational community at the CC/S/As, so they developed the CAC PIN Reset (CPR) system. The CPR system is a single-purpose client-server application that provides timely PIN resetting. The process works as follows:

1. The Certified Trusted Agent (CTA) logs in to the CPR application and asks the CAC holder to insert his or her CAC into the reader.

2. The CAC holder places a finger on the fingerprint reader.

3. If the fingerprint doesn't match the fingerprint in the DEERS database, the CTA sends the CAC holder to a DEERS/RAPIDS workstation.

4. If the fingerprint matches the fingerprint stored in the DEERS database, a picture of the CAC holder appears on the screen.

5. The CTA verifies that the individual on the screen is the individual presenting the locked CAC.

6. The CAC holder enters a new 6- to 8-digit PIN, twice. If the two entries are the same, the CAC is reset to use with the new PIN.

The original CAC had 32 KB of space on the ICC. With manufacturer overhead, PIN applets, and generic containers there is a little more than 10 KB available for PKI data. If each certificate and private key is less than 2 KB and there are two certificates, then there's plenty of room. The next-generation CAC is a 64-KB card that will comply with Homeland Security Presidential Directive (HSPD) 12. We'll talk more about this in Chapter 11.

The CAC and all of the components in the DoD and ECA architecture must use FIPS 140 evaluated cryptographic modules, as listed in Table 10-8.

The CAC also requires a card reader. Adding a card reader also means adding drivers to allow the host to communicate with the card reader and the CAC that is inserted into the reader. There's also middleware, which is a software application that serves as the interface between host applications (such as email, host logon, and web browsers) and the CAC, that needs to be added.

Applications

There are three main applications that have been implemented DoD-wide and as more web-enabled applications use security mechanisms more applications are PKI-enable every day:

Medium Grade Service (MGS).   MGS allows users to sign and encrypt email. MGS supports *individual email*, which is basically email exchange of working level information within administrative channels between individual DoD personnel that does not commit or direct an organization. Most of the implementations use Microsoft Exchange, which supports S/MIME v3. Policies are in place to require signing of all messages within the DoD and to encourage encryption.

Secure websites.   DoD uses the World Wide Web just like everybody else. They could have physically separated their servers, but this would not meet the needs of the DoD community. To make sure that only authorized users are granted access. DoD implemented a two-phase plan. The first phase required all private DoD servers to enable server-side authentication, which means that the servers need to get certificates for TLS sessions. The second phase required all private DoD servers to require client-side authentication, which means the clients use their private keys for authentication during TLS session setup. The first phase allows server administrators to rely on username and passwords over an encrypted channel. Protected passwords are far better than passwords passed in the clear or relying on other methods such as filtering IP addresses. The second phase replaces the need for the username and passwords. Obviously, the second phase can only take place once all DoD personnel have been issued CACs.

Table 10-8 FIPS   Levels

PKI ENTITY	TYPE	FIPS 140 LEVEL
DoD PKI		
CA	Hardware	Level 2
RA	Hardware	Level 2
CSA	Hardware	Level 2
Subscriber: high	Hardware	Level 2
Subscriber: medium hardware	Hardware	Level 1*
Subscriber: medium	Hardware Software	Level 1
DoD ECA		
CA	Hardware	Level 2
RA	Hardware	Level 2
CSA	Hardware	Level 2
Subscriber: medium hardware	Hardware	Level 1
Subscriber: medium	Hardware Software	Level 1

Defense Travel Service (DTS). The DTS allows DoD personnel to book travel and get reimbursed for travel expenses. It was one of the original applications targeted by the CAC and PKI. Travelers search the DTS, create an itinerary, estimate the trip's cost, and then submit it to the DTS. Submissions are signed using the CAC. The DTS then routes the submission to the Commercial Travel Office (CTO), the travel agent, for reservation booking. The CTO computes a cost and routes it through the DTS for authorization. The authorizing user accepts the cost by applying a digital signature to an approval. The approval is routed through the DTS to the CTO for final ticketing.

Success and Shortcomings

An absolute undeniable success of the DoD PKI, MGS, and CAC programs is that they used the lessons learned from the DMS program:

One size does not fit all. In DMS there was one PKI assurance level associated with the DMS application. In the DoD PKI there are a range of assurance levels to support a range of applications, in some application, like MGS, use more than one level. In DMS all messages were signed and encrypted. In MGS all messages are signed, but encrypting the messages is optional.

Leverage industry direction and open standards. DMS choose X.400 and developed MSP. MGS choose SMTP and S/MIME. DMS developed the FORTEZZA Crypto Card. DMDC and CAC choose commercial algorithms provided by the DoD PKI.

Without a doubt the DoD PKI is a shining star, that has only gotten brighter over the years. A huge deployment, it has evolved from a pilot project to a full-blown operational system generating tens of thousands of certificates a day.

The DoD PKI and CAC programs are a testament to the power of having high-level guidance bring many large and powerful organizations together, even if they are kicking and screaming about it, to work and implement a DoD enterprise solution based on commercial standards.

The biggest shortcoming is clearly the absolutely huge CRLs, which have steadily grown to over 100 MB. The CRLs have grown for practical reasons, which include revocations for normal reasons like name changes and employment status, but are magnified by the large user community and the inclusion of some certificates that were never really deployed. For example, when there is a problem issuing a CAC, the certificates generated for it are revoked, even though the private keys for the associated certificates never left the issuing station before being destroyed. Large CRLs impact certificate path validation processing times; it takes a long time to download and search the CRL for a certificate. From the users' perspective, these long processing times make them less productive, makes them think that the system is not working, and results in low user satisfaction. From an infrastructure perspective, the large CRLs take up storage space and utilize (often precious) bandwidth. Fortunately, OCSP was adopted, which allows relying parties to ask for the status of only the certificates needed for a given transaction.

Admittedly, DoD hasn't reached its goal of replacing all other DoD identification cards with a CAC, but that's partly because not everyone who gets a DoD ID card is eligible to get a CAC, not because the system couldn't support issuing cards to everyone. Also, some DoD-issued ID cards provide access to very sensitive places, and they require more strenuous identity validation than is required to obtain a CAC.

It never fails. No matter how big a program, there's always a bigger and better program coming down the pike. Enter stage left, the NIST Personal Identity Verification (PIV) requirements (discussed in Chapter 11) are applicable to the DoD CAC. Stay tuned for CAC v2.

Lessons Learned

There are number of lessons from the DoD PKI, MGS, and CAC deployments. We'll list only a few of the major ones here; listing them all would make the chapter much too long.

A powerful champion is required. In the DoD, the smart card, the PKI, and the payroll data are under the auspices of three separate programs. Without a powerful mandate and extremely strong leadership, the combination of the PKI, CAC, and DEERS/RAPIDS would never have come to pass.

Provision properly. Initially the issuance portals were problematic. In the beginning, they could not handle the load placed on them and network connections between the issuance portal, CA, and DEERS/RAPIDS, so they were not always available. This lead to user dissatisfaction and long and sleepless nights at the DoD PKI help desk and PMO. The system must be designed for growth and spikes in transaction volume and failover. Additionally, the databases that track all the interactions in the system and internally in the CA need to support tracking every audited action.

Have PIN reset mechanism available. Sometimes users forget the PIN to unlock the CACs. They couldn't remember in 2001, they can't remember now, and they probably won't be able remember in 2020. PIN resets will always be needed. Put the reset capability as close to the users as possible.

Drivers and middleware are required and they're temperamental.   Picking a PKI, smart card, and PKI-enabled application doesn't necessarily mean they're all going to work together. Care must be taken to ensure the readers, drivers, middleware, and applications all work together. Education materials for the smart cards and middleware must be available to application developers long before the applications are needed.

Understand vendor timelines.   Programs that embrace commercial offerings and open standards must rely on what vendors have to offer. Vendors make statements about when the products will be ready and the capabilities that will be provided. The products don't always perform as described in the marketing brochure. Make sure that the schedule works, with a little bit of time to deal with bugs. Make sure that the selected products can scale to meet your needs.

Modifying any part of the platform could be problematic.   Changing any part of the platform mix (operating system, card reader, application, middleware, or card) could cause the system to stop working. Extensive system testing must be performed to ensure that the upgraded component works with the other components before it is deployed.

Large CRLs don't scale.   One-hundred-MB CRLs are just too large for relying parties to download and check, even with caching. Even downloading them once a day is too much, and in some environments, once a week is too often. If the PKI is going to be very large, deploy certificate status servers based on either OCSP or SCVP.

Centralized CAs work well when coupled with widely distributed RAs. Centralized CAs mean that only a small number of CAs are actually used, but a large number of RAs will be needed to support the decentralization. If the program is enterprise-wide, make sure to indicate where the RAs are going to be located, who will staff and operate them, and what workload are they expected to handle. RA operators need to be trained to ensure that polices are enforced.

Train, train, and train some more.   If everyone in the organization is going to be issued a hardware token or software token, everyone needs to know what they are, how to use them, when and why they must be used, and how to protect them appropriately. They need to know the consequences of losing a token.

Client-side authentication is a challenge.   Implementing both client-side and server-side TLS authentication is the goal. Mutual authentication is valuable. Enabling client-side authentication continues to be problem. Until client-side authentication is omnipresent, servers are going to have support usernames and passwords over server-side authenticated TLS sessions.

It only takes two.   Initially the PKI issued three certificates: one for identity that was used for windows smart card logon, one for digital signatures that was used to sign email messages and perform TLS client authentication, and one for encryption that was used to encrypt email messages. Each certificate had extensions that limited the certificate's use and forced the separation of the identity and signature certificate. Windows 2000 required these extensions, and despite changes made in Windows XP, it took until Windows Vista for this separation to go away. It takes about two products cycles to get everyone on the same page.

Sell, sell, and sell.   Develop a comprehensive public relations effort to inform smart card users and application developers well ahead of time. This effort will facilitate the adoption and implementation process and will permit users to fully capitalize on the enhancements provided by the smart card and PKI technology.

Rolling Root CAs is hard but not impossible.   Many PKI's Root CAs are extremely long-lived. Let's be honest; many designers think "I'll be long gone before they need to roll the Root CA." This is because rolling an installed user base from one trust anchor to another takes a lot of coordination. The trust anchor needs to be instantiated, certificates need to be issued to the older trust anchor, and vice versa, old CAs need to stop issuing certificates, new CAs need to start issuing certificates, and much more. The DoD PKI has proved that it is possible to make this transition.

National Institute of Standards and Technology Personal Identity Verification

Building on the experience of the DoD, the rest of the U.S. Government has been in the process of getting into the token issuing game. President George W. Bush issued *Homeland Security Presidential Directive 12*, which is commonly referred to as HSPD-12. It provides a "Policy for a Common Identification Standard for Federal Employees and Contractors" [HSPD-12]. As its name implies, HSPD-12 aims to develop a common identification standard for all federal employees and contractors. HSPD-12 says:

> *Wide variations in the quality and security of forms of identification used to gain access to secure Federal and other facilities where there is potential for terrorist attacks need to be eliminated. Therefore, it is the policy of the United States to enhance security, increase Government efficiency, reduce identity fraud, and protect personal privacy by establishing a mandatory, Government-wide standard for secure and reliable forms of identification issued by the Federal Government to its employees and contractors (including contractor employees).*

Previously, each department and agency developed its own format for ID cards. This obviously led to issues, because the ID cards were only accepted for entry in buildings operated by a federal employee's own agency, not all government buildings, and it certainly didn't permit access to computer systems across the federal government. The goal of HSPD-12 is to eliminate these issues.

The 800-pound gorillas in the room are "How on earth are we going to implement this?" and "Get this done now." To quiet those gorillas, the National Institute of Standards and Technology (NIST) developed the *Personal Identity Verification* (PIV) process on a very short and pressure-packed timeline. All federal departments and agencies must follow the standard procedures outlined in the PIV process to authenticate the identity of their employees and contractors prior to issuing them PIV cards, which can be used for both physical and logical access. To make it easier for the federal agencies and departments to meet the deadlines for compliance, there are two phases:

PIV-I. This phase standardizes federal agency and department processes for issuing ID badges to their employees and contractors. The process, in a nutshell, requires that employees and contractors be sponsored by a designated federal employee, that their identity be verified against a list of approved documents, and that the employee undergo a background check. The line drawn in the sand for all federal agencies and departments to implement this phase was October 27, 2005.

PIV-II. This phase builds on PIV-I, issuing and using the standardized common identification card, a smart card that meets the requirements in the standard. Each federal agency and department was required to issue at least one PIV-II-compliant card by October 27, 2006. The final line in the sand is October 2008, at which time all federal employees and contractors must have a PIV-II card.

NIST produced an impressive number of documents, among them one FIPS PUB, ten Special Publications (SP), and one Interagency Report (IR), all providing the details necessary for implementing every step of the PIV process:

- PUB 201: Personal Identification and Verification for Federal Employees and Contractors. [PUB201]
- SP 800-63: Electronic Authentication Guideline. [SP800-63]
- SP 800-73: Interfaces for Personal Identity Verification (PIV). [SP800-73]
- SP 800-76: Biometric Data Specification for Personal Identity Verification. [SP800-76]
- SP 800-78: Cryptographic Algorithms and Key Sizes for Personal Identity Verification. [SP800-78]
- SP 800-79: Guidelines for the Certification and Accreditation of PIV Card Issuing Organizations. [SP800-79]
- SP 800-85: PIV Card Application and Middleware Interface Test Guidelines (SP800-73 compliance). [SP800-85]
- SP 800-87: Codes for the Identification of Federal and Federally Assisted Organizations. [SP800-87]
- SP 800-96: PIV Card to Reader Interoperability Guidelines. [SP800-96]
- SP 800-100 Information Security Handbook: A Guide for Managers. [SP800-100]
- SP 800-104: A Scheme for PIV Visual Card Topography. [SP800-104]

- NIST IR 7337: Personal Identity Verification Demonstration Summary [IR7337]

- NIST IR 7452: Secure Biometric Match-on-Card Feasibility Report. [IR7452]

NIST provided the implementation details, but they can't quiet the gorillas alone. The Office of Management and Budget (OMB), the General Services Agency (GSA),* and the Chief Information Officer (CIO) council also have produced memorandum and documents to aid purchase and deployment of the PIV process:

- OMB M-04-04: E-Authentication Guidance for Federal Agencies. [M-04-04]

- OMB M-05-24: Implementation of Homeland Security Presidential Directive (HSPD) 12 – Policy for a Common Identification Standard for Federal Employees and Contractors. [M-05-24]

- OMB M-06-18: Acquisition of Products and Services for Implementation of HSPD-12. [M-06-18]

- GSA Memorandum: Acquisitions of Products and Services for Implementation of HSPD-12. [GSAMEM]

- GSA: Government Smart Card Handbook [GSCH].

- Federal Identity Credentialing Committee: Federal Identity Management Handbook. [FIMH]

In this chapter, we present the architecture for the PIV process and discuss the lessons learned by the PIV effort.

PIV Architecture

Our discussion of the PIV architecture includes the cryptographic algorithms, certificate and CRL profiles, cards and cryptographic modules, and applications.

Cryptographic Algorithms

The PIV card is based on commercially available algorithms. It must support one asymmetric private key (the PIV authentication key in the following list), a corresponding public key certificate, and private key operations on the card. Four other keys are optional:

PIV authentication key. This key is used to authenticate the card and prove the identity of the card holder to the external entity. As mentioned earlier, this key is an asymmetric key, and it is required.

*GSA FIPS PUB 201 site is `fips201ep.cio.gov`.

Card authentication key. This key is used to authenticate the card. This key may be either an asymmetric key or a symmetric key, and it is optional.

Digital signature key. This key is used to generate digital signatures. This key is obviously an asymmetric key, and it is optional.

Key management key. This key is used for key transport or key agreement. This key is an asymmetric key, and it is optional.

Card management key. This key is used for card personalization or post issuance activities. This key is a symmetric key, and it is optional.

The digital signature and key management keys are optional, but most agencies include them on their PIV cards. The incremental cost is very low, and the opportunities to secure applications are very appealing.

The algorithms that are allowed for use with these keys are specified in [SP800-78] and summarized in Figure 11-1.

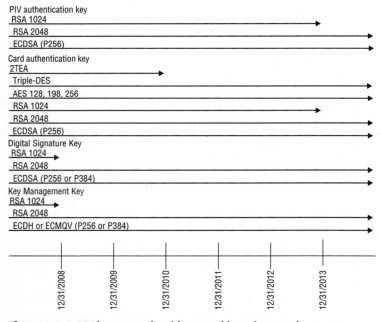

Figure 11-1 PIV key type algorithms and key size requirements

NOTE Don't be confused by the 2008 date for RSA 1024 in Figure 11-1. The Federal Identity Credentialing Committee's certificate profiles [FICCCP] indicates RSA with SHA-1 is allowed until 2010. But, if you read carefully, it says that the certificates that use RSA with SHA-1 must expire before December 31, 2010.

The message digest algorithms specified in [SP800-78] refer to the ones used to protect the information stored on the PIV card. They do not apply to the message digest algorithms used with the digital signatures generated with the digital signature certificate. Figure 11-2 shows the timeline for digital signature and message digest migration.

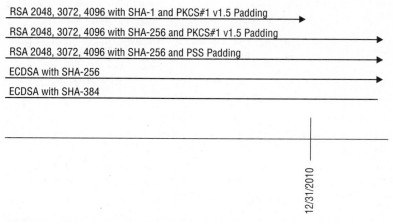

RSA 2048, 3072, 4096 with SHA-1 and PKCS#1 v1.5 Padding

RSA 2048, 3072, 4096 with SHA-256 and PKCS#1 v1.5 Padding

RSA 2048, 3072, 4096 with SHA-256 and PSS Padding

ECDSA with SHA-256

ECDSA with SHA-384

12/31/2010

Figure 11-2 PIV signature and message digest algorithm timeline

Architecture

The PIV architecture is composed of three subsystems, all of which are depicted in Figure 11-3. They are:

Front end.   Composed of the PIV card, PIV card readers, PIV card writers, PIN input device, and biometric reader, the PIV card holder uses this subsystem to gain physical, and optionally logical, access after their identity has be verified by the access control subsystem.

Issuance and management.   Composed of three processes and two components, the PIV card holder, front-end subsystem, and access control subsystem rely on outputs of this subsystem to issue cards, verify identities, and permit access.

Identity proofing and registration.   This process gathers and maintains all information required to verify the applicant's identity. Information collected includes name, date of birth, fingerprints, and so on.

Card issuance and management.   This process personalizes the visual surface of the card and loads the contents of the smart card's integrated circuit chip (ICC) before providing the PIV card to the applicant. The applicant's photo, name, employer, and other information is printed on the PIV card (more on this later in the chapter). The ICC is also loaded with PIV card applications, biometrics, and other data. The process also maintains the card after issuance.

Key management.   This process generates some of the key pairs, manages certificates, and generates certificate status information. The certificates are posted to the PKI directory component, and the certificate status information is provided to the certificate status component.

PKI directory.   This component is populated by the key management process and queried by the access control subsystem for PIV card holders.

Certificate status responder.   This component provides certificate status information to support signature verification.

Access control.   Composed of two parts, the Logical Access Control System (LACS) and the Physical Access Control System (PACS), this process is used when the PIV card is used to authenticate a PIV card holder who wishes to gain access to a logical or physical resource. Both the LACS and PACS initially verify and authenticate the PIV card holder, and then they check the PIV card holder's authorizations prior to granting access to the resource.

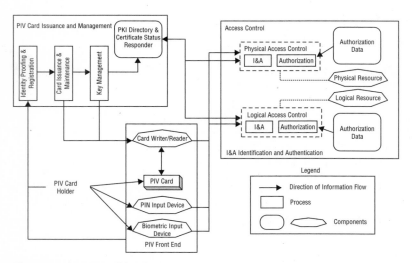

Figure 11-3 PIV architecture

Certificate Policies

The PIV specifications require certificates for each of the asymmetric keys defined for the PIV card. Certificate policies indicate the procedures required for certificate issuance and the requirements imposed on the user for protection of the private key. Rather than develop an entirely new set of policies for PIV, NIST adopted a suite of policies known as the Common Policy Framework.

These certificate polices were defined by the *Federal PKI Policy Authority Advisory* (FPKIPA), which is an interagency body established under the Chief Information Officers Council, otherwise known as the *CIO Council*. The FPKIPA enforces digital certificate standards for trusted identity authentication across federal agencies and between federal agencies and outside bodies, such as universities, state and local governments, and commercial entities. The FPKIPA originally published the Common Policy Framework support procurement of interoperable PKI services. The FPKIPA added two additional policies to enhance alignment with PIV requirements. These additional policies specifically support the PIV Authentication and Card Authentication keys.

OMB defined four assurance levels for authentication of people in [M-04-04]. The four levels are based on the degree of confidence that is placed in the process to establish the person's identity on the PIV card and the degree of confidence that the PIV card holder is actually the person to whom the PIV card was issued. The four assurance levels are described next:

1. Level 1 indicates that little or no confidence exists in the asserted identity.

2. Level 2 indicates that some confidence in the asserted identity.

3. Level 3 indicates high confidence in the asserted identity.

4. Level 4 indicates very high confidence in the asserted identity.

Technical guidance for achieving each of these levels has been published in [SP 800-63].

The latest FPKI CP is the X.509 Certificate Policy for the U.S. Federal PKI Common Policy Framework v1.3 dated 12/12/2007 [FPKICP]. There are six CPs defined in the single document, and they are listed in Table 11-1 as they are listed in the [FPKICP] along with the corresponding PIV key types. A brief summary of the applicability of each policy, and its relationship to the OMB assurance levels, is provided next:

Common-Policy. This policy is included in CA and subscriber certificates to support digital signatures or key management. Certificates asserting this policy meet the requirements for Level 3 authentication.

Common-Hardware. This policy is included in CA and subscriber certificates to support digital signatures or key management. Certificates asserting this policy meet the requirements for Level 4 authentication.

Common-Device. This policy is issued to devices. Since the OMB Memorandum 04-04 [M-04-04] applies to authentication of a person's identity, certificates asserting this policy do not correspond to the OMB levels of assurance.

Common-Authentication.   This policy is issued to subscribers supporting authentication but not digital signature. Certificates asserting this policy meet the requirements for Level 4 authentication.

Common-High.   This policy is included in CA and subscriber certificates to support digital signatures or key management. Certificates asserting this policy meet the requirements for Level 4 authentication.

Card Authentication.   This policy is issued to subscribers supporting authentication where the private key can be used without user authentication. Since these certificates are used to authenticate the PIV card, rather than the card holder, there is no correspondence to the OMB assurance levels.

Table 11-1 FPKI Certification Policy Object Identifiers

PIV KEY TYPES	OBJECT IDENTIFIER NAME	OBJECT IDENTIFIER
N/A*	id-fpki-common-policy	2.16.840.1.101.3.2.1.3.6
PIV Digital Signature Key PIB Key Management Key	id-fpki-common-hardware	2.16.840.1.101.3.2.1.3.7
PIV Content Signers**	id-fpki-common-devices	2.16.840.1.101.3.2.1.3.8
PIV Authentication Key	id-fpki-common-authentication	2.16.840.1.101.3.2.1.3.13
PIV Digital Signature Key PIV Key Management Key	id-fpki-common-high	2.16.840.1.101.3.2.1.3.16
PIV Card Authentication Key	id-fpki-common-cardAuth	2.16.840.1.101.3.2.1.3.17

*This policy is for software cryptomodules and does not apply to PIV.
**This certificate is issued to devices; therefore, it only applies when the PIV content signer is a system rather than a person. When the PIV content signer is a person, the certificate policy will be either id-fpki-common-hardware or id-fpki-common-high.

Certificate, CRL, and OCSP Profiles

The *Federal Identity Credentialing Committee*, another interagency body under CIO Council, developed the certificate and CRL profiles that CA must follow to be conformant to the FPKI CP. There are 9 worksheets: 3 for infrastructure certificates, 1 for CRLs, and 5 for EE certificates.

The infrastructure certificates are for self-signed certificate profile, self-signed CA certificate, a cross-certificate, and a CRL. All of the certificates are version 3 certificates. Tables 11-2 through 11-4 list the infrastructure certificate profile extensions.

Table 11-2 Self-Signed Certificate Extensions

EXTENSION	CRITICALITY	CONTENTS
Basic constraints	Critical	`cA=True`; path length constraints is omitted.
Key usage	Critical	The `keyCertSign` and `cRLSign` bits are asserted.
Subject information access	Non-critical	Contains `id-ad-caRepository` and `ldap://...` or `http://...` pointer.
Subject key identifier	Non-critical	Bit string identifying the public in the certificate.
Issuer alternative name	Non-critical	Optional. Includes the email address of the PKI administrator.

Table 11-3 Self-Issued CA Certificate Extensions

EXTENSION	CRITICALITY	CONTENTS
Basic constraints	Critical	`cA=True`; path length constraints is omitted.
Key usage	Critical	The `keyCertSign` and `cRLSign` bits are asserted.
Certificate policies	Non-critical	Includes one or more policies from Table 11-1.
CRL distribution point	Non-critical	Identifies the X.500 directory entry with an X.500 DN. It also includes two pointers: `ldap://...` and `http://...`
Authority information access	Non-critical	Contains `id-caIssuers` with both the `ldap://...` and `http://...` access methods.
Subject information access	Non-critical	Contains `id-ad-caRepository` and `ldap://...` or `http://...` access methods.

(continued)

Table 11-3 (*continued*)

EXTENSION	CRITICALITY	CONTENTS
Authority key identifier	Non-critical	Bit string identifying the key used to sign the certificate.
Subject key identifier	Non-critical	Bit string identifying the public in the certificate.
Issuer alternative name	Non-critical	Optional. Includes the email address of the PKI administrator.

Table 11-4 Cross-Certificate Profile Extensions

EXTENSION	CRITICALITY	CONTENTS
Basic constraints	Critical	`cA=True`; path length constraints is optional.
Key usage	Critical	The `keyCertSign` and `cRLSign` bits are asserted.
Certificate policies	Non-critical	Includes one or more policies from Table 11-1.
CRL distribution point	Non-critical	Identifies the X.500 directory entry with an X.500 DN. It also includes two pointers: `ldap://...` and `http://...`
Authority information access	Non-critical	Contains `id-caIssuers` with both `ldap://...` and `http://...` access methods.
Subject information access	Non-critical	Contains `id-ad-caRepository` and `ldap://...` or `http://...` access methods.
Authority key identifier	Non-critical	Bit string identifying the key used to sign the certificate.
Subject key identifier	Non-critical	Bit string identifying the public in the certificate.
Issuer alternative name	Non-critical	Optional. Includes the email address of the PKI administrator.
Policy mappings	Non-critical	Optional. Includes mapped certificate policies.
Name constraints	Critical	Optional. May include excluded and permitted subtrees.

The CRLs are version 2 and include one mandatory CRL entry extension (reason code to indicate why the certificate was revoked) as well as one optional CRL entry extension (invalidity date if the invalidity date proceeds the revocation date). The CRLs also include the authority key identifier and

CRL number CRL extensions, and it may include the issuing distribution point extension to support segmented CRLs.

The end entity certificates are all X.509v3 certificates. The end entity certificate profiles are as listed in Tables 11-5 through 11-9. The PIV authentication and card authentication certificates include two new pieces of information. The first piece of information is the *Federal Agency Smart Credential Number* (FASC-N), which is provided as a general name within the other name choice. This uses the ASN.1 syntax specified in [FIPS201], but the string format is specified in [FASC-N]. The FASC-N is the standard numbering scheme used to uniquely identify the PIV card. It is used in the PIV authentication and card authentication certificates to support physical access procedures. It is not modified during the lifetime of the PIV card, which means that it can be used to track the card throughout its lifetime.

Table 11-5 Digital Signature Certificate Extensions

EXTENSION	CRITICALITY	CONTENTS
Key usage	Critical	The `digitalSignature` and `nonRepudiation` bits are asserted.
Certificate policies	Non-critical	`id-fpki-common-policy`, `id-fpki-common-hardware`, `id-fpki-common-high` are allowed.
CRL distribution points	Non-critical	Identifies the X.500 directory entry with an X.500 DN. It also includes two pointers: `ldap://...` and `http://...`
Authority information access	Non-critical	Contains `id-caIssuers` with both `ldap://...` and `http:/...` access methods.
Authority key identifier	Non-critical	Bit string identifying the key used to sign the certificate.
Subject key identifier	Non-critical	Bit string identifying the public key in the certificate.
Subject alternative name	Non-critical	Includes the email address of the subject.
Extended key usages	Optionally Critical	Optional. Includes either the `id-PIV-content-signing` or `id-anyExtendedKeyUsages`.
Issuer alternative name	Non-critical	Optional. Contains the email address of the PKI administrator.
Subject alternative name	Non-critical	Optional. Contains the email address of the subject.

Table 11-6 Key Management Certificate Extensions

EXTENSION	CRITICALITY	CONTENTS
Key usage	Critical	Either `keyEncipherment` (for RSA) or `keyAgreement` for (ECDH or ECMQV) bit are asserted.
Certificate policies	Non-critical	`id-fpki-common-policy,` `id-fpki-common-hardware,` `id-fpki-common-high` are allowed.
CRL distribution points	Non-critical	Identifies the X.500 directory entry with an X.500 DN. It also includes two pointers: `ldap://...` and `http://...`
Authority information access	Non-critical	Contains `id-caIssuers` with both `ldap://...` and `http://...` access methods.
Authority key identifier	Non-critical	Bit string identifying the key used to sign the certificate.
Subject key identifier	Non-critical	Bit string identifying the public key in the certificate.
Issuer alternative name	Non-critical	Optional. Contains the email address of the PKI administrator.
Subject alternative name	Non-critical	Optional. Contains the email address of the subject.

Table 11-7 Devices Certificate Extensions

EXTENSION	CRITICALITY	CONTENTS
Key usage	Critical	May assert digitalSignature and either `keyEncipherment` with RSA or keyAgreement with EC.
Certificate policies	Non-critical	`id-fpki-common-devices` is asserted.
CRL distribution points	Non-critical	Identifies the X.500 directory entry with an X.500 DN. It also includes two pointers: `ldap://...` and `http://...`
Authority information access	Non-critical	Contains `id-caIssuers` with both `ldap://...` and `http://...` access methods.
Authority key identifier	Non-critical	Bit string identifying the key used to sign the certificate.
Subject key identifier	Non-critical	Bit string identifying the public key in the certificate.

(continued)

Table 11-7 (*continued*)

EXTENSION	CRITICALITY	CONTENTS
Extended key usage	Optionally critical	Optional. Indicates `id-PIV-content-signing` or `id-anyExtendedKeyUsage`.
Issuer alternative name	Non-critical	Optional. Contains the email address of the PKI administrator.
Subject alternative name	Non-critical	Optional. Includes the email or IP address of the subject.

Table 11-8 Card Authentication Certificate Extensions

EXTENSION	CRITICALITY	CONTENTS
Key usage	Critical	May assert `digitalSignature` and either `keyEncipherment` with RSA or `keyAgreement` with EC.
Certificate policies	Non-critical	`id-fpki-common-devices` is asserted.
CRL distribution points	Non-critical	Identifies the X.500 directory entry with an X.500 DN and it identifies the LDAP directory entry with either `ldap://...` or `http://...` that contains the CRL.
Authority information access	Non-critical	Contains the `id-caIssuers` access method with either and `ldap://...` or `http://...` pointer.
Authority key identifier	Non-critical	Bit string identifying the key used to sign the certificate.
Subject key identifier	Non-critical	Bit string identifying the public key in the certificate.
Extended key usage	Optionally critical	Indicates `id-PIV-content-signing` or `id-anyExtendedKeyUsage`.
Subject alternative name	Optionally critical	Criticality depends on presence of subject field. Must include the FASC-N `other-name`.
PIV Interim	Non-critical	Boolean indicating whether the National Criminal History Fingerprint Check has been completed successfully and the NACI has been successfully completed (`FALSE`) or the NACI has been initiated (`TRUE`).
Issuer alternative name	Non-critical	Optional. Contains the email address of the PKI administrator.

Table 11-9 PIV Card Authentication Certificate Extensions

EXTENSION	CRITICALITY	CONTENTS
Key usage	Critical	May assert `digitalSignature` and either `keyEncipherment` with RSA or `keyAgreement` with EC.
Certificate policies	Non-critical	`id-fpki-common-devices` is asserted.
CRL distribution points	Non-critical	Identifies the X.500 directory entry with an X.500 DN and it identifies the LDAP directory entry with either `ldap://...` or `http://...` that contains the CRL.
Authority information access	Non-critical	Contains the `id-caIssuers` access method with either and `ldap://...` or `http://...` pointer.
Authority key identifier	Non-critical	Bit string identifying the key used to sign the certificate.
Subject key identifier	Non-critical	Bit string identifying the public key in the certificate.
Subject alternative name	Optionally critical	Criticality depends on presence of subject field. Must include the FASC-N `other-name`.
PIV Interim	Non-critical	Boolean indicating whether the National Criminal History Fingerprint Check has been completed successfully and the NACI has been successfully completed (`FALSE`) or the NACI has been initiated (`TRUE`).
Extended Key Usages	Non-critical	Optional. Includes either the `id-PIV-content-signing` or `id-anyExtendedKeyUsages`.
Issuer alternative name	Non-critical	Optional. Contains the email address of the PKI administrator.

The second piece of information is the PIV National Agency Check with Inquires (NACI) indicator certificate extension. It indicates whether the PIV card holder's background check has been completed at the time of PIV card's issuance. The extension is set to FALSE if the Federal Bureau of Investigation (FBI) National Criminal History Fingerprint Check has been completed successfully and the NACI has been successfully adjudicated, whereas it is set to TRUE if the NACI has been initiated but not completed. The PIV NACI indication extension's syntax, which is always non-critical, is as follows:

```
piv-interim  EXTENSION ::= {
   SYNTAX          NACI_indicator
```

```
         IDENTIFIED BY  id-piv-NACI}

id-piv-NACI  OBJECT IDENTIFIER ::= { 2 16 840 1 101 3 6 9 1}

NACI_indicator ::= BOOLEAN DEFAULT FALSE
```

There are also three defined extended key usages:

`id-PIV-content-signing`. This extended key usage indicates that the public key contained in the certificate can be used to verify signatures on PIV Card Holder Unique Identifiers (CHUIDs) and PIV Biometrics, which will be discussed in the next section. This extension can be included in digital signature certificates for both humans and devices. It's only included when the EE is a trusted participant in the PIV issuing process.

`id-anyExtendedKeyUsage`. From [RFC3280], this extended usage indicates that the private key is not restricted to a particular key usage. In fact, it can be used for any extended key usage. This extension can be included in digital signature certificates for both humans and devices.

`id-PIV-cardAuth`. This extended key usage indicates that the public key in the certificate authenticates the PIV card rather than the PIV card holder. This extension must be present in card authentication certificates.

Cards and Cryptographic Modules

All of the components in the PIV architecture must use FIPS 140-2 (or later) evaluated cryptographic modules. Depending on which PKI entity the cryptographic module may be implemented in hardware or software. Table 11-10 lists the requirements for each PKI entity.

Physical access means two things: that the card can be read by a card reader and that the card can be examined by humans. [PUB201, SP800-104] standardizes the PIV card's "visual topography," which uses a 10-cent word to describe the card's printed surfaces. There are 20 printing zones identified

Table 11-10 FIPS 140 Levels

PKI ENTITY	TYPE	FIPS 140 LEVEL
CA*	Hardware	Level 3
CA	Hardware	Level 2
RA	Hardware	Level 2
EE**	Hardware	Level 2

*If the CA issues certificates that contain `id-fpki-common-high` certificate policy.
**All PIV cards are required to be FIPS 140 Level 2 with Level 3 physical security.

on the card, with 7 of the zones are required, while the remaining 10 zones are optional (some of them are background for required layers). There are several configurations available. Figure 11-4 shows a typical government PIV card, both the front and back, including all of the mandatory zones. The mandatory zones are:

- Photograph
- Name
- Employee affiliation
- Organizational affiliation
- Agency card serial number
- Issuer identification.

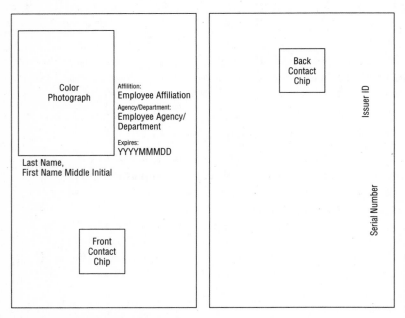

Figure 11-4 PIV card physical layout

The PIV card's ICC is required to support the following:

Personal identification number (PIN).   The PIN is used to gain access to other items stored on the PIV card. For example access to the biometric fingerprint data and PIV authentication data requires the user to authenticate to the PIV card prior to the PIV card providing this data.

Card Holder Unique Identifier (CHUID).   The CHUID is used by the PACS to support physical access to federal agency and department buildings. Activation of the CHUID does not require the PIV card holder enter their PIN. The requirements for the CHUID are found in [SP800-73] and [TIG-SCEPAS]. The FASC-N, *Global Unique Identifier* (GUID), expiration date, and issuer asymmetric signature are required, while an agency code, an organization identifier, a Data Universal Numbering System (DUNS), and authentication key map are optional. To make sure that the CHUID isn't modified on the card, it is included in a CMS `SignedData`. The structure is:

- `version` is set to 3.

- `digestAlgorithms` identifies the algorithm used to compute the `message-digest` attribute.

- `eContentInfo` represents a detached signature by including an `eContentType` set to `id-PIV-chuidSecurityObject`, and the `econtent` is omitted.

- `certificates` includes the CHUID signer's certificate.

- `crls` is omitted.

- `singerInfos` includes one `SignerInfo` and the following signed attributes:

  - `message-digest` includes a hash value that is calculated from the CHUID, excluding the asymmetric signature field.

  - `piv-Signed-DN` includes the DN of the CHUID signer.

PIV authentication data.   The PIV authentication data is the PIV authentication key and the PIV authentication certificate. It must be activated by the PIV card holder by entering his or her PIN.

Two biometric fingerprints.   The two fingerprints are collected to support PACs (more about this in the next section). A facial scan and a full set of fingerprints are taken as part of the identity proofing and PIV registration process, but only two of the fingerprints are required to be stored on the PIV card. To make sure that the fingerprints aren't modified on the card, they are included in a CMS `SignedData`. The structure is:

- `version` is set to 3.

- `digestAlgorithms` identifies the algorithm used to compute the `message-digest` attribute.

- `eContentInfo` represents a detached signature by including an `eContentType` set to `id-PIV-chuidSecurityObject`, and the `econtent` is omitted.

- `certificates` includes the biometric signer's certificate, but only if it's different than the CHUID signer's certificate.

- `crls` is omitted.
- `singerInfos` includes one `SignerInfo` and the following signed attributes:
  - `message-digest` includes a hash value that is calculated from of the biometric data, excluding the asymmetric signature field.
  - `pivFASC-N` includes FASN-C of the PIV card.
  - `piv-Signed-DN` includes the DN of the biometric signer.

> **NOTE** The PIV card actually holds the CHIUD string and biometrics and an asymmetric signatures physically on the PIV card. Since detached signatures are used, the stored data is not encapsulated in a `SignedData` content type.

The ICC on the PIV card supports both a contact and a contactless interface. The NIST requirements tell which pieces of information stored on the ICC are allowed to be provided through the contact and contactless interfaces.

The ICC on the PIV card may also support other optional elements such as the other keys and algorithms listed the "Cryptographic Algorithms" section of this chapter.

Applications

PIV cards support both physical and logical access when the PIV card holder is authenticated. There are five options, each providing different levels of assurance.

The first option, which is referred to as VIS authentication, involves authenticating the PIV card holder using the PIV visual credentials, which is the information printed on the PIV card. The process requires a guard to check the physical description information on the PIV card against the PIV card holder. Access is only granted after the guard performs the visual checks.

The second option, which is referred to as CHUID authentication, involves authenticating the PIV card holder using the CHUID stored on the PIV card. The process checks the expiration date in the CHUID and one or more CHUID elements. The card reader may also support checking the digital signature on the CHUID. Access is granted only after it has been verified that the CHUID has not expired and that the CHUID elements authorize the PIV card holder's access.

The third option, which is referred to as BIO authentication, involves authenticating the PIV card holder, using the biometrics stored on the PIV card. The process requires an electronic card reader, a PIN input device, and a biometric reader. The electronic card reader reads the CHUID; the PIN reader accepts the PIN, and the biometric reader obtains the PIV card holder's

Table 11-11 Authentication for Physical Access

PIV ASSURANCE LEVEL REQUIRED BY APPLICATION/RESOURCE	APPLICABLE PIV AUTHENTICATION MECHANISM
SOME CONFIDENCE	VIS, CHUID
HIGH CONFIDENCE	BIO
VERY HIGH CONFIDENCE	BIO-A, PKI

fingerprint(s). The PIV card must not be expired, the PIN must be correct, the biometric must match, the CHUID FASC-N must match the FASC-N in the `SignedData`, and one or more CHUID elements must permit the PIV card holder access. The signature on the biometric can optionally be verified.

The fourth option, which is referred to as BIO-A authentication, involves authenticating the PIV card holder with biometrics stored on the card, but this time the PIN is entered in front of an attendant. The difference in this process as compared to the BIO authentication process is that the PIN is entered in front of the attendant to ensure liveness.

The fifth option, which is referred to PKI authentication, involves authenticating the PIV card holder with the PKI. The process requires an electronic card reader and a PIN input device. The card reader reads the PIV card, and the PIN input device allows the PIV card holder to input his or her PIN. The card reader then issues a challenge to the card; the card responds with a signed response computed with the PIV authentication key; the card reader verifies the signature on the response and the response value, and the subject's DN and FASC-N are passed to the authorization function. Access is only granted after the authorization function returns a successful response.

Obviously, VIS authentication is only applicable to physical access, but the other four are applicable to both physical and logical access. Table 11-11 lists the authentication requirements for physical access, and Table 11-12 lists the requirements for logical access.

Table 11-12 Authentication for Logical Access

PIV ASSURANCE LEVEL REQUIRED BY APPLICATION/RESOURCE	APPLICABLE PIV AUTHENTICATION MECHANISM	
	LOCAL WORKSTATION ENVIRONMENT	REMOTE NETWORK ENVIRONMENT
SOME CONFIDENCE	CHUID	PKI
HIGH CONFIDENCE	BIO	PKI
VERY HIGH CONFIDENCE	BIO-A, PKI	PKI

NOTE Federal agencies and departments that don't have card readers will initially rely upon visual inspection of the PIV card, but will eventually be required to implement PIV card readers. The various assurance levels allow agencies and departments the ability to implement the right solution at the building, floor, and door.

If the digital signature and key management certificates are populated on the PIV card, they can support secure email (i.e., S/MIME), secure web, and other secure applications.

Lessons Learned

NIST caged the gorillas, but it took longer than anticipated. There are many lessons learned from the PIV effort. The following are some points you should take home from this case study:

- Physical security systems are not Internet applications. Each facility makes their own rules for access, so a PIV card issuance process might satisfy some but not all of these rules. Also, PIV card status information is hard to leverage across organizations.

- Physical security is very concerned with speed, so vendors are very reluctant to go beyond FASC-N checks to ensure that their system is responsive. Digital signatures on CHUID and data are rarely used.

- Contactless interface is faster, but the communication channel is generally insecure. Biometrics are not available over the contactless interface to ensure privacy constraints imposed in HSPD-12 are met.

- In practice, PIV cards are not updated at the user's desktop. This means that agencies issue PIV cards with a three year lifetime rather than a five year lifetime. As a result, certificates require renewal.

- Interoperability concerns have deterred agencies from deploying ECC, in spite of the obvious performance implications. No one wants to be the pioneer.

- The initial version of SP 800-78 specified six different ECC curves, which amplified interoperability concerns. The first revision of SP 800-78 reduced the set to two ECC curves, which has resulted in increased interest.

- Agencies prefer RSA 1024 since it is much faster than 2048 bit RSA. When deployments are forced to choose between 2048 bit RSA and ECC-256 for the PIV Authentication keys, ECC may prove more attractive.

Expectations
for the Future

CHAPTER 12

Future Developments

This book has focused on features that are widely available in today's email, such as secure email, PKI, and tokens. Some of these fields have been around for a while, but they are continuing to evolve. With our Magic 8 Ball we can't predict which features will prove important, but we'll make some educated guesses in this chapter.

This chapter examines features that may become important over the next few years and is organized to mirror the presentation of material in this book, rather than the relative order of importance of the various topics.

Email

Email has been around for about 50 years, and it's been evolving continually. The saying "evolve or die" is definitely applicable to email because it has been around for so long. New features keep appearing, and there is little doubt that email will continue to be around for many more years.

The two key things we expect to see in the future are the continuing evolution of messaging and increasing interest in stopping *spam*.

Evolution of Messaging

It's interesting that the term *messaging* has started to encompass more than just email. Now *instant messaging* (IM), which is commonly referred to as *chatting*, and *Short Message Service* (SMS), which is commonly referred to as *texting*, are referred to in the same breath as email. To be honest, it's only the people that run the infrastructure that really care about the difference, except when there is a price difference. Users don't care which method they use as long as they can communicate with their friends, family, and colleagues.

Instant messaging has been around for as long as email. It's different from email because it is session-oriented, which means that both parties must be available (well, at least both devices need to be available) at the same time. On the other had, email is store-and-forward, which allows the parties (and their devices) to be connected to the network at vastly different times. Depending on how it's implemented, IM seems instant because of the session, even if a stored-and-forwarded network is used behind the scenes. The first IM specification for the Internet was published in 1993; it was the *Internet Relay Chat* (IRC) protocol [RFC1459] and later updated by [RFC2810-2812]. It worked by opening a window on your computer where you typed and could see what the other person typed. IRC was popular with many techies but was never widely adopted outside of that community.

The first IM commercial success was a program called ICQ, which provided this feature along with a graphical user interface (GUI) and a presence indicator, which indicates whether the user is available. The GUI made it easier for non-techies to use, while the presence indicator let you know whether or not your contacts were available. If ICQ started the craze, then America Online (AOL) Instant Messenger (AIM) took it to the next level, which was quickly followed by Microsoft MSN Messenger and Yahoo! Messenger, each wanting to make sure that their user base had the same functionality. Guess what: they didn't interoperate because they were all proprietary solutions. Now, there are two sets of open standards that are vying for dominance in this space:

- *Extensible Messaging and Presence Protocol* (XMPP), which gives homage to its root with the Extensible Markup Language (XML) community, and is documented in [RFC3920-3923].

- *Session Initiation Protocol for Instant Messaging and Presence Leveraging Extensions* (SIMPLE), which uses the Session Initiation Protocol (SIP) protocol and is documented in about 30 different documents [SIMPLE].

We're not sure which one will ultimately win out, but we're hoping that the interoperability mess will be sorted out.

SMS is part of Global System for Mobile communication or GSM for short. GSM is defined by the GSM Association as ''an open, digital cellular technology used for transmitting mobile voice and data services.'' SMS allows short message of up to 160 characters to be sent between mobile phones. It's wildly popular. The Multimedia Messaging Service (MMS) is an evolution of SMS that also supports multimedia messages.

IM and SMS/MMS won't replace email anytime soon. In fact, they might never do so, especially since they are being touted as a part of enterprise messaging services. IM and SMS/MMS are in fact aimed at providing different services than email, which is considered by many to be more formal, whereas texting and chatting are considered less so. There are a number of reasons for this social difference. One reason is that email has been around for longer and has been integrated into business processes. Another related reason is that email is more often archived in records management systems. Another possible reason is that some people don't want to be "instant," preferring to take their time when responding to correspondence (i.e., they want to sit and think before responding). With some IM applications, there's also the problem of not having subjects or an inbox for storing messages in any kind of related way. Of course, IM is developing work flow and sharing applications, so it's not sure how it'll all turn out. Some enterprises have started to archive all IM traffic because it is becoming business critical.

Until very recently IM security was unavailable. There was some security for SMS because it uses the telephone network. In future, we expect that security for IM, and the phone network, will continue to improve and become more standard. IM and SMS/MMS do provide some of the same functionality, but we don't think SMS/MMS is going to be replaced by IM because SMS/MMS is part of the GSM standard. However, gateways between the two are already beginning to appear.

While email might not be replaced by IM, we do see email and IM merging. Gateways will move shorter email messages through instant messaging and vice versa. Larger messages will be sent to the inbox, with notifications of its arrival being sent through IM. Users will get to choose the delivery method based on presence information.

People are just beginning to think about security for the presence information. As the presence information expands to include geographic location, this kind of security will become more important.

Just as we have seen text and voice capabilities come together on mobile phones, we can expect to see further integration. A single application that provides email, IM, voice, and video to the desktop is coming, and the email address book will be combined with IM buddy lists and voice address books. And to cut down on unwanted email traffic (spam), the application will also support subscriptions to various information feeds, using the Atom Publishing Protocol [RFC5023].

Stopping spam

Some studies suggest that about half of all email delivered to a user's inbox is spam. The amount of spam on the Internet backbone is even higher because it is addressed to mailboxes that don't exist. It's generated by bots that have infected unsuspecting home and office computers and sent by unscrupulous individuals and businesses. The good thing is that everybody wants to stop it. Spam costs money by consuming unnecessary bandwidth, leads to fraud, and damages the reputations of both people and organizations.

There have been a number of efforts to stop spam, including *DomainKeys* [RFC4870], *Sender ID* [RFC4406], and *Sender Policy Framework* [RFC4408]. These three standards are either historic or experimental specifications.

One specification that is on the standards track and is gaining traction is *Domain Key Identified Mail* (DKIM) [RFC4871]. DKIM wants to provide an authentication mechanism for the email domain that sent the email. DKIM can be deployed without MUA upgrades, does not require a large infrastructure or trusted third parties, and can be implemented at low cost.* DKIM works by allowing the MTA representing a domain, such as *your-company.com*, to hash and sign both the message contents and header fields. Verification can then be performed by MTAs representing other domains to see if the message contents and header fields have been modified. The intent is to have domains sign only those messages for which they are accepting responsibility. Signers can decide what to do if they won't sign email, and verifiers can decide what to do if email isn't signed. In any case, not accepting them and not delivering them is allowed. Put this all together, and it's a way to stop masquerading open relay mail bots that fill everyone's inboxes with spam. DKIM allows verifiers to verify an identity, determine whether the identity is known, and determine whether a known identity is trusted.

Figure 12-1 shows the DKIM architecture. It shows two message paths from Alice to Matt and Bob; all of whom are all in different MTAs. Alice's message to Bob goes from her MTA #1, transits through MTA #2, and is delivered to Bob's MTA #3. Alice's message to Matt goes from her MTA #1, to MTA #4, and finally to Matt's MTA #5. MTAs can be arranged in an almost arbitrary way: MTA #2 is a transit for MTA #3, while MTA #5 is a subdomain of MTA #4.

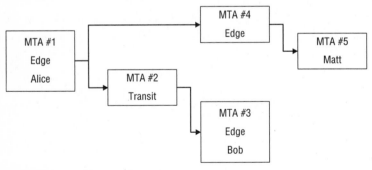

Figure 12-1 DKIM architecture

The DKIM signature structures, as well as the signature generation and verification rules, are specified in [RFC4871]. The DKIM signature is added in the DKIM-Signature header. An example DKIM-Signature header is listed

---

*The DKIM working group in the IETF scoped their work and they purposefully choose to not address message content encryption.

in Listing 12-1. The following is a summary of the DKIM-Signature fields and their support requirements:

v=This indicates the DKIM-Signature version. It must be included.

a=This identifies the signature algorithm. It must be included.

b=This is the signature value. It must be included.

bh=This is the hash of the message body. It must be included.

d=This identifies the domain that performed the signature. It must be included.

h=This lists the header fields that were included in the. It must be included, but the From field is the only required header field required to be signed.

s=This subdivides the name space of the domain. It must be included.

t=This indicates when the message was signed. It is recommended that this field be included.

x=This indicates the date after which the signature should not be considered valid. It is recommended that this field be included.

c=This indicates the canonicalization scheme used on the message body and header fields. This field is optional. The default if not included is for simple canonicalization.

i=This indicates the identity of the end user. This field is optional.

l=This indicates the number of octets of the message body that was used as input to the hash algorithm. This field is optional. The default is the entire message body.

q=This indicates methods to retrieve the public key. This field is optional. There is only one mechanism defined dns/text, which indicates the public key is retrieved from the DNS.

z=This includes headers the original headers and their values. This field is optional.

```
DKIM-Signature: v=1; a=rsa-sha256; s=brisbane;
  d=example.com; c=simple/simple; q=dns/txt;
  i=joe@football.example.com;
  h=Received : From : To : Subject : Date : Message-ID;
  t=1117574938; x=1118006938;
  bh=2jUSOH9NhtVGCQWNr9BrIAPreKQjO6Sn7XIkfJVOzv8=;
  b=AuUoFEfDxTDkHlLXSZEpZj79LICEps6eda7W3deTVFOk4yAUoqOB
    4nujc7YopdG5dWLSdNg6xNAZpOPr+kHxt1IrE+NahM6L/LbvaHut
    KVdkLLkpVaVVQPzeRDI009SO2Il5Lu7rDNH6mZckBdrIx0orEtZV
    4bmp/YzhwvcubU4=;
```

Listing 12-1 DKIM-Signature Heading Field Example

The private keys are retained by the signer, whereas the public keys* are stored and distributed by the DNS in a *resource record* (RR). A RR is the format for data stored in the DNS; DKIM uses the unstructured TXT RR. Domain keys are stored in subdomains named "_domainkey" to allow verifiers to use the q=, d=, and s= to format a DNS query for the correct key. DKIM defines the following key tags for use in the unstructured text:

p=This is the public key. This field is required.

v=This indicates the version of the DKIM key record. This field is optional.

g=This indicates the granularity of the key. This field is optional. The default is all.

h=This indicates the acceptable hash algorithms. This field is optional, but both the SHA-1 and SHA-256 algorithms must be supported. The default is all.

k=This indicates the key type. This field is optional. The default is RSA and it uses the syntax for RSAPublicKey from [RFC3447].

n=This includes notes that humans might find interesting. This field is optional.

s=This indicates the service type to which this key applies. This field is optional. The default is all.

t=This includes flags. This field is optional. The default is no flags.

Large email service providers are pushing to implement DKIM because users are being inundated with spam and phishing messages. DKIM increases the chance that email comes from the indicated originator, but this won't completely work until everyone implements it. If DKIM is widely implemented, users might not even see the spam when their spam filter is configured to delete messages that aren't signed. DKIM doesn't provide authentication of the message originator because the private key is not controlled by the originator. There's also no support for confidentiality, but that was a conscious decision. An improper setting of the l= field can cause some interesting results. Namely, if the length is shorter than the full length of the message, then it's possible that an attacker could modify the part of the message that wasn't used as an input to the message digest. This capability cannot be removed because text is sometimes legitimately added to the end of message. For example, when people send to a mail list, the mail list server might add information to the end of every message that it processes. The other thing is that there's no visible indication in mail clients even though the message was actually authenticated. The DKIM-Signature header is often hidden, so if you want to know that it

---

*There's no certificate it's just the public key.

was signed you have to enable verbose/full headers. A visible indication of a DKIM signed message would be very helpful.

As DKIM becomes widely deployed, sending domains will develop reputations as sources of spam or useful messages. Since DKIM provides authentication of the domain, this reputation will be useful. For example, banks are not the real source of phishing messages. Once you are able to authenticate your bank's domain, you will be able to distinguish the phishing messages from messages that really originate with your bank.

Cryptography

The recent focus in the cryptography field has been two fold: hash and elliptic curve algorithms. This section addresses both.

Competing Hash Algorithms

In the not-too-distant past, there was a huge push to transition encryption algorithms from DES to Triple-DES and then to AES. Now the focus has turned to message digest algorithms (recall that these are also called one-way hash functions). The reason for this is the cryptographic attacks that have been theorized against SHA-1.*

Hash algorithms need to have two important properties: being collision-free and being one-way. To show that an algorithm is weaker, an attack must show that it will take less than the optimal number of operations to produce a collision or that the function is not one-way.

Collision attacks occur when two messages result in the same hash value. For a strong hash algorithm, the number of operations necessary to find these two messages is supposed to be $2^{L/2}$, where L is the number of bits in the resulting hash value.

Attacks on the one-way property occur either when the attacker has a hash value and tries to find a message that returns the same hash value or when the attacker has a message and tries to find another message that has the same hash value. For a strong hash algorithm, the number of operations necessary to find either the hash or message is 2^L. The first attack on the one-way property is called a *first-preimage* attack, and the second attack is called a *second-preimage attack*.

Figure 12-2 shows three types of attacks against hash algorithms. Table 12-1 shows the number of operations necessary to find collision and image attacks against the SHA-1 and SHA-2 hash algorithms.

*It's a theorized attack because there are no known verifications of the attack. Though the computation is very large, NIST surmised that it is not out of the realm of possibility for a highly motivated and highly resourced attacker; therefore, they accept that the attack deserves serious consideration.

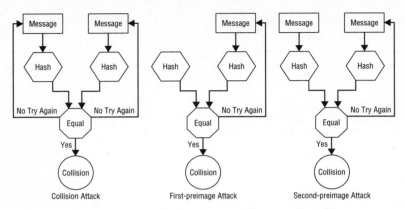

Figure 12-2 Hash algorithm attacks: collision, first-preimage, second-preimage

Table 12-1 Number of Operations to Find Hash Collision or Image

ALGORITHM	OPERATIONS TO FIND COLLISION	OPERATIONS TO FIND IMAGE
SHA-1	2^{63}	2^{80}
SHA-224	2^{112}	2^{224}
SHA-256	2^{128}	2^{256}
SHA-384	2^{192}	2^{384}
SHA-512	2^{256}	2^{512}

In 2005, Professor Xiaoyun Wang announced a collision attack against SHA-1 that lowered its strength from 2^{80} to 2^{63} [WANG].* Other collision attacks have also been published that further lower the number of operations. With the handwriting on the wall, NIST has developed a three phase plan to develop the next family of hashing algorithms, which they are referring to as the SHA-3 family. The three steps are as follows:

1. **Migrate to SHA-2 algorithms.** This strategy is a "walk towards the exit" strategy as opposed to a "run towards the exit" strategy. There is every indication that the SHA-2 family of algorithms will be secure for at least the next decade. It's a prudent strategy because the number of operations necessary to compute the attacks is so large that there's still time to develop a replacement before any real problems emerge. The strategy is also smart because there is always significant lag time between the announcement of a new algorithm, standards being updated that include the new algorithm, and products becoming available that implement

*The attacks do not seem to affect HMACs or KDFs based on SHA-1.

the standard. By allowing a transition period and backing the timeline up with NIST documents, NIST helps stimulate a market, and provides time for vendors to develop and test their products. This kind of strategy should come as no surprise, as NIST is part of the U.S. Department of Commerce.

2. **Encourage hash function research.**   NIST does this by hosting workshops. (They've held two so far.) The first was held in late 2005, addressing, among other things, the status the status of SHA-1 and SHA-256, deployment challenges for new algorithms, and potential replacement options. The second was held in mid-2006, addressing mathematical foundations, analysis and design, and practical uses and pitfalls. The workshop outputs were used to develop the minimum acceptability requirements, submission requirements, and evaluation criteria. On November 2, 2007 the formal announcement was published, requesting algorithm submissions and listing their requirements and evaluation criteria.

3. **Host hash function competition.**   The AES selection process worked well, and it is being used as the model for selecting the SHA-3 hash algorithms. The selection process will accept submissions until the fourth quarter of 2008, and then three hash function candidate conferences will be held. They are scheduled to take place in the second quarter of 2009 and the second quarter of 2010, with the final one taking place in the first quarter of 2012.

Adopting Elliptic Curve Cryptography

The other focus in the field of cryptography is on adopting Elliptic Curve Cryptography (ECC). After AES was announced, work began to establish public key algorithms offering the same strength as the new symmetric cipher. NIST published [SP800-57] to provide some guidance.* As you can see in Table 12-2, as the number of bits of security increases so does the public key size. For AES-128, the key size of equal strength using the RSA or Diffie-Hellman algorithm is 3200 bits, which doesn't seem too unreasonable, but the equivalents for AES-192 and AES-256 are well beyond the capabilities of small, cheap cryptographic tokens. It's not the storage that will be the problem; the issues will be the key pair generation and the time needed to perform private key operations. Therefore, we expect to see more tokens that support the Elliptic Curve Digital Signature Algorithm (ECDSA) to be developed and deployed. One indication of this transition is the support in Microsoft Windows Vista for ECDSA with the CNG (Cryptographic Next Generation).

*We added SKIPJACK to the 80-bit row.

Table 12-2 Comparative Algorithm Strength

BITS OF SECURITY	SYMMETRIC ALGORITHM	ONE-WAY HASH FUNCTION	RSA/DSA DIFFIE-HELLMAN KEY LENGTH	PRIME FIELD ELLIPTIC CRUVE KEY LEGNTH	BINARY FIELD ELLIPTIC CURVE LENGTH
80	SKIPJACK	SHA-1	1,024	$\|p\| = 192$	$m = 163$
112	Triple-DES	SHA-224	2,048	$\|p\| = 224$	$m = 233$
128	AES-128	SHA-256	3,200	$\|p\| = 256$	$m = 283$
192	AES-192	SHA-384	7,500	$\|p\| = 384$	$m = 409$
256	AES-256	SHA-512	15,000	$\|p\| = 512$	$m = 571$

The one issue with ECC is intellectual property rights (IPR). There are lots of IPR statements and patents in this space dealing with some specific curves, issuance, and optimizations. The U.S. Government has done their part and bought the rights for many patents under these two conditions:

- With elliptic curves over GF(p), where p is a prime number greater than 2^{255}

- When the product is approved by the U.S. National Security Agency or is used for national security and is compliant with FIPS 140-2 or its successors

There is also some interesting research into making RSA friendlier to the limited processing capabilities of tokens, especially smart cards. Multi-Prime RSA [PKCS1v21] also offers hope by using more than two prime factors, making the RSA private key operations become less processor intensive. If this research becomes widely accepted and deployed, then the uptake of ECC will take longer.

Public Key Infrastructure

The amount of experience gained in small-, mid-, and large-scale PKI deployments over the last five years has been substantial. All of the architectures described in Chapter 5 have been implemented.

The basic certificate structure remains unchanged, but new extensions are defined for by many different communities. The base IETF PKI standard has been published twice, and it is being readied for a third publication. The basic certificate structure is unchanged, but a few new extensions, matching rules, and processing rules have been added. Additional extensions have also been defined in other documents. We don't expect that the base certificate structure will change in the next five years, but we do expect more and more extensions.

Interconnecting the different enterprise PKIs has lead to some interesting trends that will likely continue. Revocation checking has actually started to occur on a regular basis.

Unfortunately, authorization information is continuing to creep into certificates. We see two ways that authorization information can be addressed: attribute and proxy certificates. We also think that large enterprises will start to demand that they mange their own trust stores. We discuss all of these next.

Trending Architectures

We believe there will be more PKIs but fewer CAs within any given large-enterprise PKI. Initially, CAs were going to be distributed to every organization so that the organization could maintain control, but after spreading out the CAs the organizations found the cost was too high for training, equipping, and maintaining their CA. As a result, CAs are now being centralized. If the CAs are properly provisioned to support the needed operations with high availability, then they are more than adequate to do the job. The catch is that more RAs are needed to help with the registration process. This separation of duties is better for the organization because they can concentrate their efforts on a relatively smaller number of CAs by getting higher-assurance infrastructure components.

Bridge CAs are being used for the interoperability of enterprise PKI. Enterprises were developing CPs, but then the concern about all the comparisons necessary to cross-certify has resulted in everyone moving towards bridges with the same assurance-based CPs being used by large communities. We believe this trend will continue.

At some point, though, the number of bridges could get out of control. Bridges for bridges would lead to extremely complex certification path development. When relying parties start to go through three or four bridge CAs, we predict that we'll start to see them consolidate.

Checking Certificate Status

When PKIs first emerged very few clients checked the certificate status. When certificate status checking was finally implemented, CRLs issued by some CAs were growing at an alarming rate. The result was interest in online certificate status checking. OCSP has started to take off, and we expect continued growth of online certificate status checking, eventually replacing CRLs. Granted, CRLs will still be produced, but relying parties won't be checking them directly. The CRLs will provide information to OCSP responders and in the not-too-distant future also to SCVP servers.

Online Certificate Status Protocol

The Online Certificate Status Protocol (OCSP) is defined in [RFC2560]. OCSP enables applications to determine the status of a particular certificate by querying an OCSP responder. An OCSP client issues a status request to the OCSP responder and suspends acceptance of the certificate in question until the OCSP responder provides a reply. The OCSP responder sends the certificate status information to the requester. Support for OCSP in included in a certificate using the authority information access certificate extension. CAs may host this service locally or delegate this responsibility to an OCSP responder operated by someone else.

Figure 12-3 depicts a simple OCSP response. The request from Bob shown here includes four data items. The certID field describes the certificate that Bob is interested in and it includes the hash algorithm, issuer name hash, issuer key hash, and serial number. The issuer name hash is the result of hashing the certificate issuer name field. Similarly, the issuer key hash is the result of hashing the issuer public key, as obtained from the subject public key field in the issuer's certificate. The hash algorithm used for both these hashes is identified in the hash algorithm field. The serial number is the serial number of the certificate for which status is being requested. In Figure 12-3, the certificate of interest has serial number 2560. Bob has included a nonce in an extension field to guard against replay.

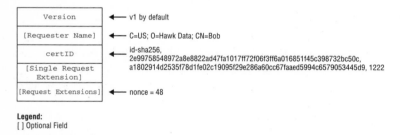

Legend:
[ ] Optional Field

Figure 12-3 An OCSP request message

When using CRLs, the pairing of issuer name and serial number identifies a certificate, whereas OCSP uses the more complicated certificate identifier structure. In the absence of a global directory system, it is possible that two CAs could choose the same name. Since an OCSP responder may provide service for multiple CAs, the OCSP responder must be able to distinguish CAs with the same issuer name. Two CAs will not have the same public key. By using the hash of the issuer public key in addition to the hash of the issuer name to identify the issuer, the possibility of collisions is removed.

As shown in Figure 12-3, Bob has requested status information for one certificate. The OCSP request format supports requesting status for multiple certificates in a single request. In that case, the CertID and the optional single request extension fields appear for each certificate. Bob may optionally sign his

OCSP request. By omitting the signature, lightweight clients may reduce the number of expensive signature operations they perform. However, an OCSP responder may insist on signed requests for billing or access control purposes.

An OCSP response includes the version, the responder identifier, the time the message was produced, the certificate identifier, the certificate status, the time that the status was last updated, and the time when the next status update for this certificate is expected. In the single extensions, the OCSP responder includes additional information about that particular certificate. If the response conveys information about more than one certificate, the certificate identifier, status, update information, and single extension appear for each certificate. The response extensions include additional information for the entire response. Every OCSP response is digitally signed by the OCSP responder.

Figure 12-4 depicts the data in the OCSP response to Bob's request. The response came from the Hawk Data's OCSP1 server. The message was produced at 2:12 P.M. Greenwich Mean Time on February 2, 2008. The certificate was revoked on January 17, 2008, at 8 P.M. Greenwich Mean Time. The last update for this certificate's status was 8 A.M. that same morning. The next update is expected at 8 A.M. the following morning.

Figure 12-4 An OCSP response message

OCSP is often described as providing revocation information in a more timely fashion than CRLs. An OCSP responder can provide the most up-to-date information it possesses without repository latency. If the OCSP responder is also the CA, the most up-to-date information will be provided. With CRLs, the CA may have additional information that it cannot provide to certificate users. However, in practice, there has been little difference in freshness of the certificate status information provided by an OCSP responder and a CRL.

Most OCSP responders are not CAs. Rather, they are single-purpose machines that handle certificate status requests for a large number of CAs. Typically, these servers obtain their revocation information periodically in the form of CRLs. The information obtained by the requester is no fresher than if they obtained the same CRLs themselves.

When the OCSP response is returned to the requestor, it is digitally signed. The requestor must validate the signature on the response. How can the requestor determine if the OCSP responder has been revoked? To do this, the requestor needs to ask the OCSP responder for status information on itself or validate the certification path of the OCSP responder, including CRL checks. Of course, asking the OCSP responder about itself is rather silly, and the point of OCSP is to avoid CRL checks. Therefore, the actions needed to revoke OCSP responders that use the noCheck extension [RFC2560] are similar to the actions needed to remove a trust anchor from a certificate trust list.

The real utility of OCSP lies in the single-response extension fields. If Bob is checking a signature on a purchase order, he could request approval for this signature and a particular dollar amount. The OCSP responder could provide a response stating that the certificate status was good and whether the signature could be accepted for the stated dollar amount. This is the added functionality provided to the credit card companies through the online request. This is the functionality that CRLs cannot deliver.

Coupling business decisions with certificate validation has significant advantages. The organization can administer one OCSP responder and be assured that all clients are applying the same business rules for all transactions.

If there is a need for transaction-specific authorization information, then OCSP may be the best choice. If not, the advantages of CRL caching may outweigh the benefits of online checking.

Another benefit arises if CRLs are very large. In this situation, the OCSP traffic for several days may be much less than the download of a single CRL. Very large CRLs can be a big burden on network bandwidth and user patience. Users are often unaware of the processing that is taking place when a CRL is being fetched; after all, they were simply trying to open a digitally signed email message when the hourglass appeared.

Server-Based Certificate Validation Protocol

The Server-Based Certificate Validation Protocol (SCVP) is defined in [RFC5055]. SCVP enables applications to delegate both certification path construction and certificate path validation. The services are characterized as follows:

Delegated Path Validation.   The delegated path validation (DPV) service targets at applications that want to allow a trusted server to do all the work. SCVP clients request that the server confirm that the public key belongs to the identity named in the certificate and confirmation that the public key can be used for the intended purpose.

Delegated Path Discovery.   The delegated path discovery (DPD) service targets applications that want to offload certification path construction.

SCVP clients request that the server construct a valid certification path and return it to them and they'll do the certification path validation.

This protocol evolved out of the growing concern with the complexity of constructing and then validating X.509v3 certification paths. Certification path validation was relatively straightforward in X.509v1 and X.509v2. Each certificate in the sequence had to be within its validity period and a CRL checked for each certificate. The names and signatures needed to chain for each subsequent certificate in the path. If these checks passed, the chain started at a known trust anchor, and the client could determine that each issuer was a CA, then the certification path was valid.

X.509v3 added both functionality and complexity to certification path validation. Now, certificates identify CAs explicitly. They also include limitations on subject names, the appropriate use of public keys, and certificate policies. The concept of criticality added additional processing requirements. Initially, different vendors supported different sets of standard extensions. This led to inconsistent results, as valid certification paths were rejected when unrecognized critical extensions were encountered. The Internet Certificate and CRL Profile [RFC3280] has generated greater consensus but inconsistent results persist because implementers have interpreted non-critical extensions differently. If one implementation ignores a constraint in a non-critical extension and another implementation honors the constraint, the two implementations can return different results.

SCVP uses CMS as its protective wrapper; `SignedData` and `Authenticated Data` allowed.* Requests use the `CVRequest` content type. Figure 12-6 shows the syntax of the `CVRequest`. There are two mandatory fields: the version and the query. There are eight optional fields: a requestor reference to detect looping in relay environments, a requestor nonce to stop replays, the requestor's name, the name of the requested responder, request extensions, the signature algorithm, the hash algorithm, and arbitrary text added by the requestor. The query must contain the certificates to be checked, what checks are to be performed, and what policy is applied during these checks. Queries may also include additional information that the requestor wants back from the responder (e.g., the valid certification path), information from previous request-responses (e.g., nonces), the time at which the validation should be performed (this time can be in the past), intermediate certificates, revocation information, an indication that caches responses are allowed, and extensions for this query. In Figure 12-5, Bob includes Alice's certificate and wants the path built, checked, and returned using the default validation policy. He also includes a nonce to protect against replay attacks.

---

*It is up to the SCVP server whether the client certificate needs to included the `id-kp-scvpClient` extended key usage.

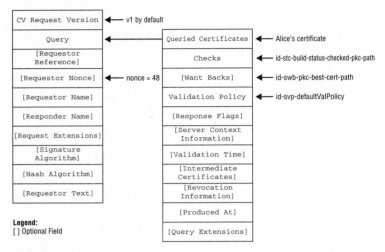

Figure 12-5 An SCVP request

SCVP responses use the `CVResponse` content, as shown in Figure 12-6. The four required fields indicate the version, the configuration of the server, the time the response was produced, and the status of the response. There are a number of optional fields to indicate the policy that was used during validation, a reference to the request, the requestor reference from the request, the requestor's name, the reply objects, a server nonce, server context information returned from the request, extensions, and text returned from the request. The reply objects include the information the requestor wanted including the certificate being checked, the status of this reply, the time the reply was validated, the checks that were performed, and the want backs. Optional validation errors, a next update time, and extensions can also be included. In Figure 12-6, the SCVP responder replies to Bob's request from Figure 12-5. The response includes a server configuration identifier, the time the response was produced, the response status of okay, and a responder nonce. The reply objects include Alice's certificate, a reply status of success, a reply validation time of February 2, 2008 at 2:12 P.M., an indication that the entire path was checked and is valid, and the entire certification path.

As with OCSP responders, an SCVP responder can also be a CA or be a separate entity. Also like OCSP responses, the SCVP response is signed and the requestor must validate the signature on the response. To do this, the requestor needs to ask the SCVP responder for status information on itself or validate the certification path of the SCVP responder, including CRL checks. Of course, asking the SCVP responder about itself is rather silly, and the point of SCVP is to avoid path construction and CRL checks. Therefore, the actions needed to revoke SCVP responders that are configured as trust anchors are similar to the actions needed to remove a trust anchor from a certificate trust list.

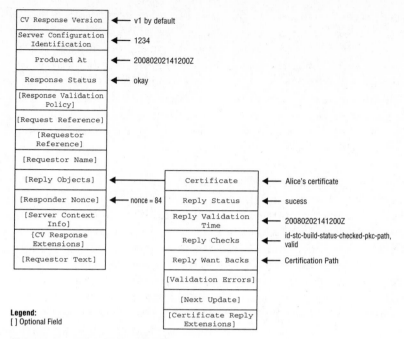

Figure 12-6 An SCVP response

The IETF took a very long time to finish the SCVP specification. We think SCVP will eventually replace OCSP because the whole path can be validated in one request. Further, SCVP supports delegating path validation so that devices that don't have the wherewithal to do path validation can hand it off to an SCVP server. This ability may allow the bridge CA environments to become more complex than might otherwise be possible.

Authorizing with Attribute Certificates

The certificates we've been talking about so far in this book have been public key certificates. Public key certificates bind the subject and the public key. Establishing and maintaining this binding was the focus of Chapter 5. However, the relationship between the subject and public key ought to be long-lived. Most end-entity certificates include a validity period of less than three years.

Organizations seek to improve access control. Public key certificates can be used to authenticate the identity of a user, and this identity can be used as an input to access control decision functions. However, in many contexts, the identity is not the criterion used for access control decisions. The access control decision may depend upon role, security clearance, group membership, or ability to pay.

Authorization information, such as membership in a group, often has a shorter lifetime than the binding of the identity and the public key. Authorization information could be placed in a public key certificate extension. However, this is not a good strategy for two reasons. First, the certificate is likely to be revoked because the authorization information needs to be updated. Revoking and reissuing the public key certificate with updated authorization information is quite expensive. Second, the CA that issues the public key certificates is not likely to be authoritative for the authorization information. This results in additional steps for the CA to contact the authoritative authorization information source.

The X.509 attribute certificate (AC) binds attributes to an AC *holder* [X50997, RFC3281]. Since the AC doesn't contain a public key, the AC is used in conjunction with a public key certificate. An access control decision function may make use of the attributes in an AC, but it is not a replacement for authentication. The public key certificate must first be used to perform authentication, then the AC is used to associate attributes with the authenticated identity.

ACs may also be used in the context of a data origin authentication service and non-repudiation service. In these contexts, the attributes contained in the AC provide additional information about the signing entity. The information can be used to make sure that the entity is authorized to sign the data. This kind of checking depends either on the context in which the data is exchanged or on the data that had been digitally signed.

An AC resembles a public key certificate. The AC is an ASN.1 DER encoded object and is signed by the issuer. An AC contains nine fields: version, holder, issuer, signature algorithm identifier, serial number, validity period, attributes, issuer unique identifier, and extensions. The AC holder is similar to the public key certificate subject, but the holder may be specified with a name, the issuer and serial number of a public key certificate, or the one-way hash of a certificate, public key, or an arbitrary object. The attributes describe the authorization information associated with the AC holder. The extensions describe additional information about the AC and how it may be used.

The contents of an AC are shown in Figure 12-7, wherein the AC permits Alice to administer the VPN for four hours. As a result of the short validity period, the AC issuer does not need to maintain revocation information. By the time the revocation information could be compiled and distributed, the AC would expire. So, with short-lived ACs, revocation information is not distributed. In this example, Hawk Data accepts the risk for that four-hour window rather than maintain CRLs for attribute certificates. If an AC has a longer life span (for example, weeks or months), then Hawk Data would need to maintain AC status information.

The Hawk Data VPN server can obtain Alice's AC in two different ways, as shown in Figure 12-8. Alice may provide the AC to the server when she initiates a connection. This is knows as the *push* model. Alternatively, Hawk

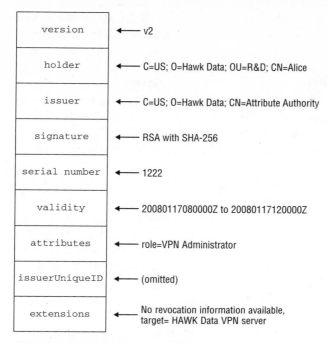

version	◄── v2
holder	◄── C=US; O=Hawk Data; OU=R&D; CN=Alice
issuer	◄── C=US; O=Hawk Data; CN=Attribute Authority
signature	◄── RSA with SHA-256
serial number	◄── 1222
validity	◄── 20080117080000Z to 20080117120000Z
attributes	◄── role=VPN Administrator
issuerUniqueID	◄── (omitted)
extensions	◄── No revocation information available, target= HAWK Data VPN server

Figure 12-7 An attribute certificate for Alice

VPN server can request the AC from the AC issuer or a repository when Alice initiates the connection. This is known as the *push* model. A major benefit of the pull model is that it can be implemented without changes to the client or the client-server protocol. The pull model is especially well suited for interdomain communication where the client's rights are assigned with in the server's domain rather than within the client's domain.

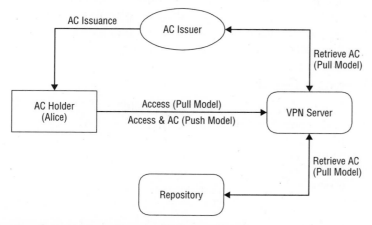

Figure 12-8 An attribute certificate architecture

Returning to the AC in Figure 12-7, the AC specifies the Hawk VPN server as the target through an AC extension. The intent of this extension is to specify the servers or services that may use this AC. This means that a trustworthy server that is not listed a target will reject the AC.

The X.509 specification supports a broader definition of authorization than the IETF AC profile. X.509 defines authorizations as the "conveyance or privilege from one entity that holds such privilege, to another entity." The privilege could be further delegated by the AC holder if he or she chose to do so. X.509 allows for the construction and validation of an attribute certificate path that describes the delegation of authority.

Assume that all of Hawk Data privileges derive from the CEO. The CEO could delegate authority for all network access decisions to the corporate security officer. The corporate security officer could delete authority to manage VPN access to the VPN administrator, Alice. The VPN administrator could delegate the privileges to use the VPN to employees who are authorized to telecommute. In the extreme case, an AC represents each of these delegations of privilege.

The Hawk Data VPN server's access control function must construct a path of four ACs to verify an employee VPN access. The Hawk server will also need to construct a path for the employee's public key certificate so that it can perform authentication. In fact, the Hawk Data VPN server must construct a certification path for each link in the delegated privilege chain, so they can verify the signature on each AC!

This adds considerable complexity, and our experience with ACs is quite limited. As a result, the IETF developed [RFC3281] and does not recommend use of AC chains. This is good advice, at least for the near term. The simple case, where a single authority issues all of the ACs for a particular attribute, adds considerable functionality without adding considerable complexity. There are also scenarios in which more than one AC is required. For example, Alice might need an AC to demonstrate membership in the R&D group and another AC to assert a managerial role. Different authorities issue each of these ACs. Implementations should be ready to support such scenarios.

Delegating with Proxy Certificates

Another option for delegation is proxy certificates, which are defined in [RFC3820]. The idea came from the Grid community. In a nutshell, proxy certificates allow Alice to grant Bob the rights for Bob to be authorized with others as if Bob were Alice. Alice does not need to offer Bob all of her authorizations; she can provide an explicit subset of her authorizations. In other words, Bob acts as a proxy on behalf of Alice. It doesn't have to be a person; Alice could allow her proxy to be an application running on a particular host connected to the Internet. For example, Alice wants to synchronize her VPN access databases between her servers on Hawk's intranet-based grid. She wants to do this from her laptop and wants to submit the requests and then go offline without waiting for it to complete. Alice's will leave an agent running on her laptop that will check on the process of the synchronization by contacting the application. She also wants to do this securely and so does her company that requires she use her smart card. For all this to happen:

- Alice needs to mutually authenticate with the synchronization application to ensure that she's allowed to perform the operation.

- The synchronization application needs to mutually authenticate with the databases on the different servers, and it needs to do this on behalf of Alice.

- The master and slave databases need to mutually authenticate each other.

- The agent running on Alice's laptop must mutually authenticate with the synchronization application in order to check the progress of the operation.

NOTE Grid computing can be thought of as a group of computers working on the same task. A popular one is the Search for Extraterrestrial Intelligence (SETI), where they've listened to the stars with a radio telescope. Processing the data is a huge task. What they've done is write a small application that uses spare computing time to process the data. Volunteers load this application onto their machines and then churn on the data doing whatever processing is necessary. Other programs targeted at more worldly endeavors include: protein folding, drug candidates, and cancer research.

A proxy certificate allows Alice to proxy her rights to the agent for performing synchronization of the databases. Only one access to the smart cards is required if the agent acts as her proxy. Proxy certificates can also allow the agent, servers, and remote processes need to be proxies for Alice.

A proxy certificate is an X.509 public key certificate that is issued from a *proxy issuer*. A proxy issuer is either an entity with an EE certificate or a proxy certificate that issues other proxy certificates. The proxy issuer's certificate must include the key usage extension, and it must have the digital signature bit set. The proxy certificate is signed with the private key associated with the proxy issuer. The proxy certificate has its own distinct private public key pair, but this private key cannot be used to sign EE certificates. The subject of the proxy certificate is name of the proxy issuer with an additional CN attribute appended to the end of the proxy issuer's name. The serial number is unique, and the validity period is assigned by the proxy issuer. The key usage digital signature bit must be set in the proxy certificate. A proxy certificate also contains the critical *Proxy Certificate Information* certificate extension. This extension indicates the allowed depth of proxy certificate hierarchy. It's like the path length constraints within the basic constraints certificate extension; a value of zero indicates that no more proxy certificates are allowed. The extension also indicates the proxy certificate policies. An example proxy certificate hierarchy that allows two proxy certificates is depicted in Figure 12-9.

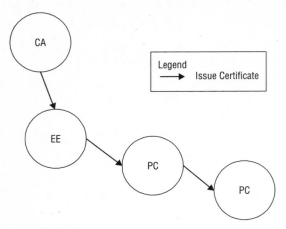

Figure 12-9 Proxy certificates

Like X.509 public key certificates, proxy certificates also have certification path validation rules. They're very similar to X.509 public key certificates except that that the path ends with the EE and not with the CA. Granted, the EE certificate must also be valid and that involves validating its certification path.

The difference between delegating with proxy certificates and attribute certificates is that proxies delegate the identity, whereas attributes delegate a particular set of authorizations for an identity.

Managing Trust Anchors

Currently, the most widely implemented architecture is trust lists. They're in every operating system and in every browser (Mozilla, Opera, and Safari), as well as in many other applications. There are 40 or more trusted root CAs in each store. In most cases, these stores are now updated via software updates.

If an enterprise wishes to constrain the contents of the trust store, then they need to work with the operating system, browser, or application developer to ensure that only the trusted root CAs the enterprise wants installed on their desktops are included in the software distribution. If users can install whatever certificates they want in the trust store, then it's hard for the enterprise to make sure that they can control the enterprise trust relationships.

For devices, it's a little more interesting, since many don't support features like automatic software updates and they don't have the storage capacity for a huge list of trust anchors. These devices really need is a simple mechanism to know what trust anchor is allowed to do what.

We see the need for a protocol to manage trust anchors. Administrators should be able to remote query for what's in their users trust lists and add and remove the trust anchors from their user's trust list. Work is just beginning on such a protocol in the IETF. We seriously hope this protocol emerges much more rapidly than SCVP.

Security

CMS was designed for flexibility. If a new class of algorithm comes along all that needs to be done to support the new class is to define a new content type. For example, authenticated-enveloped data was defined to support authenticated encryption algorithms like AES-GCM and AES-CCM. Therefore, we don't see the need for any major changes to CMS in the near future.

Work on S/MIME will continue as long as algorithms evolve. S/MIME 3.2 won't be the last update.

S/MIME has embraced algorithm agility. It is much more algorithm agile than most protocols. As noted in Chapter 6, parallel signatures are supported by one or more signers. In the near feature, we expect one signer to start applying two signatures: one with SHA-1 and one with SHA-256. To make sure that a downgrade attack isn't performed, which is where an attacker removes the signature applied with the stronger algorithm, the multiple-signatures signed attribute was defined. It protects a signer who applies two signatures in parallel to ensure detection if one of the signatures is removed. The signed attribute is fairly straightforward: every `SignerInfo` includes a pointer to every other `SignerInfo` created by a particular signer. If a multiple-signatures attribute is removed the verifier can detect it because the number of `SignerInfo` doesn't match the expected number of multiple-signatures attributes. This is shown in Figure 12-10.

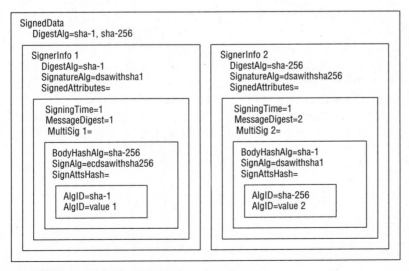

Figure 12-10 Multiple signers signed attribute

There have been numerous attempts to protect email heading information. S/MIME has a mechanism, as does DKIM. We expect more work on this issue.

Tokens

In the next couple of years, feedback on large-scale token deployments will become available. We expect that PCMCIA tokens for end users will disappear and that smart cards and USB tokens will be widely deployed. As the processing power and storage capacity increases on the ICC, we'll see more and more cryptographic operations being performed on the token.

We expect that wireless card readers will become the norm and possibly be included in laptops and desktops natively. This will reduce the wear and tear on tokens from insertions in the reader.

In terms of form factor, there has been some discussion about using cell phones as tokens. You might be wondering why, and the reason is that almost everybody has a cell phone, and they have it with them almost all the time. The processing power of a phone is beyond that of a smart card or USB token. As yet, it is unclear which protocol will be used to get the data to the phone for private key operations. The protocol would need to be secure, so that the phone isn't tricked into using the private key when it shouldn't. Many cell phones support TLS/SSL, so maybe this will be used to secure the protocol. Maybe Bluetooth can be used. Maybe this is a place for proxy certificates. Needless to say, we expect research and innovation in this area.

Physical Access Control

The proximity tokens used for physical access today offer much less security than the PKI-enabled alternatives, such as the NIST PIV card. Today, the proximity transmits its card identifier to the reader mounted by the door, the card identifier is checked against an access control list (ACL), and then, as shown in Figure 12-11, if the card identifier is on the ACL, open the door. The ACL is normally updated on a daily basis. The transmission of the card identifier to the reader occurs over an unsecure radiofrequency. So, one straightforward attack is to record the transmission of a legitimate card, and then simply replay the transmission to gain access at any time in the future.

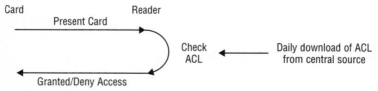

Figure 12-11 Today's card architecture

One important design consideration is latency. The door lock must open quickly for legitimate users. The system will be perceived as broken or worse if legitimate users have a long wait at the door.

PKI-enabled tokens offer two significant improvements. First, revocation of the certificate will deny access to all doors, regardless of the number of controller systems. With today's systems, the revoked user must be removed from the ACLs in each controller system by their individual administrators. Second, a challenge-response protocol is used, completely eliminating the record-and-retransmit attack.

We envision a physical access system based on PKI-enabled tokens with these capabilities:

- Enrollment involves presenting the token to the controller. At this time, the controller validates the certificate, and the card identifier and the certificate are stored in a local database to be revalidated at regular intervals. If the certificate is revoked, this periodic revalidation will detect it. This procedure ensures certificate validity without spending any time on certificate status checking while the user is trying to get in the door.

- The controller provides the card identifiers and public keys to the reader as part of the upgraded ACL structure.

- When a token is presented at the reader, a challenge is generated and transmitted to the token. Next, the token digitally signs the challenge and returns this response to the reader. Then, the reader checks the digital signature with the public key associated with the card identifier. If the signature is valid the door opens; otherwise, it remains locked.

Conclusion

Some of the technologies discussed in this book are considered mature, and some are still young and up and coming. All continue to evolve. We have made some predictions about the new features that will appear in products in the next few years. We've used our Magic 8 Ball; hopefully it's not lying. We're hoping that these technologies emerge sooner rather than later, but only time will tell.

ABNF Primer

The Backus-Naur Form (BNF), first invented by John Backus and later improved by Pater Naur [BNF], is a formal notation that describes the syntax of a language. Many IETF specifications adopted some version of BNF. There's BNF, Extended BNF, and Augmented BNF (ABNF). They all can be used to specify a formal language, because, as the ABNF standard [RFC4234] indicates, "It balances compactness, simplicity with reasonable representational power." We'll focus on ABNF for two reasons. First, because it's used to define email protocols and MIME. Second, it's formally documented.

While we didn't include any ABNF in this book, we figured it was worth giving you a quick primer on the topic in case you actually decided to take a look at the email protocol or MIME references. They are all online and easy to find. The ABNF standard [RFC4234] is relatively short at only 16 pages. We recommend this as the best place to go for more information.

Rules

All rules have names. The names are case-insensitive, and they must begin with alphabetic characters. The rest of the rule name may contain alphanumeric characters and dashes. Angle brackets, composed of the less-than sign (<) and the greater-than sign (>), are optional.

The rules themselves include the *rulename* followed by an equal sign (=), the *elements*, and a CRLF, which is a carriage-return character followed by a line-feed character, not shown. *elements* are either another rule or a string of terminals. Terminals can be printable characters as well as binary, decimal, and hexadecimal values. Some examples are listed next; all of these examples are for the same rule.

```
rulename = elements
RuleName = elements
<rulename> = elements
```

Operators

Like all good computer languages, rules must be able to be operated on, and ABNF does not disappoint. The rules can be:

Combined.   Rules can contain multiple elements. When including multiple elements, which is referred to as *concatenated*, more than one rule is listed after the equal sign. The date rule shown next, from [RFC2822], concatenates the day, month, and year elements.

```
date = day month year
```

ORed.   Rules need to allow for alternative elements, which are indicated by the forward slash (/) used to separate the different alternative elements. The day-name rule shown next, from [RFC2822], offers the three-letter abbreviations of the seven days of the week.

```
day-name = "Mon" / "Tue" / "Wed" / "Thu" / "Fri" / "Sat" / "Sun"
```

Expanded.   Rules can be expanded by using the same rule name followed by the forward slash and equal sign (/=) and the new element or elements. Say that the day-name rule originally only included Monday but was later expanded to include the other days of the week, as shown next.

```
day-name = "Mon"
day-name /= "Tue" / "Wed" / "Thu" / "Fri" / "Sat" / "Sun"
```

Ranged.   Rules can be assigned numeric ranges by using a dash (-). The DIGIT rule shown next, from [RFC4234], restricts the values of DIGIT to the ASCII characters for 0 through 9.

```
DIGIT = %30-39
```

Grouped.   Rules can group elements together using the parenthesis: (and). The carOrTruck rule below evaluates to either sports car or sports utility-vehicle.

```
carOrTruck = sports (car / utility-vehicle)
```

Repeated. Multiple elements are included in one of two ways, referred to as *variable* and *specific repetitions*. Both variable and specific repetitions use the asterisk (*) to indicate the repetition. Variable repetition indicates a minimum and maximum amount of elements. Specific repetition indicates a specific number of elements that must be present. The rules shown next provide two examples. The first example shows variable repetition where there is *either* one or two elements. The second example shows specific repetition where there are *exactly* two elements. The default for the number before the asterisk is zero, and the default for the number following the asterisk is infinity.

```
rulename = 1*2element
rulename = 2element
```

Optioned. Optional elements are enclosed in square brackets: [and]. The `rulename` in the rule shown next requires `this` and `that` be present, but `other` can be omitted. Note that, repetition can be used to do much the same thing by placing `*1` or `0*1` before `other` the element and removing the square brackets.

```
rulename = this that [ other ]
```

Commented. Comments can be added by including a semicolon followed by the comment. If the comment is more than one line long, another semicolon is needed on the second line because the first comment ends `CRLF`.

Operator Precedence

Precedence is assigned to the operators in following order:

1. Strings, Names formation
2. Comment
3. Value range
4. Repetition
5. Grouping, optional
6. Concatenation
7. Alternative

ASN.1 Primer

The reader must have a fundamental understanding of ASN.1 to fully understand the data structures presented in this book, including CMS content types, X.509 certificates, and certificate revocation lists (CRLs). For this reason, we've included this primer as an appendix. We do not attempt to cover ASN.1 completely. Rather, we present just enough material to provide you with an understanding of the data structures presented in this book. For a more complete coverage of ASN.1, we suggest a few sources. Kaliski [KALI93a] provides a tutorial of ASN.1-1988 [X20888] aimed at programmers and standards developers, and it is available online as a Microsoft Word document at `ftp://ftp.rsasecurity.com/pub/pkcs/doc/layman.doc`. Steedman [STEE90] provides a complete discussion of ASN.1-1988. Larmouth [LARM00] provides a complete discussion of ASN.1-1997 [X68097], and he covers ASN.1-1988 as well. We use ASN.1-2003 [X68003] throughout this book. The features we use are identical to those in ASN.1-1997.

Much of the discussion in this appendix is adapted with permission from Kaliski [KALI93a]; we updated the material to conform to ASN.1-2003.

Open Systems Interconnection (OSI, defined in [IS7498]) describes a widely accepted architecture for the interconnection of computers. It defines seven protocol layers, from the physical layer up to the application layer. Abstract Syntax Notation One (ASN.1, defined in [X68003]) is a tool for specifying the syntax of data objects used in the application layer. The semantics of the data elements within the data structures aren't covered by ASN.1; generally, prose is used to specify the semantics. ASN.1 is a flexible notation, permitting the definition of a variety of data types. Simple types, such as integers and bit strings, are provided as primitive types. Structured types, such as sets and sequences, can be constructed from a collection of these primitive types.

ASN.1 encoding is the set of rules for representing data structures as a stream of bits. The output for each type consists of a type identifier, a length, and a value. The Basic Encoding Rules (BER, defined in [X69003]) describe how to represent values of each ASN.1 type as a string of octets. Unfortunately, there is almost always more than one way to BER-encode any given value. BER-encoded objects are not suitable for digital signatures, since the signature will only be valid for one of the legal encodings. This property led to the creation of a subset of BER that only permits a single encoding. This subset is called the Distinguished Encoding Rules (DER).

ASN.1 has two flavors: old and new. The older syntax is specified in ASN.1-1988. The newer syntax emerged in 1993, and updates were published in 1997 and 2003, respectively. The newer syntax is referred to as ASN.1-2003. ASN.1-2003 is used exclusively in this book. Many programming tools are available that support ASN.1-1988, but recently freeware compilers have become available for both ASN.1-1988 and ASN.1-2003. Fortunately, experts can define a data structure in ASN.1-1988 and in ASN.1-2003, such that the resulting DER-encoded output is identical.

Syntax Definition

ASN.1 is a notation for describing abstract types and values. Some types permit a finite number of values; others permit an infinite number of values. ASN.1 has four type classes: simple, structured, tagged, and other. Simple types are primitive; they have no additional components. Structured types have components; they are sets or sequences of other types. Tagged types are derived from any of the other types. Other types are special ones that do not fit in the first three categories; CHOICE and ANY are examples of other types. Types are given names with the ASN.1 assignment operator (::=), and then those names can be used in defining other types.

ASN.1 types, except CHOICE and ANY, have tags. There are four tag classes: universal, application, private, and context-specific.

Universal tags.   These tags are associated with types whose meaning is the same in all applications; these types are only defined in the ASN.1 specification.

Application tags.   These tags are associated with types whose meaning is specific to one application. For example, application tags are used in the specification of directory names. Care must be exercised with these tags;

two different applications may have the same application-specific tag but with completely different meanings.

Private tags. These tags are associated with types whose meaning is specific to a given enterprise. No private tags are used in this book. Context-specific tags are associated with types whose meaning is specific to a given structured type.

Context-specific tags. These tags are used to distinguish components within a set or sequence that would otherwise be indistinguishable. For example, if a sequence includes two optional integer types, a context-specific tag is used to remove ambiguity when an instance only includes one of the optional integers.

Types with universal tags are assigned universal tag numbers. Types with other tags are always obtained by either implicit or explicit tagging.

ASN.1 uses a notation that is very similar to a programming language. Comments start with a pair of hyphens (--). Comments end with another pair of hyphens or at the end of the line. Identifiers must begin with a lowercase letter, and type references must begin with uppercase letters.

Simple Types

Simple types are primitive; they have no additional components. The simple types used in this book are briefly described next.

BIT STRING. This is a string of bits. The length in bits does not have to be a multiple of eight.

BMPString. This is a multilingual string. BMPString is a subtype of UniversalString that models the Basic Multilingual Plane of ISO/IEC 10646-1. This universal type is not part of ASN.1-1988, but most tools that support ASN.1-1988 allow it to be easily added.

BOOLEAN. This is a single bit value, either TRUE or FALSE.

GeneralizedTime. This is a coordinated universal time value, including the date and the time of day. The year is represented with four digits.

IA5String. This is a string of ASCII characters.

INTEGER. This is an integer. The value may be positive, zero, or negative.

NULL. This is a null (or empty) value.

NumericString. This is a string of digits.

OBJECT IDENTIFIER. This is a sequence of integer components that identify an object. Object identifiers are often used to name cryptographic algorithms, attributes, name components, and extensions.

OCTET STRING.   This is a string of octets. The length in bits must be a multiple of eight.

PrintableString.   This is a string of printable characters.

TeletexString.   This is a string of teletext characters.

T61String.   This is a string of T.61 characters. Each character is 8 bits long.

UniversalString.   This is a multilingual string. This universal type is not part of ASN.1-1988, but most tools that support ASN.1-1988 allow it to be easily added.

UTCTime.   This is a coordinated universal time value, including the date and the time of day. The year is represented with two digits; the century digits are omitted.

UTF8String.   This is a multilingual string. The content of this type conforms to RFC 2279. This universal type is not part of ASN.1-1988, but most tools that support ASN.1-1988 allow it to be easily added.

Structured Types

Structured types are those consisting of components. The structured types used in this book are briefly described next.

SEQUENCE.   This is an ordered collection of one or more types. Some or all of the types may be optional.

SEQUENCE OF.   This is an ordered collection of zero or more instances of the same type.

SET.   This is an unordered collection of one or more types. Some or all of the types may be optional.

SET OF.   This is an unordered collection of zero or more instances of the same type.

Implicit and Explicit Tagging

Tagging is commonly used to distinguish component types within a structured type. Often, optional components within a set or sequence are given distinct context-specific tags to avoid ambiguity. There are two ways to tag a type: implicitly and explicitly. Implicitly tagged types are derived from other types by changing the tag of the underlying type. Implicit tags are denoted by [number] IMPLICIT. Explicitly tagged types are derived from other types by adding an additional tag (or prefix tag) to the underlying type. Think of explicitly tagged types as structured types with a single component of the underlying type. Explicit tags are denoted by [number] EXPLICIT.

Explicit tags may be required to avoid ambiguity if the tag of the underlying type is indeterminate. That is, explicit tags may be required if the underlying type is CHOICE or ANY.

CHOICE is another ASN.1 type. The CHOICE type provides a list of alternative types. Only one of the alternative types may be selected for a particular instance.

In ASN.1-1988, the ANY type was used to denote an arbitrary value of an arbitrary type. An object identifier or an integer value was often used to define the syntax within the arbitrary type. In the more recent versions of ASN.1, information object class definitions provide this functionality and also offer a way to include a table of supported values and component relation constraints.

Other Types

Other types in ASN.1 include CHOICE and ANY. The CHOICE type provides a list of alternative types. Only one of the alternative types may be selected for a particular instance. The ANY type denotes an arbitrary value of an arbitrary type. An object identifier or an integer value is often used to define the syntax within the arbitrary type.

Basic Encoding

The ASN.1 Basic Encoding Rules (BER) provide one or more unambiguous ways to represent any ASN.1 value as a stream of octets. BER provides three ways to encode an ASN.1 value, depending on the type and whether the length of the value is known. Simple string types employ any of the methods, but structured types employ either of the constructed methods. The three methods are as follows:

Primitive, definite-length method. This method applies to simple types and implicitly tagged types that are derived from simple types. This method requires that the length of the value be known in advance. Simple nonstring types employ this method.

Constructed, definite-length method. This method applies to simple string types, structured types, implicitly tagged types that are derived from simple string types and structured types, and any explicitly tagged types. This method requires that the length of the value be known in advance.

Constructed, indefinite-length method. This method applies to simple string types, structured types, implicitly tagged types that are derived from simple string types and structured types, and any explicitly tagged types. It does not require that the length of the value be known in advance.

In each method, the BER encoding has three or four parts:

Identifier.   These octets identify the class (universal, application, context-specific, or private), indicate whether the type is primitive or constructed, and include the tag number of the ASN.1 value. If the tag number is between 0 and 30, then the identifier is a single octet.

Length.   For definite-length methods, these octets contain the number of octets within the contents. If the length is between 0 and 127, then the length is a single octet. For the constructed, indefinite-length method, these octets contain a flag (a value of '80' hexadecimal) that indicates that the length is indefinite.

Contents.   For the primitive, definite-length method, these octets contain a representation of the value. For the constructed methods, these octets contain the concatenation of the BER-encoded components.

End-of-contents.   For the constructed, indefinite-length method, these two octets denote the end of the contents. The two octets contain a value of '00 00' hexadecimal. For the other methods, these octets are absent.

Distinguished Encoding Rules

The ASN.1 Distinguished Encoding Rules (DER) are a subset of BER, providing exactly one way to represent any ASN.1 value. DER is intended for applications in which a unique (or distinguished) octet stream encoding is needed. For example, a distinguished octet stream is needed when a digital signature is computed on an ASN.1 value, such as the CMS signed attributes or the contents of an X.509 certificate. DER was originally defined in Section 8.7 of [X50988], but DER is now defined in [X69003].

DER requires that definite-length encoding always be used. When the length is between 0 and 127, the length must be encoded as a single octet. When the length is 128 or greater, the length must be encoded in the minimum number of octets. For simple string types and implicitly tagged types that are derived from simple string types, the primitive, definite-length method must be employed. For structured types, implicitly tagged types that are derived from structured types, and any explicitly tagged types, the constructed, definite-length method must be employed.

Other restrictions are defined for particular types. These rules ensure that there is only one way to encode any ASN.1 value. In general, the fewest possible number of octets is used to represent the value using definite-length encoding.

MIME Primer

The reader must have a fundamental understanding of Multipurpose Internet Mail Extensions (MIME) to fully understand the email and S/MIME data structures presented in this book. For this reason, we include this primer as an appendix. We do not attempt to cover MIME completely; rather, we present just enough material to understand the data structures presented in this book. For a more complete coverage of MIME, we suggest Marshall Rose's *The Internet Message* [MR]. Rose provides a more detailed look at the syntax of MIME, and he also addresses rendering and storage issues. MIME is based on a series of five RFCs:

MIME Part One: Format of Internet Message Bodies. [RFC2045].

MIME Part Two: Media Types. [RFC2046].

MIME Part Three: Message Header Extensions for Non-ASCII Text. [RFC2047].

MIME Part Four: Media Type specification and Registration Procedures. [RFC2048].

MIME Part Five: Conformance Criteria and Examples. [RFC2049].

In these five RFCs, MIME defines support for four important concepts:

1. Character sets other than US-ASCII in text messages.

2. Different formats for non-text messages.

3. Multipart message bodies.

4. Character sets other than US-ASCII in text headers.

The four concepts are intertwined. For example, you can't support additional character sets without a new header to indicate the character set, and you also need a new transfer encoding scheme to convey the characters. We'll skip discussions about registration and conformance criteria and cover the four main concepts: character sets, transfer encodings, MIME types, and multipart messages. But first, email messages that include MIME indicate their support with the `MIME-Version` email heading field. Version 1.0 is the only defined value.

Character Sets

Character sets are actually quite a complicated subject. Think about all the languages in the world and then think about every single character needed to write those languages. Needless to say there are thousands of characters, numbers, and punctuation marks. A few things need to be done to support multiple character sets:

Collect characters for character set.   The individual characters need to be collected in order to recognize what the character set. The most famous one is the printable portion of the US ASCII character set.

Punctuation marks.   !''#$%&'()*+,-./:;<=>?@[\]^_'{|}~ and space

Digits.   0–9

Characters.   a–z and A–Z

Register character set.   This value will be used in the protocol to indicate which character set is being used.

Assign characters a value.   Characters are not transmitted; rather binary representations of them are transmitted. The US ASCII table includes 128 entries, there are also nonprintable characters. For example, the space has a decimal value of 32, and tilda (~) has a decimal value of 126. In binary, you only need 7 bits to encode these values — hence the name 7bit encoding. If you've got more characters you're going to need more bits.

Determine character's transfer encoding.   Determine the character's encoding based on the supported transport mechanism, which we'll get in to in the next section.

Indicate character set in message.   An indication is needed for the recipient so that their MUA will know how to process the character set, which we'll get into in the content type section.

Transfer Encoding

Email messages traverse the Internet. Because the Internet has evolved over time, it should come as no surprise that it is not a uniform network and there are multiple mechanisms to transport email messages. MIME acknowledged this by defining the `Content-Transfer-Encoding` email heading extension. It indicates one of five transfer encodings:

7bit. `7bit` is the default and indicates that the data is represented with lines of 998 octets or less. Each line is separated by a sequence of carriage return and line feed characters (CRLF). Carriage return (CR) and line feed (LF) are only allowed as part of the CRLF. Null characters are not allowed. Each octet must have a decimal value less than 127.

8bit. `8bit` is the same as `7bit`, except that octets may have a decimal value larger than 127, up to 255.

binary. `binary` allows arbitrary octets to be transferred, including an octet of all zero bits.

quoted-printable. `quoted-printable` allows 8-bit octets to be conveyed over 7-bit transport via a conversion process. The mechanism is relatively simple: an equal sign (=) followed by hexadecimal representation from the character table. For example, the British Pound sign (£) is represent by =A3, where the decimal value of 163 is converted to hexadecimal A3. The US ASCII characters are represented by themselves, except for tab and space. There are also special rules for line breaks, as well as tab and the space that appears at the end of lines. Lines are limited to 76 characters.

base64. `base64`, like `quoted-printable`, allows 8-bit octets to conveyed over 7-bit transport via a conversion process; this conversion process is different from the `quoted-printable` conversion process. The process converts arbitrary data to the base64 encoding, and all you need to know is how to convert from the string of characters to binary and back again. We'll use an US ASCII example: convert each character to decimal value from the standard US ASCII table, convert each character's decimal value to binary, take 6 bits, convert to decimal, do a base64 table lookup, and assign a base64 encoding value (from RFC2035). In Figure C-1, the original text is "S/MIME" and the base64-encoded value is "Uy9NSU3F".

x-token. `x-token` allows private non-standard transfer encodings.

Text	S/MIME
Convert to character to decimal value from ASCII Table	S converts to 83 / converts to 47 M converts to 77 I converts to 73 M converts to 77 E converts to 69
Convert each charcter's decimal value to binary	010100110010111101001101010010010100110101000101
Convert to base64: Take 6 bits, convert to decimal, assign encoding from base64 table	010100 converts to U 110010 converts to y 111101 converts to 9 001101 converts to N 010010 converts to S 010100 converts to U 110101 converts to 3 000101 converts to F

Figure C-1 Base64 encoding example

Content Type

To support more than just text in email messages, there needs to be a mechanism to indicate the type of the message content. MIME defines what it refers to as MIME types or content types. The Content-Type email heading has three parts:

1. **type:** This indicates the MIME media type or the general type of data. It is either a discrete-type or a composite-type. The composite-type is either message or multipart, which we'll discuss in the next section. The discrete-type content types are opaque as far as MIME is concerned. Some examples are:

    Content-type: application. This is the catch-all type for content that don't fit in another category. The content must be processed by an application, which is specified by the sub-type, before it is useful to the user.

    Content-type: audio. This indicates that the content type contains audio data.

    Content-type: image. This indicates that the content type contains image data.

    Content-type: message. This indicates that the content type contains message data.

    Content-type: text. This indicates that the content type contains text data.

Content-type: video. This indicates that the content type has video
  data.

2. **sub-type:** This indicates the subtype of the MIME media type or the
   specific format for the data. It is required, and it follows the content type
   and a forward slash (/). Some examples, which include the type, are:

   ```
   Content-type: application/pkcs7-mime
   Content-type: application/pkcs7-signature
   Content-type: audio/basic
   Content-type: image/jpeg
   Content-type: message/rfc822
   Content-type: text/plain
   Content-type: video/mpeg
   ```

3. **parameters:** Indicates additional information about the sub-type. Some
   examples are:

   ```
   Content-type: text/plain; charset=us-ascii
   Content-type: application/pkcs7-mime; smime-type=enveloped-data;
   name=p7m
   Content-type: application/pkcs7-mime; smime-type=signed-data; name=p7m
   ```

Listing C-1 provides a complete example that includes many of the EHLO
commands discussed in this book and a Multipart Message and discrete-type
data.

```
S: 220 pleasantville.ca.us
C: EHLO washington.dc.us
S: 250-pleasantville.ca.us greets washington.dc.us
S: 250-8BITMIME
S: 250-SIZE
S: 250-DSN
S: 250 HELP
S: 250 AUTH CRAM-MD5
C: AUTH CRAM-MD5
S: 334 PENCeUxFREJoU0NnbmhNWitOMjNGNndAZWx3b29kLmlubm9zb2Z0LmNvbT4=
C: ZnJlZCA5ZTk1YWVlMDljNDBhZzJiODRhMGMyYjNiYmFlNzg2ZQ==
S: 235 Authentication successful
C: MAIL FROM: <aadams@washington.dc.us>
S: 250 sender <aadams@washington.dc.us> OK
C: RCPT TO:<bburton@pleasantville.ca.us>
S: 250 recipient <bburton@pleasantville.ca.us> OK
C: RCPT TO:<mrogers@pleasantville.ca.us>
S: 250 recipient <mrogers@pleasantville.ca.us> OK
C: DATA
S: 354 Start mail input; end with <CRLF>.<CRLF>
C: Date: Mon, 11 Feb 2008 09:55:06 -0400
C: MIME Version: 1.0
```

Listing C-1 Signed-Only Message Example

```
C: From: Alice <aadams@washington.dc.us>
C: Subject: Meeting Date and Time
C: To: Bob <bburton@pleasantville.ca.us>
C: Cc: Matt <mrogers@pleasantville.ca.us>
C: Message-ID: <1234@washington.dc.us>

Content-Type: application/pkcs7-mime; smime-type=signed-data;
  name=smime.p7m
Content-Transfer-Encoding: base64
Content-Disposition: attachment; filename=smime.p7m

567GhIGfHfYT6ghyHhHUujpfyF4f8HHGTrfvhJhjH776tbB9HG4VQbnj7
77n8HHGT9HG4VQpfyF467GhIGfHfYT6rfvbnj756tbBghyHhHUujhJhjH
HUujhJh4VQpfyF467GhIGfHfYGTrfvbnjT6jH7756tbB9H7n8HHGghyHh
6YT64V0GhIGfHfQbnj75
C: .
S: OK
C: QUIT
S: 221 pleasantville.ca.us closing transmission channel
```

Listing C-1 (*continued*)

Multipart Messages

There are a plethora of content types, and more are registered every year. So it's obvious that there needs to be a way of conveying more than one content type at a time. Otherwise, you would need messages to send a portable document format (PDF) file of the contract and the note to say when it needs to be returned. The `multipart` `composite-type` fulfills this need. One additional part that is required is a mechanism to indicate where each content type begins and ends. The boundary parameter indicates the start and end of each content type within the message. Listing C-2 provides a complete example that includes many of the EHLO commands discussed in this book and a Multipart Message:

```
S: 220 pleasantville.ca.us
C: EHLO washington.dc.us
S: 250-pleasantville.ca.us greets washington.dc.us
S: 250-8BITMIME
S: 250-SIZE
S: 250-DSN
S: 250 HELP
```

Listing C-2 Multipart-Signed Example

```
S: 250 AUTH CRAM-MD5
C: AUTH CRAM-MD5
S: 334 PENCeUxFREJoU0NnbmhNWitOMjNGNndAZWx3b29kLmlubm9zb2Z0LmNvbT4=
C: ZnJlZCA5ZTk1YWVlMDljNDBhZjJiODRhMGMyYjNiYmFlNzg2ZQ==
S: 235 Authentication successful
C: MAIL FROM: <aadams@washington.dc.us>
S: 250 sender <aadams@washington.dc.us> OK
C: RCPT TO:<bburton@pleasantville.ca.us>
S: 250 recipient <bburton@pleasantville.ca.us> OK
C: RCPT TO:<mrogers@pleasantville.ca.us>
S: 250 recipient <mrogers@pleasantville.ca.us> OK
C: DATA
S: 354 Start mail input; end with <CRLF>.<CRLF>
C: Date: Mon, 11 Feb 2008 09:55:06 -0400
C: MIME Version: 1.0
C: From: Alice <aadams@washington.dc.us>
C: Subject: Meeting Date and Time
C: To: Bob <bburton@pleasantville.ca.us>
C: Cc: Matt <mrogers@pleasantville.ca.us>
C: Message-ID: <1234@washington.dc.us>

Content-Type: multipart/signed;
  protocol="application/pkcs7-signature";
  micalg=sha256; boundary=HereIsTheBoundary

--HereIsTheBoundary
Content-Type: text/plain

This is a clear-signed message.

--HereIsTheBoundary
Content-Type: application/pkcs7-signature; name=smime.p7s
Content-Transfer-Encoding: base64
Content-Disposition: attachment; filename=smime.p7s

ghyHhHUujhJhjH77n8HHGTrfvbnj756tbB9HG4VQpfyF467GhIGfHfYT6
4VQpfyF467GhIGfHfYT6jH77n8HHGghyHhHUujhJh756tbB9HGTrfvbnj
n8HHGTrfvhJhjH776tbB9HG4VQbnj7567GhIGfHfYT6ghyHhHUujpfyF4
7GhIGfHfYT64VQbnj756

--HereIsTheBoundary--
C: .
S: OK
C: QUIT
S: 221 pleasantville.ca.us closing transmission channel
```

Listing C-2 (*continued*)

RFC Summaries

We reference over 80 RFCs in this book and we thought it would be useful to summarize them. We don't note the RFC track, but remember that there are three of them: information, standards, and experimental. Many of these summaries are taken from the RFC's abstract section. The following standards-track RFCs are referenced in this book:

RFC 768 – User Datagram Protocol.   This RFC defines the User Datagram Protocol (UDP). UDP is a transaction-oriented (sometimes referred to as datagram-oriented) transport layer protocol. UDP provides no reliability, and it provides no guarantee of ordering. As a result, packets can be dropped, duplicated, or arrive out of order. UDP assumes that the Internet Protocol (IP) is used as the underlying protocol. It's used by network applications like the Domain Name System (DNS) and Voice over IP (VoIP), which require speed more than reliability.

RFC 791 – Internet Protocol.   This RFC defines the Internet Protocol (IP). While this remains the workhorse of the Internet, a new version has been specified. RFC 791 specifies IPv4, and the new version is IPv6. IPv5 was never really deployed. IPv4 is an unreliable, connectionless, transaction-oriented network layer protocol. IPv4 also provides an addressing scheme that identifies sources and destinations for the packets.

RFC 793 – Transmission Control Protocol.   This RFC defines the Transmission Control Protocol (TCP). TCP is a connection-oriented transport layer protocol. Unlike UDP, TCP provides a reliable service that guarantees packet ordering. This protocol assumes that the IP is used as the underlying protocol. It's used by applications like email, the File Transfer Protocol (FTP), and the Hypertext Transfer Protocol (HTTP).

RFC 1035 – Domain Names – Implementation and Specification.   This RFC defines the Domain Name System (DNS). The DNS is the system that resolves domain names (e.g., `www.ieca.com`) into an IP address (e.g., 196.196.0.0).

RFC 1321 – The MD5 Message-Digest Algorithm.   This RFC describes the MD5 message-digest algorithm. MD5 returns a 128-bit message digest or hash regardless of the size of the input message.

RFC 1421 – Privacy Enhancement for Internet Electronic Mail: Part I: Message Encryption and Authentication Procedures.   This RFC, which is the first in a set of four Privacy Enhanced Mail (PEM) RFCs, defines the PEM message encryption and authentication procedures.

RFC 1422 – Privacy Enhancement for Internet Electronic Mail: Part II: Certificate-Based Key Management.   This RFC, which is the second in a set of four PEM RFCs, specifies PEM key management mechanisms based on public key certificates.

RFC 1423 – Privacy Enhancement for Internet Electronic Mail: Part III: Algorithms, Modes. And Identifiers.   This RFC, which is the third in a set of four PEM RFCs, specifies algorithms, modes, and associated identifiers used when processing PEM messages.

RFC 1424 - Privacy Enhancement for Internet Electronic Mail: Part IV: Key Certification and Related Services.   This RFC, which is the last in a set of four PEM RFCs, specifies services used in conjunction with the key management infrastructure, including conventions for certificate requests.

RFC 1459 – Internet Relay Chat.   This RFC defines the Internet Relay Chat (IRC) protocol. The IRC is a text-based protocol that allows users to "chat" among themselves. It is a client-server-based protocol.

RFC 1652 – SMTP Service Extensions for 8bit-MIMEtransport.   This RFC defines the 8BITTIME extension to the Simple Mail Transport Protocol (SMTP) service. The extension indicates that server supports SMTP content bodies that include arbitrary lines of octet-aligned material, including characters outside of the US-ASCII octet range.

RFC 1847 – Security Multiparts for MIME: Multipart/Signed and 0 Multipart/Encrypted.   This RFC defines two subtypes of the `multipart` content type: `signed` and `encrypted`. The `multipart/signed` and `multipart/encrypted` content types support the application of security services to Multipurpose Internet Mail Extension (MIME) body parts. Both `multipart/signed` and `multipart/encrypted` have two body parts: one for the protected data and one for the control information that is needed to remove the protection.

RFC 1848 – MIME Object Security Services.   This RFC defines the MIME Object Security Services (MOSS), which is a protocol that uses the two content subtypes from RFC 1847, to support digital signature and encryption services.

RFC 1854 – SMTP Service Extensions for Command Pipelining.   This RFC defines the `PIPELINIG` extension to the SMTP service. The extension indicates that server supports the ability to accept multiple SMTP commands in a single TCP send operation.

RFC 1869 – SMTP Service Extensions.   This RFC defines the `EHLO` extension to the SMTP service and responses to it. The extension allows the client to indicate that it supports SMTP service extensions. The server then responds with the SMTP service extension(s) that it supports.

RFC 1870 – SMTP Service Extension for Message Size Declaration.   This RFC defines the `SIZE` extension to the SMTP service. The extension indicates the maximum message size the server is willing to support.

RFC 1891 – SMTP Service Extension for Delivery Status Notifications.   This RFC defines the `DSN` extension to the SMTP service. It also defines two optional parameters for the `RCPT` command, `NOTIFY` and `ORCPT`, and two optional parameters for the `MAIL` command, `RET` and `ENVID`. The extension indicates the server supports Delivery Service Notifications (DSNs), which indicate whether or not the message was delivered to the destination MTA. `NOTIFY` indicates whether success, failure, or both; `ORCPT` indicates the originators address; `RET` indicates whether upon failure the entire message or just the headers should be returned; `ENVID` propagates an identifier known to the sender for correlation with any returned DSNs.

RFC 1939 – Post Office Protocol – Version 3.   This RFC documents the Post Office Protocol (POP) version 3 (commonly called POP3). SMTP clients use POP3 to retrieve their email messages from SMTP servers. It does not provide a mechanism to manage the mailbox. POP3 supports deleting email after retrieval, retaining email permanently on the server, or deleting the email after a specified time.

RFC 1991 – PGP Message Exchange Formats.   This RFC defines the Pretty Good Privacy (PGP) security protocol and associated procedures. PGP supports confidentiality and digital signature services for email message content.

RFC 2045 – Multipurpose Internet Mail Extensions (MIME) Part One: Format of Internet Message Bodies.   This RFC, which is the first in a set of five MIME RFCs, defines the structure of MIME message bodies. The RFC includes: MIME header definitions using Augment Backus-Naur Form (ABNF), 7-bit, 8-bit, and binary transport procedures; and BASE64 content transfer encoding scheme. Note that Appendix C contains more information on the MIME content transfer encoding.

RFC 2046 – Multipurpose Internet Mail Extensions (MIME) Part Two: Media Types.   This RFC, which is the second in a set of five MIME RFCs, specifies the `content-type` MIME header's media types. Five discrete top-level media types are defined: `text`, `image`, `audio`, `video`, and `application`. Two composite top-level media types are defined: `multipart` and `message`.

RFC 2047 – MIME (Multipurpose Internet Mail Extensions) Part Three: Message Header Extensions for Non-ASCII Text.   This RFC, which is the third in a set of five MIME RFCs, describes extensions to SMTP to allow non-US-ASCII text data in email header fields.

RFC 2048 – Multipurpose Internet Mail Extensions (MIME) Part Four: Registration Procedures.   This RFC, which is the fourth in a set of five MIME RFCs, specifies the Internet Assigned Numbers Authority (IANA) registration procedures for MIME-related facilities. These procedures are used to register new MIME types and subtypes.

RFC 2049 – Multipurpose Internet Mail Extensions (MIME) Part Five: Conformance Criteria and Examples.   This RFC, which is the last in a set of five MIME RFCs, describes MIME conformance criteria and provides examples of MIME message formats.

RFC 2104 – HMAC: Keyed-Hashing for Message Authentication.   This RFC defines the Hash Message Authentication Code (HMAC) algorithm. It uses any one-way hash function (e.g., SHA-256) and a secret key to compute a message authentication code (MAC).

RFC 2131 – Dynamic Host Configuration Protocol.   This RFC defines the Dynamic Host Configuration Protocol (DHCP). DHCP is a client-server protocol that allows clients to obtain IP addresses from a server. This dynamic allocation allows service providers to give clients IP addresses for a period of time as opposed to permanently.

RFC 2195 – IMAP/POP AUTHorize Extensions for Simple Challenge/ Response.   This RFC defines the `AUTH` extension to the POP3 service. The extension allows the client to indicate that it wishes to perform two-way authentication with the server using the prescribed mechanism. The Challenge Response Authentication Mechanism (CRAM) MD5 (commonly called CRAM-MD5) mechanism is defined in this RFC.

RFC 2246 – The TLS Protocol Version 1.0. This RFC defines the Transport Layer Security (TLS) protocol version 1.0. This client-server protocol allows servers to authenticate themselves to clients, and it allows clients and servers to mutually authenticate each other. TLS also provides an encrypted and integrity-protected session between the client and server.

RFC 2311 – S/MIME Version 2 Message Specification. This RFC defines the Secure MIME (S/MIME) version 2 format for message specification. It defines the protocol to convey digital signatures and encryption services as well as the process to create a protected MIME body part.

RFC 2315 – PKCS #7: Cryptographic Message Syntax Version 1.5. This RFC defines PKCS #7 version 1.5. PKCS #7 is a general-purpose syntax for cryptographic protection of data, including digital signatures and encryption. It supports an enveloping scheme that allows the protecting content types to be nested inside another. Attributes can also be applied to some of the content types to support additional services.

RFC 2407 – The Internet IP Security Domain of Interpretation for ISAKMP. This RFC defines the Internet IP Security (IPsec) Domain of Interpretation (DOI). The IPsec DOI instantiates the Internet Security Association and Key Management Protocol (ISAKMP) for use with IP when ISAKMP is used to negotiate security associations.

RFC 2408 – Internet Security Association and Key Management Protocol (ISAKMP). This RFC defines the Internet Security Association and Key Management Protocol (ISAKMP), which defines the authentication procedures for communicating peers, creation and management of security associations, key generation techniques, and threat mitigation.

RFC 2409 – The Internet Key Exchange (IKE). This RFC defines the Internet Key Exchange (IKE) protocol. IKE is used in conjunction with ISAKMP to obtain authenticated keying material for use with ISAKMP. It is also used in the IPsec DOI for to establish security associations used by other IPsec protocols, especially Authentication Header (AH) and Encapsulating Security Payload (ESP).

RFC 2412 – The OAKLEY Key Determination Protocol. This RFC defines the OAKLEY key establishment algorithm. OAKLEY allows two authenticated parties to agree on secure and secret keying material.

RFC 2554 – SMTP Service Extension for Authentication. This RFC defines the AUTH extension to the SMTP service. The extension allows the client to indicate that it wishes to perform two-way authentication with the server using the prescribed mechanism. It supports the CRAM-MD5 mechanism from RFC 2195.

RFC 2560 – X.509 Internet Public Key Infrastructure Online Certificate Status Protocol – OCSP. This RFC defines the Online Certificate Status Protocol (OCSP). OCSP is a client-server protocol that allows the client to query the server on the status of a digital certificate without requiring the client to process CRLs.

RFC 2595 – Using TLS with IMAP, POP3, and ACAP. This RFC defines the "STARTTLS" extension to the Internet Mail Access Protocol (IMAP), the Application Configuration Access Protocol (ACAP), and POP3 services. In POP3, the STLS extension allows the client to indicate that it wishes to use TLS when communicating with the server.

RFC 2630 – Cryptographic Message Syntax. This RFC defines the Cryptographic Message Syntax (CMS), and it is the successor to PKCS#7 version 1.5. CMS provides a general-purpose syntax for the cryptographic protection of data, including digital signatures and encryption. It supports an enveloping scheme that allows the protecting content types to be nested inside another. Attributes can also be applied to some of the content types to support additional services.

RFC 2632 – S/MIME Version 3 Certificate Handling. This RFC specifies the certificate formats and certificate-processing rules to be used with S/MIME version 3.

RFC 2633 – S/MIME Version 3 Message Specification. This RFC specifies S/MIME version 3. It makes RFC 2311 obsolete.

RFC 2634 – Enhanced Security Services for S/MIME. This RFC defines four additional services for S/MIME. Additional content types and attributes are defined to support signed receipts, security labels, secure mailing lists, and signing certificates.

RFC 2810 – Internet Relay Chat: Architecture. This RFC documents the Internet Relay Chat (IRC) architecture as of 2000.

RFC 2811 – Internet Relay Chat: Channel Management. This RFC defines the IRC channel mechanism, which allows multiple users to communicate in a forum. This RFC specifies how channels, their characteristics, and their properties are managed by IRC servers.

RFC 2812 – Internet Relay Chat: Client Protocol. This RFC defines the IRC client protocol. IRC is a simple text-based conferencing client-server protocol.

RFC 2821 – Simple Mail Transfer Protocol. This RFC defines the protocol electronic mail transport. It defines SMTP commands and the responses that are used by SMTP clients and servers.

RFC 2822 – Internet Message Format. This RFC defines the syntax for the electronic mail transported with the SMTP. Header fields like TO, FROM, and SUBJECT are defined, along with supported characters.

RFC 2831 – Using Digest Authentication as a SASL Mechanism. This RFC defines to use the HTTP Digest Authentication mechanism with the Simple Authentication and Security Layer (SASL). It's an improvement over the CRAM-MD5 mechanism.

RFC 3114 – Implementing Company Classification Policy with the S/MIME Security Label. This RFC explains how a company's security policy for data classification might be mapped to the S/MIME ESS security label. Multiple examples are provided.

RFC 3161 – Internet X.509 Public Key Infrastructure Time-Stamp Protocol (TSP). This RFC defines the Time-Stamp Protocol (TSP). The TSP is client-server protocol that allows the client to request that a server attest to a piece of data existence at a given time.

RFC 3207 – SMTP Service Extensions for Secure SMTP over Transport Layer Security. This RFC defines the STARTTLS extension to the SMTP services. The STARTTLS extension allows the client to indicate that it wishes to use TLS when communicating with the server.

RFC 3274 – Compressed Data Content Type for Cryptographic Message Syntax (CMS). This RFC defines the compress-data content type. This content type can be used to compress encapsulated data.

RFC 3280 – Internet X.509 Public Key Infrastructure Certificate and Certificate Revocation List (CRL) Profile. This RFC defines the Internet profile for X.509 certificates and CRLs. It includes requirements on format and processing of X.509 certificates and CRLs.

RFC 3281 – An Internet Attribute Certificate Profile for Authorization. This RFC defines the Internet profile for X.509 attribute certificates. It includes requirements on format and processing of attribute certificates.

RFC 3370 – Cryptographic Message Syntax (CMS) Algorithms. This RFC documents the algorithms, their identifiers, and their use with the CMS.

RFC 3447 – Public-Key Cryptographic Standards (PKCS) #1: RSA Cryptography Specifications Version 2.1. This RFC defines the recommended implementation for public key cryptography based on the RSA algorithm. RSA is most often used as specified in PKCS#1 version 1.5, and that information in repeated in this document, but it also provides alternatives that are likely to be widely adopted in the future.

RFC 3546 – Transport Layer Security (TLS) Extensions. This RFC defines extensions to the TLS protocol that may be used to add functionality.

RFC 3566 – The AES-XCBC-MAC-96 Algorithm and Its Use With IPsec.
This RFC defines the use of the AES-XCBC-MAC-96 algorithm. This algorithm is used to secure messages of varying lengths. It is especially useful in the IPsec AH and ESP protocols.

RFC 3647 – Internet X.509 Public Key Infrastructure Certificate Policy and Certification Practices Framework. This RFC provides a framework that writers of certificate policies and certificate practice statements can use to develop better certificate policies and certificate practice statements. With a common framework it's easier to evaluate certificate policies and certificate practice statements.

RFC 3820 – Internet X.509 Public Key Infrastructure (PKI) Proxy Certificate Profile. This RFC defines a certificate profile for Proxy certificates. Proxy certificates, which are based on X.509 public key certificates, allow an end entity to delegate some or all of its rights to another entity allowing that entity to act as if it were the delegating entity.

RFC 3851 – Secure Multipurpose Internet Mail Extensions (S/MIME) Version 3.1 Message Specification. This RFC specifies S/MIME version 3.1. This RFC makes RFC 2633 obsolete.

RFC 3852 – Cryptographic Message Syntax (CMS). This RFC defines the Cryptographic Message Syntax (CMS). This RFC makes RFC 2630 obsolete.

RFC 3920 – Extensible Messaging and Presence Protocol (XMPP): Core.
This RFC defines the Extensible Messaging and Presence Protocol (XMPP). The XMPP is a close-to-real-time protocol that supports streaming Extensible Markup Language (XML) elements in order to exchange structured information between any two network endpoints.

RFC 3921 – Extensible Messaging and Presence Protocol (XMPP): Instant Messaging and Presence. This RFC defines extensions to the XMPP. These extensions provide basic instant messaging and presence functionality.

RFC 3922 – Mapping Extensible Messaging and Presence Protocol (XMPP) to Common Presence and Instant Messaging (CPIM). This RFC defines a mapping between the Common Presences and Instant Messaging (CPIM) specification and the XMPP.

RFC 3923 – End-to-End Signing and Object Encryption for the Extensible Messaging and Presence Protocol (XMPP). This RFC defines the mechanisms to sign and encrypt XMPP exchanges. It is based on CMS.

RFC 4073 – Protecting Multiple Contents with the Cryptographic Message Syntax (CMS). This RFC defines the content-with-attributes and content-collection content types. The content-with-attributes content type can be used to add attributes to any other content type. The content-collection content type can be used to collect more than one content type together.

RFC 4234 – Augmented BNF for Syntax Specifications: ABNF.   This RFC defines the Augmented Backus-Naur Form (ABNF). ABNF is a formal notation that describes the syntax of a language. It is used to specify the syntax of many IETF protocols.

RFC 4262 – X.509 Certificate Extension for Multipurpose Internet Mail Extensions (S/MIME) Capabilities.   This RFC defines the S/MIME capabilities certificate extension. This extension indicates the S/MIME capabilities of the certificate's subject.

RFC 4301 – Security Architecture for the Internet Protocol.   This RFC describes the Security Architecture for IP. It makes RFC 2401 obsolete.

RFC 4302 – IP Authentication Header.   The RFC defines the IP Authentication Header (AH). The AH provides authentication services in both IPv4 and IPv6.

RFC 4303 – IP Encapsulating Security Payload (ESP).   This RFC defines the Encapsulating Security Payload (ESP). The ESP provides confidentiality, data origin authentication, connectionless integrity, an anti-replay service, and limited traffic flow confidentiality in both IPv4 and IPv6.

RFC 4305 – Cryptographic Algorithm Implementation Requirements for Encapsulating Security Payload (ESP) and Authentication Header (AH).   This RFC defines the mandatory-to-implement algorithms in ESP and AH. This RFC makes RFCs 2404 and 2406 obsolete.

RFC 4306 – Internet Key Exchange (IKEv2) Protocol.   This RFC defines IKE v2. This RFC makes RFCs 2407, 2408, and 2409 obsolete.

RFC 4307 – Cryptographic Algorithms for Use in the Internet Key Exchange Version 2 (IKEv2).   This RFC defines the mandatory-to-implement algorithms for IKEv2.

RFC 4346 – The Transport Layer Security (TLS) Protocol Version 1.1.   This RFC defines the Transport Layer Security (TLS) protocol version 1.1. This client-server protocol allows servers to authenticate themselves to clients, and it allows clients and servers to mutually authenticate each other. TLS also provides for encrypted links between the client and server. This RFC makes RFC 2246 obsolete.

RFC 4347 – Datagram Transport Layer Security.   This RFC defines the Datagram Transport Layer Security (DTLS) protocol. The DTLP is a client-server protocol that provides communications privacy for datagram protocols. It's based on TLS and provides similar security services without requiring a reliable transport protocol like TCP.

RFC 4366 – Transport Layer Security (TLS) Extensions.   This RFC defines extensions to the TLS protocol that may be used to add functionality. It makes RFC 4366 obsolete.

RFC 4406 – Sender ID: Authenticating Email.   This RFC defines a mechanism that allows receiving Mail Transfer Agents (MTAs), Mail Delivery Agents (MDAs), and/or Mail User Agents (MUAs) to determine whether the received message was used with the permission of the owner of the domain contained in that email address.

RFC 4408 – Sender Policy Framework (SPF) for Authorizing User of Domains in Email, Version 1.   This RFC defines the Sender Policy Framework (SPF) protocol. The SPF protocol allows a domain to explicitly authorize hosts that are allowed to use its domain name. The SPF protocol also allows a receiving host to check these authorizations.

RFC 4870 – Domain-Based Email Authentication Using Public Keys Advertized in the DNS (DomainKey).   This RFC defines a mechanism that permits emails to be signed on a per-domain basis. With this mechanism, receiving MTAs can determine whether the mail originated in a domain or whether the headers have been spoofed.

RFC 4871 – DomainKeys Identified Mail (DKIM) Signatures.   This RFC defines the DomainKeys Identified Mail (DKIM) signature mechanism. DKIM is a mechanism that allows domains to apply a digital signature over the email message headers. Receiving MTAs and MUAs can then use this digital signature to determine whether the email message came from an authorized domain.

RFC 4880 – OpenPGP Message Format.   This RFC defines the Open Pretty Good Privacy (PGP) message format. It makes RFC 1991 obsolete.

RFC 5023 – The Atom Publishing Protocol.   This RFC defines the Atom Publishing (AtomPub) Protocol. AtomPub is protocol that is used to publish and edit Web resources.

RFC 5035 – Enhanced Security Services (ESS) Update: Adding CertID Algorithm Agility.   This RFC defines an update to the ESS `CertID` structure. ESS certificate identifiers originally only supported SHA-1, but this update allows for hash algorithm agility.

RFC 5055 – Server-Based Certificate Validation Protocol (SCVP).   This RFC defines the Server-Based Certificate Validation Protocol (SCVP). SCVP is a client-server protocol that allows a client to delegate certification path construction and certification path validation to a server.

RFC 5083 – Cryptographic Message Syntax (CMS) Authenticated-Enveloped-Data Content Type.   This RFC defines the authenticated-enveloped-data content type. This content type is defined for use with authenticated encryption algorithms.

References

Chapter 2

[IANAM] www.iana.org/assignments/mail-parameters
[ISOC00] www.isoc.org/internet/history/brief.shtml
[RFC0791] www.ietf.org/rfc/rfc791.txt
[RFC0793] www.ietf.org/rfc/rfc793.txt
[RFC1035] www.ietf.org/rfc/rfc1035.txt
[RFC1652] www.ietf.org/rfc/rfc1652.txt
[RFC1854] www.ietf.org/rfc/rfc1854.txt
[RFC1869] www.ietf.org/rfc/rfc1869.txt
[RFC1870] www.ietf.org/rfc/rfc1870.txt
[RFC1891] www.ietf.org/rfc/rfc1891.txt
[RFC1939] www.ietf.org/rfc/rfc1939.txt
[RFC2045] www.ietf.org/rfc/rfc2045.txt
[RFC2046] www.ietf.org/rfc/rfc2046.txt
[RFC2047] www.ietf.org/rfc/rfc2047.txt
[RFC2048] www.ietf.org/rfc/rfc2048.txt
[RFC2049] www.ietf.org/rfc/rfc2049.txt
[RFC2131] www.ietf.org/rfc/rfc2131.txt
[RFC2821] www.ietf.org/rfc/rfc2821.txt
[RFC2822] www.ietf.org/rfc/rfc2822.txt
[ROSE92] Rose, Marshall, *The Internet Message: Closing the Book With Electronic Mail*. New York: Prentice Hall, 1992, ISBN 978-0130929419.

Chapter 3

[ASSESS] Landoll, Douglas J., *Performing an Information Security Risk Assessment*. Boca Rotan, FL: CRC, 2005, ISBN 978-0849329982.
[BROWN] http://i.a.cnn.net/cnn/2005/images/11/03/brown.emails.pdf
[DOJ] http://www.usdoj.gov/usao/gan/press/2006/07-05-06.pdf
[HP] http://www.msnbc.msn.com/id/14687677/site/newsweek
[HACK] Beaver, Kevin and Stuart McClure. *Hacking For Dummies,* 2nd Edition, Hoboken, NJ: Wiley, 2007, ISBN 978-0-470-05235-8.

[IDTHFT] Collins, Judith M., *Investigating Identity Theft: A Guide for Businesses, Law Enforcement, and Victims.* Hoboken, NJ: Wiley, 2006, ISBN: 978-0-471-75724-5.

[ISO7498] ISO/IEC Part 2 "Security Architecture for Open Systems Interconnection for CCITT Applications," 1991.

[KAHN67] Kahn, D., *The Codebreakers: The Story of Secret Writing*, New York: Macmillan, 1967.

[PHISH] Lininger, Rachael and Russell Dean Vines. *Phishing: Cutting the Identity Theft Line*, Indianapolis, IN: Wiley, 2006, ISBN: 978-0-7645-8498-5.

[RISK] Jones, Andy and Debi Ashenden, *Risk Management for Computer Security.* Burlington, MA: Butterworth-Heinemann, 2005, ISBN 978-0750677950.

[SCHN00] Schneier, Bruce. *Email Security: How to Keep Your Electronic Messages Private.* Indianapolis, IN: Wiley, 1995, ISBN 978-0-471-05318-7.

[SPOOK] Peneberg, Adam and Marc Barry. *Spooked: Espionage in Corporate America*, New York: HarperCollins, 2000, ISBN 978-0738205939.

Chapter 4

[CNSS] http://www.cnss.gov/Assets/pdf/cnssp_15_fs.pdf

[DIFF76] Diffie, W., and M. Hellman. "New Directions in Cryptography", *IEEE Transactions on Information Theory*, vol. IT-22, no. 6, 1976, pp. 644–654.

[EFF98] Electronic Frontier Foundation. *Cracking DES*, Sebastopol: O'Reilly & Associates, Inc., 1998.

[FIPS46] *U.S. Department of Commerce. Data Encryption Standard, Federal Information Processing Standards*, Publication 46, 1977.

[FIPS180a] U.S. Department of Commerce. *Secure Hash Standard, Federal Information Processing Standards*, Publication 180-1, 1995.

[Supersedes FIPS PUB 180 published in 1993.]

[FIPS180b] U.S. Department of Commerce. *Secure Hash Standard, Federal Information Processing Standards*, Publication 180-2, 2002.

[Supersedes FIPS PUB 180-1 published in 1995.]

[FIPS186a] U.S. Department of Commerce. *Digital Signature Standard (DSS), Federal Information Processing Standards*, Publication 186, 1994.

[FIPS186b] U.S. Department of Commerce. *Digital Signature Standard (DSS), Federal Information Processing Standards*, Publication 186, 1994.

[Supersedes FIPS PUB 186 published in 1994 and 186-1 published in 1998.]

[FIPS197] U.S. Department of Commerce. *Advanced Encryption Standard, Federal Information Processing Standards*, Publication 197, 2001.

[FIPS198] U.S. Department of Commerce. *The Keyed-Hash Message Authentication Code (HMAC), Federal Information Processing Standards*, Publication 198, 2002.

[KAHN67] Kahn, D., *The Codebreakers: The Story of Secret Writing.* New York: Macmillan, 1967.

[KRAW97] Krawczyk, H., M. Bellare, and R. Canetti. "HMAC: Keyed-Hashing for Message Authentication," RFC 2104, 1997.

[MENE97] Memezes, A., P. vanOorschot, and S. Vanstone, *Handbook of Applied Cryptography.* New York: CRC Press LLP, 1997.

[NIST1] http://csrc.nist.gov/groups/ST/hash/statement.html

[NIST2] http://csrc.nist.gov/groups/ST/hash/policy.html

[NIST3] http://csrc.nist.gov/groups/ST/hash/documents/
SecondHashWshop%202006%20Report.pdf

[RFC3447] www.ietf.org/rfc/rfc3447

[RIVE78] Rivest, R., A. Shamir, and L. Adleman. A Method for Obtaining Digital Signatures and Public-Key Cryptosystems, *Communications of the ACM*, vol. 21, no. 2, 1978, pp. 120–126.

[SCHN96] Schneier, B., *Applied Cryptography: Protocols, Algorithms, and Source Code in C*, 2nd ed. Indianapolis, IN: Wiley, 1996.

[SEC1] "Standards for Efficient Cryptography, Elliptic Curve Cryptography, SEC1 Version 1," 2000, http://www.secg.org/collateral/sec1_final.pdf.

[SP800-38a] U.S. Department of Commerce. *Recommendations for Block Cipher Modes - Methods and Techniques*, FIPS SP800-38A, 2001.

[SP800-38b] U.S. Department of Commerce. *Recommendations for Block Cipher Modes: The CMAC Mode of Authentication.* FIPS SP800-38B, 2005.

[SP800-38c] U.S. Department of Commerce, *Recommendations for Block Cipher Modes: The CCM Mode for Authentication and Confidentiality.* FIPS SP800-38C, 2004.

[SP800-38d] DRAFT U.S. Department of Commerce. *Recommendations for Block Cipher Modes: The Galois/Counter Mode (GCM) for Confidentiality and Authentication*, FIPS SP800-38C, 2001.

[TUCH79] Tuchman, W. "Hellman Presents No Shortcut Solutions to DES", *IEEE Spectrum*, vol. 6, no. 7, July 1979, pp. 40–41.

[X392] *American National Standards Institute. Data Encryption Algorithm*, ANSI X3.92, 1981. [Most recently reaffirmed in 1998.]

[X942] American National Standards Institute. *Public Key Cryptography Using Irreversible Algorithms for the Financial Services Industry, Part 2: The Secure Hash Algorithm (SHA-1)*, ANSI X9.30-2, 1997.

[X952] American National Standards Institute. *Triple Data Encryption Algorithm Modes of Operation*, ANSI X9.52-1998, 1998.

[X9302] American National Standards Institute. *Public Key Cryptography Using Irreversible Algorithms for the Financial Services Industry, Part 2: The Secure Hash Algorithm (SHA-1)*, ANSI X9.30-2, 1997. (Originally published in 1993.)

Chapter 5

[CL] Carlyle, A., and Lloyd, S., *Understanding PKI: Concepts, Standards, and Deployment Considerations*, Second Edition. Boston, MA: Addison-Wesley, 2002.

[FIPS140] U.S. Department of Commerce, *Security Requirements for Cryptographic Modules*, Federal Information Processing Standards Publication 140-1, 1994. [Supersedes FIPS 140 *General Security Requirements for Equipment Using the Data Encryption Standard.*]

[HP] Housley, R., and Polk, T. *Planning for PKI.* New York: John Wiley & Sons, Inc, 2001.

[RFC3161] www.ietf.org/rfc/rfc3161.txt

[RFC3280] www.ietf.org/rfc/rfc3280.txt

[RFC3851] www.ietf.org/rfc/rfc3851.txt

[X955] American National Standards Institute, "Public Key Cryptography For The Financial Services Industry: Extensions To Public Key Certificates And Certificate Revocation Lists," ANSI X9.55, 1995.

[X50900] ITU-T, The Directory — Authentication Framework, Recommendation X.509, 2000.

[X50997] ITU-T, *The Directory — Authentication Framework*, Recommendation X.509, 1997.

Chapter 6

[HOUS1] Housley, Russell. "Electronic Message Security: A Comparison of Three Approaches". In *Fifth Annual Computer Security Applications Conference Proceedings*, December 1989, pp 29.

[NISTMSPR] NISTIR 90-4250, "Secure Data Network System (SDNS) Network, Transport, and Message Security Protocols," Charles Dinkel, Editor, February 1990.

[RFC1421] www.ietf.org/rfc/rfc1421.txt

[RFC1422] www.ietf.org/rfc/rfc1422.txt

[RFC1423] www.ietf.org/rfc/rfc1423.txt

[RFC1424] www.ietf.org/rfc/rfc1424.txt

[RFC1847] www.ietf.org/rfc/rfc1847.txt

[RFC1848] www.ietf.org/rfc/rfc1848.txt

[RFC1991] www.ietf.org/rfc/rfc1991.txt

[RFC2311] www.ietf.org/rfc/rfc2311.txt

[RFC2315] www.ietf.org/rfc/rfc2315.txt

[RFC2630] www.ietf.org/rfc/rfc2630.txt

[RFC2632] www.ietf.org/rfc/rfc2633.txt

[RFC2633] www.ietf.org/rfc/rfc2632.txt
[RFC2634] www.ietf.org/rfc/rfc2634.txt
[RFC3114] www.ietf.org/rfc/rfc3114.txt
[RFC3274] www.ietf.org/rfc/rfc3274.txt
[RFC3280] www.ietf.org/rfc/rfc3280.txt
[RFC3370] www.ietf.org/rfc/rfc3370.txt
[RFC3851] www.ietf.org/rfc/rfc3851.txt
[RFC3852] www.ietf.org/rfc/rfc3852.txt
[RFC4073] www.ietf.org/rfc/rfc4073.txt
[RFC4262] www.ietf.org/rfc/rfc4262.txt
[RFC4880] www.ietf.org/rfc/rfc4880.txt
[RFC5035] www.ietf.org/rfc/rfc5035.txt

Chapter 7

[FIPS180] U.S. Department of Commerce, Secure Hash Standard, Federal Information Processing Standards Publication 180-2, 2002. [Supersedes FIPS PUB 180 published in 1995.]
[RESC] Rescorla, E., SSL and TLS: Designing and Building Secure Systems, Boston, MA: Addison-Wesley, 2000, ISBN 978-0201615982.
[RFC768] www.ietf.org/rfc/rfc768.txt
[RFC793] www.ietf.org/rfc/rfc793.txt
[RFC1321] www.ietf.org/rfc/rfc1321.txt
[RFC2104] www.ietf.org/rfc/rfc2104.txt
[RFC2195] www.ietf.org/rfc/rfc2195.txt
[RFC2246] www.ietf.org/rfc/rfc2246.txt
[RFC2407] www.ietf.org/rfc/rfc2407.txt
[RFC2408] www.ietf.org/rfc/rfc2408.txt
[RFC2409] www.ietf.org/rfc/rfc2409.txt
[RFC2412] www.ietf.org/rfc/rfc2412.txt
[RFC2554] www.ietf.org/rfc/rfc2554.txt
[RFC2595] www.ietf.org/rfc/rfc2595.txt
[RFC2831] www.ietf.org/rfc/rfc2831.txt
[RFC3207] www.ietf.org/rfc/rfc3207.txt
[RFC3546] www.ietf.org/rfc/rfc3546.txt
[RFC3566] www.ietf.org/rfc/rfc3566.txt
[RFC4301] www.ietf.org/rfc/rfc4301.txt
[RFC4302] www.ietf.org/rfc/rfc4302.txt
[RFC4303] www.ietf.org/rfc/rfc4303.txt
[RFC4305] www.ietf.org/rfc/rfc4305.txt
[RFC4306] www.ietf.org/rfc/rfc4306.txt
[RFC4307] www.ietf.org/rfc/rfc4307.txt

[RFC4346] www.ietf.org/rfc/rfc4346.txt

[RFC4366] www.ietf.org/rfc/rfc4366.txt

[RFC4347] www.ietf.org/rfc/rfc4347.txt

[SSL] Freier, A., P. Karlton, and P. Kocher, The SSL Protocol, Version 3.0, Netscape Communications, 1996. [http://home.netscape.com/eng/ssl3/draft302.txt]

[TLS12] www.ietf.org/internet-drafts/draft-ietf-tls-rfc4346-bis-07.txt

Chapter 8

[CC] www.commoncriteriaportal.org/public/files/CCPART1V3.1R2.pdf

www.commoncriteriaportal.org/public/files/CCPART2V3.1R2.pdf

www.commoncriteriaportal.org/public/files/CCPART3V3.1R2.pdf

[CCPPL2] www.niap-ccevs.org/cc-scheme/pp/PP_OS_SL_MR2.0_V1.91.pdf

Dreifus, Henry, and J. Thomas Monk. *Smart Cards: A Guide to Building and Managing Smart Card Applications.* New York: John Wiley & Sons, Inc, 1998.

[FIPS140] http://csrc.nist.gov/publications/fips/fips140-2/fips1402.pdf

[ISO15408] http://standards.iso.org/ittf/PubliclyAvailableStandards/c040612_ISO_IEC_15408-1_2005(E).zip

http://standards.iso.org/ittf/PubliclyAvailableStandards/c040612_ISO_IEC_15408-2_2005(E).zip

http://standards.iso.org/ittf/PubliclyAvailableStandards/c040612_ISO_IEC_15408-3_2005(E).zip

[Nielsen] R. Nielsen, "Observations from the Deployment of a Large Scale PKI", Proceedings of the 4th Annual PKI Research Workshop, pp. 159–165, August 2005.

[PKCS11] ftp://ftp.rsasecurity.com/pub/pkcs/pkcs-11/v2-20/pkcs-11v2-20.pdf

[PKCS12] ftp://ftp.rsasecurity.com/pub/pkcs/pkcs-12/pkcs-12v1.pdf

[Marchesini] J. Marchesini, S.W. Smith, M. Zhao, "Keyjacking: Risks of the Current Client-side Infrastructure", Proceedings of the 2nd Annual PKI Research Workshop, pp. 128–144, April 2003.

[Whitten] A. Whitten and J.D. Tygar, "Why Johnny Can't Encrypt: A Usability Evaluation of PGP 5.0", Proceedings of the 8th USENIX Security Symposium, pp. 169–184, August 1999

[WOLFGANG] Hoboken, NJ: Wiley, ISBN 978-0470856680.

Chapter 9

[ASAFE] "AstraZeneca Implementation of SAFE Digital Signature," Version 1, 25 February 2007.

[NISTSP] http://csrc.nist.gov/publications/nistpubs/800-57/SP800-57-Part1.pdf

[PSAFE] "Pfizer Implementation of SAFE Digital Signature for Electronic Lab Notebook," Version 1, 23 July 2007.

Chapter 10

[DODCP] http://iase.disa.mil/pki/dod-cp-v90-final-9-feb-05-signed.pdf

[ECACP] http://iase.disa.mil/pki/eca/docs/ECA_CP_V3.1_30Aug2006_Final_Signed.pdf

[RFC2527] www.ietf.org/rfc/rfc3647.txt

[RFC3647] www.ietf.org/rfc/rfc3647.txt

Chapter 11

[FASC-N] www.smartcard.gov/information/TIG_SCEPACS_v2.2.pdf

[FICCCP] www.cio.gov/ficc/documents/CertCRLprofileForCP.pdf

[FIMH] www.cio.gov/ficc/documents/FederalIdentityManagement-Handbook.pdf

[FPKICP] www.cio.gov/fpkipa/documents/CommonPolicy.pdf

[GSCH] www.smartcard.gov/information/smartcardhandbook.pdf

[GSAMEM] http://fips201ep.cio.gov/documents/GSA_HSPD-12_Acquisition_Guidance.pdf

[HSPD-12] www.whitehouse.gov/news/releases/2004/08/20040827-8.html

[IR7337] http://csrc.nist.gov/publications/nistir/ir7337/NISTIR-7337.pdf

[IR7452] http://csrc.nist.gov/publications/nistir/ir7452/NISTIR-7452.pdf

[M-04-04] www.whitehouse.gov/omb/memoranda/fy2004/m04-04.pdf

[M-05-24] www.whitehouse.gov/omb/memoranda/fy2005/m05-24.pdf

[M-06-18] www.whitehouse.gov/omb/memoranda/fy2006/m06-18.pdf

[PUB201] http://csrc.nist.gov/publications/fips/fips201-1/FIPS-201-1-chng1.pdf

[RFC3280] www.ietf.org/rfc/rfc3280.txt

[SP800-63] http://csrc.nist.gov/publications/nistpubs/800-63/
   sp800-63V1_0_2.pdf

[SP800-73] http://csrc.nist.gov/publications/nistpubs/800-73-1/
   sp800-73-1v7-April20-2006.pdf

[SP800-76] http://csrc.nist.gov/publications/nistpubs/800-76-1/
   SP800-76-1_012407.pdf

[SP800-78] http://csrc.nist.gov/publications/nistpubs/800-78-1/
   SP-800-78-1_final2.pdf

[SP800-79] http://csrc.nist.gov/publications/nistpubs/800-79/
   sp800-79.pdf

[SP800-85] http://csrc.nist.gov/publications/nistpubs/800-85A/
   SP800-85A.pdf

http://csrc.nist.gov/publications/nistpubs/800-85B/SP800-85b-
   072406-final.pdf

[SP800-87] http://csrc.nist.gov/publications/nistpubs/800-87/
   sp800-87-Final.pdf

[SP800-96] http://csrc.nist.gov/publications/nistpubs/800-96/
   SP800-96-091106.pdf

[SP800-100] http://csrc.nist.gov/publications/nistpubs/800-100/
   SP800-100-Mar07-2007.pdf

[SP800-104] http://csrc.nist.gov/publications/nistpubs/800-104/
   SP800-104-June29_2007-final.pdf

[TIG-SCEPAS] www.smart.gov/information/TIG_SCEPACS_v2.2.pdf

Chapter 12

[PKCS1v21] PKCS #1 v2.1: RSA Cryptography Standard, June 14, 2002.

[RFC1459] www.ietf.org/rfc/rfc1459.txt

[RFC2560] www.ietf.org/rfc/rfc2560.txt

[RFC2810] www.ietf.org/rfc/rfc2810.txt

[RFC2811] www.ietf.org/rfc/rfc2811.txt

[RFC2812] www.ietf.org/rfc/rfc2812.txt

[RFC3280] www.ietf.org/rfc/rfc3280.txt

[RFC3281] www.ietf.org/rfc/rfc3281.txt

[RFC3447] www.ietf.org/rfc/rfc3447.txt

[RFC3820] www.ietf.org/rfc/rfc3820.txt

[RFC3920] www.ietf.org/rfc/rfc3920.txt

[RFC3921] www.ietf.org/rfc/rfc3921.txt

[RFC3922] www.ietf.org/rfc/rfc3922.txt

[RFC3923] www.ietf.org/rfc/rfc3923.txt

[RFC4870] www.ietf.org/rfc/rfc4870.txt

[RFC4406] www.ietf.org/rfc/rfc4406.txt

[RFC4408] www.ietf.org/rfc/rfc4408.txt
[RFC4871] www.ietf.org/rfc/rfc4871.txt
[RFC5023] www.ietf.org/rfc/rfc5023.txt
[RFC5055] www.ietf.org/rfc/rfc5055.txt
[SIMPLE] http://ietf.org/html.charters/simple-charter.html
[SP800-57] http://csrc.nist.gov/publications/nistpubs/800-57/
   SP800-57-Part1.pdf
[WANG] http://csrc.nist.gov/groups/ST/hash/documents/
   Wang_SHA1-New-Result.pdf
[X50997] ITU-T, *The Directory — Authentication Framework*, Recommendation
   X.509, 1997.

Appendix A

[BNF] Naur, P. (ed.), 1963, "Revised report on the algorithmic language
   ALGOL 60", *Communications of the ACM* 6:1, pp 1–17
Nnaur, Peter (ed.), "Revised Report on the Algorithmic Language ALGOL
   60", *Communications of the ACM*, Vol. 3 No.5, pp. 299–314, May 1960.
[RFC2822] www.ietf.org/rfc/rfc2822.txt
[RFC4234] www.ietf.org/rfc/rfc4234.txt

Appendix B

[KALI93a] Kaliski, B., *A Layman's Guide to a Subset of ASN.1, BER, and DER*, An
   RSA Laboratories Technology Note, 1993. [ftp://ftp.rsasecurity.
   com/pub/pkcs/doc/layman.doc]
[LARM00] Larmouth, J., *ASN.1 Complete*, San Diego: Morgan Kaufmann Aca-
   demic Press, 2000.
[IS7498] ISO/IEC, *Information Technology - Information Processing Systems -
   Open System Interconnection - Basic Reference Mode - The Basic Model*, ISO/IEC
   7498-1: 1994.
[STEE90] Steedman, D., *Abstract Syntax Notation One (ASN.1): The Tutorial and
   Reference*, Twickenham: Technology Appraisals Ltd., 1990.
[X20888] CCITT, *Specification of Abstract Syntax Notation One (ASN.1)*, Recom-
   mendation X.208, 1988.
[X50988] CCITT, *The Directory - Authentication Framework*, Recommendation
   X.509, 1988.
[X68097] ITU-T, *Information Technology - Abstract Syntax Notation One (ASN.1):
   Specification of Basic Notation*, Recommendation X.680, 1997.
[X68003] ITU-T, *Information Technology - Abstract Syntax Notation One (ASN.1):
   Specification of Basic Notation*, Recommendation X.680, 2003.

[X69003] ITU-T, *Information Technology - Abstract Syntax Notation One (ASN.1) Encoding Rule: Specification of Basic Encoding Rules (BER), Canonical Encoding Rules (CER) and Distinguished Encoding Rules (DER)*, Recommendation X.690, 2003.

Appendix C

[MR] Marshall Rose, *The Internet Message*, New York: Prentice Hall, 1992, ISBN 978-0130929419.

[RFC2045] www.ietf.org/rfc/rfc2045.txt

[RFC2046] www.ietf.org/rfc/rfc2046.txt

[RFC2047] www.ietf.org/rfc/rfc2047.txt

[RFC2048] www.ietf.org/rfc/rfc2048.txt

[RFC2049] www.ietf.org/rfc/rfc2049.txt

Index